# RED THRUST

# RED THRUST
## Attack on the Central Front, Soviet Tactics and Capabilities in the 1990s

Steven J. Zaloga

**PRESIDIO**

Quality Printing and Binding by:
Orange Graphics
P.O. Box 791
Orange, VA 22960 U.S.A.

**To Marlene and Paul**
For their encouragement and support

# CONTENTS

# RED THRUST

# INTRODUCTION

How good is the Soviet Army? Certainly it is large. With a tank inventory in excess of 55,000 vehicles, more than 200 divisions, and quantitative superiority over NATO in nearly every type of conventional weapon, it is an imposing force. But would these numbers directly translate into combat power on the modern battlefield?

These questions are impossible to answer. The Soviet Army has not fought a conventional land war in forty-five years. Attempts to answer these questions based on Soviet performance in World War II are growing increasingly irrelevant with the passage of time and the advent of new military technologies. But even if these questions are impossible to answer, some tentative conclusions can be suggested on the basis of a careful examination of what is known about today's Soviet Army.

This book examines the combat power of the Soviet Union in a unique fashion. Each chapter is devoted to a particular aspect of the modern Soviet armed forces: the tanks, motor rifle troops, special forces, attack helicopters, and so on. Each chapter begins with a fictional scenario of this element of the Soviet military forces in combat in a conventional war in Europe in the early 1990s. These fictional scenarios are complemented by an analytic essay about current and future trends in that branch of the Soviet armed forces. It is not the point of this book to suggest that such a war in Europe is likely. Rather, the Soviet Army is configured and deployed primarily for such an eventuality, and it is in this context in which it should be judged.

The perspective of this book is mainly from the tactical viewpoint. It examines the tactics and equipment of small units: squads, platoons, companies, and battalions. It is not the aim of this book to predict whether the Soviet Army would win in a conventional war against NATO. Rather, it is a more modest attempt to describe how the Soviet Army would be likely to fight.

There are three underlying themes in this book. The first is that quantitative advantages in weapons and hardware do not necessarily translate into real advantages on the battlefield. Superior tactics, better training, and technological advantages can overcome mere numbers. The second theme is that the contemporary battlefield is likely to be extremely lethal, even by World War II standards. Firepower density and accuracy at all levels has increased enormously since 1945. Many of the Soviet units depicted in the fictional scenarios are decimated in relatively brief encounters. This should not be misunderstood. This is not an attempt to portray the Soviets as a bunch of bumbling military incompetents. Modern warfare at the small unit level is likely to be extremely destructive of men and machines. The fictional scenarios attempt to show why this is so, and where particular weaknesses in Soviet training, tactics, or equipment may exacerbate these trends.

The third underlying theme is the issue of the likelihood of such a European war. This book tries to avoid directly addressing this issue. The decision to go to war is more in the realm of grand diplomacy and military strategy than the muddy world of small unit tactics, which is the focus of this book. But the scenarios attempt to show that the Soviet Union cannot be assured of a cheap or easy victory in a conventional European land war, in spite of its substantial numerical advantages. The Tsar's army of

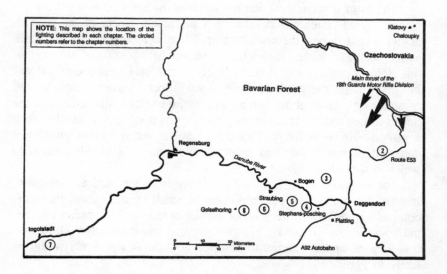

1914 and Stalin's army of 1941 were substantially larger than their opponents but were soundly trounced. Anxiety over possible shortcomings in the performance of the modern Soviet Army and any effort on the part of the Kremlin to use its military power in Europe will continue to worry the Soviet Union.

Indeed, as this book was being written, Mikhail Gorbachev announced unprecedented, unilateral cuts in Soviet conventional forces. After over forty years of armed tension, the Cold War seems to be finally abating. This book attempts to show how internal pressures in the Soviet armed forces helped to promote these unilateral cuts. It also explores some of the changes that may be seen in the Soviet Army over the next few years.

The setting for the fictional scenarios has been confined to one area in southern Germany, in the Bavarian countryside to the northeast of Munich. The fictional scenarios examine the progress of several related Soviet units during the first week of the war as they attempt to break through frontier defenses and push across the Danube River into the Bavarian plains beyond. Although the time of this war is the early 1990s, the equipment, organization, and tactics are not markedly different from those of the Soviet Army today, with some minor exceptions.

The fictional accounts are entirely from the Soviet perspective. Soviet terms have been used in favor of NATO code names or expressions. This extends to many small details, such as the use of metric measurements when referring to distances, which may be a bit awkward for some American readers. But Soviet troops do not refer to their weapons by their NATO names, such as Saggers, Fulcrums, or ACRVs, but by their Soviet names, such as Malyutka, MiG-29, or 1V12. For readers unaccustomed to these terms, explanatory notes have been provided. For readers interested in pursuing further reading about the contemporary Soviet armed forces, the bibliography should provide a good starting point.

# CHAPTER 1

## Plan Buran:
## The Invasion of Western Europe

0730, 22 September, Moscow

Colonel Stepan Kucherenko stepped out of his army limo in the interior entrance of Moscow Military District headquarters at Chapayevskskiy Lane. Normally the wartime STAVKA[1] high command would meet in its own central headquarters. The district headquarters had been selected to attract less attention from the prying eyes of NATO intelligence.

Kucherenko had never spent much time in the district headquarters. As a staff officer in the operations directorate of the General Staff, he spent most of his time at the Ministry of Defense offices. It didn't matter, as at the security entrance, there was a young NCO assigned to escort the STAVKA officers to the proper meeting rooms. Kucherenko's task today would be to brief fellow staff officers of the Southwestern Front[2] regarding the forthcoming operations. He knew many of the officers quite well, having attended the General Staff Academy with several of them. The hallways were filled with other officers scurrying to meetings. Many wore the camouflage battle dress of the air assault helicopter pilots, which had become fashionable in the late 1980s, when the uniforms had been first

---

1. STAVKA is the traditional Russian term for the high command of the armed forces in time of war.

2. Front is the Soviet term for a military formation containing several armies. Soviet terms for higher military formations differ from their NATO counterparts. A Soviet army (two to three divisions) is roughly the equivalent of a NATO corps; a Soviet front (two to three armies) is similar to a NATO army.

issued to aircrews in Afghanistan. Kucherenko disdained such affectations, even though he had served a tour fighting the Afghan rebels. Staff positions, even in the Soviet Army, attracted fops and political opportunists. Wearing battle dress at a time like this seemed not only tasteless, but provocative, since the NATO intelligence snoops might notice.

On his way to the meeting hall, Kucherenko ran into an old friend, Col. Yevgeniy Burlatskiy, who would be attending the briefing.

"So, Stepan Romanovich, it will be you giving us the briefing today. Nice to see you again."[3]

"Welcome back, Yevgeniy Pavlovich. I see your German comrades are giving us some serious trouble. How was Berlin?"

Burlatskiy grimaced. The situation in East Germany was far worse than anyone could have expected, even an astute officer like Stepan Kucherenko. It seemed certain that the deteriorating situation in Germany would lead to war.

## The German Crisis

The troubles had begun in the spring. A fire had started at a large GSFG (Group of Soviet Forces-Germany) storage area near the Saale rail yard. The local commander was convinced he could bring the fire under control and did not evacuate local civilian factories or the local elementary school. It was a costly mistake. In the afternoon, the fire reached the missile and ammunition reserves, setting off a huge explosion, which devastated several nearby factories and part of the school. Casualties were made worse by a large cloud of noxious gas. The Soviets claimed the cloud was created by dispersal of rocket propellant chemicals. Local residents were convinced it was from some sort of chemical weapons. Total casualties were 405 killed and nearly three times as many injured.

What ignited the troubles was the decision by the German Communist party to allow newspaper and television to run the story instead of suppressing it per usual policy. They realized that the underground samizdat press would cover it anyway, and the West German television stations as

---

3. The traditional Russian greeting uses a person's given name and patronymic. The patronymic is a form of the father's name. Stepan Kucherenko's father's name was Roman, hence Stepan Romanovich.

well. Running the story would give the party a bit of badly needed credibility with an audience weary of the numbing socialist press. The German Democratic Republic was coming down with a bad case of the "Polish disease" that summer, on the fortieth anniversary of the East Berlin riots of 1953.

The story captured nationwide attention and led to a series of protest marches outside the Saale *kaserne*,[4] led by a coalition of unofficial antiregime groups. It is doubtful that the Soviets could have done much to defuse the situation. Even had they hung the offending officers at the gate of the garrison, the local citizenry wouldn't have been much placated. German patience had finally worn too thin. All spring, they had been subjected to the usual obsequious television and radio programs about the valiant Soviet soldiers protecting freedom-loving mankind during the Great Patriotic War. Heroes of Kursk! Heroes of Stalingrad! Liberators of Germany! For nearly fifty years, East Germany had been one big Soviet military camp, with German ambitions and dreams suppressed and ridiculed by the Russians and their Communist party puppets. The Germans wanted the Soviets out, and for that matter they wouldn't be unhappy to see the Americans go from the Federal Republic next door. They were sick of hearing of the threat from NATO, the military mischief of the Bundeswehr (the West German Army), and the heinous machinations of American politicians. After fifty years, they wanted to forget about World War II, and they wanted the Russians and Americans to forget about it too. The Germans were ashamed of having acted so passively for the past decades. It was finally a time for action.

No one expected what happened. The Americans had long dismissed the East Germans as the most passive of the Warsaw Pact states. The German economy was relatively prosperous. The Germans had long accepted the sacrifice of political freedom and honor for well-stocked shops. At least they were better off than the Poles and the Czechs, who usually had neither. The East German Army was rated by NATO analysts as the best trained and best motivated of the Warsaw Pact armies. The Soviet military shared this opinion. The East German NVA (National Peoples Army) was the only Warsaw Pact army to figure in Soviet war operations plans. Soviet plans assumed that the Germans would fight in any direct confrontation

---

4. *Kaserne* is the German word for a garrison or military base. It is widely used by other NATO forces as well, including American and British forces.

with NATO. The Poles and the Czechs would be expected to fight, but in peripheral theaters like Denmark or Austria. What happened in the summer had shattered these preconceptions.

The demonstrations and public meetings spread through East Germany. The Wildner regime responded in the reflexive socialist fashion, using police and tear gas. This infuriated most East Germans, who had been promised a more humane regime as part of recent reforms. It was not the escalating scale of the demonstrations that worried the Soviets; it was something more serious. In early June, a bomb was set off in a restaurant in Dresden frequented by Soviet officers. Sixteen officers were killed and nearly fifty more injured. For the first time since the Soviet occupation of Central Europe in 1945, the Soviets were facing a serious terrorist threat in Central Europe. A group calling itself the National Committee for a Free Germany (NKFD) claimed responsibility. The name of the group was particularly insulting; it was the same as the organization of German prisoners of war formed by the Soviets in 1943, which formed the basis of the communist East German state. Neither the Poles nor the Czechs had ever resorted to violence during the disturbances there. The Soviets began suspecting outside agitators, namely West Germans. Bombings and shootings of Soviet officials and soldiers continued through June, and Soviet troops were confined to their base areas. In two separate acts of sabotage, two large ammunition dumps exploded on 21 June. German police arrested at least seven members of the group, and found that two were West German citizens who had been providing arms and explosives to the NKFD terrorists through hideouts in West Berlin. On 27 June, the commander of the 2d Guards Tank Army and his chauffeur were ambushed outside of Fuerstenberg.

## Martial Law

The East German militia proved incapable of counteracting the rising violence. General Rostislav Belov, at GSFG headquarters in Zonsen-Wunstorf, called in his staff people to begin planning a martial law crackdown patterned on the successful Polish operation a decade earlier. They were unprepared for the German response. Their "colleagues" in the East German Army stated categorically that they doubted the army would be any more effective than the police. The army had just inducted the usual semiannual crop of draftees, many of whom weeks earlier had been on the protest lines themselves. Calling out the troops might backfire. They might support the protestors and cause a tragic escalation in the civil violence. After consulting with a high-ranking delegation from the Politburo in Moscow, the GSFG commander informed his colleague in the East German Army that they would be expected to "perform their socialist mission" or the Soviets would be obliged to call in Czech and Polish troops to assist in suppressing civil disturbances. The thought of Polish or Czech troops being used in East Germany infuriated the German officers even further.

The GSFG staff had been surprised by the German Army's response. The East German Army was the one Warsaw Pact army most thoroughly integrated into the Soviet command structure. But the close contact between the two forces came at a price. The Germans were utterly contemptuous of their Soviet counterparts. The East Germans viewed themselves as real soldiers, and the Soviets as country bumpkins. They were appalled by the slovenly Soviet maintenance practices, the disgusting food, and the ignorance and backwardness of the common soldiers. The Germans boasted that they spoke better Russian than a lot of the Soviet Central Asian troops! The East German soldiers were well educated, listened regularly to West German television, and had a less provincial view of the world outside the bloc than average Soviet troops. Few of the young German soldiers enjoyed soldiering, but they took pride in a job well done. This was an attitude alien to most of the Soviet troops. The tragic fire at Saale was symptomatic of the Soviet forces' casual attitude toward safety. The Soviet Ground Forces recruited mainly out of the rural areas. Any Russian kid with brains got a posting with the Air Force, Navy, or some technical branch. Serving with the motor rifle troops or tanks was two years of backbreaking work, poor food, humiliation, and confinement. As a result, there were a lot of non-Slavic ethnic troops in the ground forces, more than 40 percent. Thousands of miles from home, with no chance for leave in the local towns, they were a sorry bunch.

Like the community around them, the young German troops were fed up with the Soviet presence in their country. They quickly grew tired of the endless lectures about maintaining fraternal relations with their brothers-in-arms, the Soviets. The dim German view of the Russians was exacerbated by the sheer number of Soviet troops in Germany. In Poland, Soviet troops were hardly ever seen in the major city, only in a few towns in the western provinces. Even in Czechoslovakia, the Soviet presence was confined to a few regions. But in Germany, it was hard to escape the thousands of kasernes and bases of the GSFG.

Having had martial law duty foisted on them by the Soviets, the East German military treated the matter with uncharacteristic casualness. All orders were dutifully conveyed, but it didn't take long for the average soldier to understand that the officers had little sympathy for their forthcoming "socialist duty." Martial law was declared on 15 July and a curfew was imposed in most cities. The new situation was enforced without enthusiasm, and large public protests were met with ineffective army actions. A pattern of small-scale mutiny began, compounded by large-scale desertion by troops stationed on curfew duty. What was especially alarming was that the soldiers were deserting with their weapons. With Soviet troops largely confined to the kasernes, the NKFD terrorists began striking at strategic targets, especially military rail links into the bases. This was not amateur high jinks: Military-grade high explosive was being used. Soviet investigations found that it was Soviet explosives used in the attacks, but the Soviet press pointed an accusing finger at West Germany as being behind the NKFD activities. The propaganda campaign became so shrill that the West German government withdrew its ambassador from Berlin in late July "for consultations."

## The Leipzig Troubles

The situation continued to degenerate. Enraged by the halfhearted response of the East German Army to the martial law crisis, the GSFG commander, General Belov, decided to employ Soviet troops for crowd control for the first time. On 29 July, special Interior Army (security force) regiments brought in from the Ukraine were used to confront a large "peace" rally in Leipzig. The Soviet troops were taunted by the crowd, and bottles and rocks were thrown. The Soviet soldiers did not have shields, tear gas, or any of the usual riot gear paraphernalia. They carried ordinary assault rifles. After nearly twenty minutes of abusive behavior by the irate German crowds, shots rang out. A Soviet investigation stated that German provocateurs had begun sniping at the Soviet troops from rooftops. But many Soviet officers present knew that the situation had simply gotten out of hand, and isolated soldiers had fired for fear of losing their lives to an angry mob. Several dozen Germans were killed.

East German troops on the outskirts of the city, on hearing of the massacre, mutinied. With many of their junior officers in the lead, they headed into the center of the city to settle some old scores. Sporadic street fighting broke out in a confusing battle between Soviet Interior Army troops, German police, and German soldiers. It was not clear who was fighting whom, but it was obvious that the two regiments of Soviet troops were inadequate to pacify the city. A motor rifle division from neighboring kasernes was rushed in the next morning to prevent any further fighting. The German troops did not give up easily, but they did not have an adequate supply of antiarmor weapons. In two days of street fighting, the Soviets finally managed to restore a measure of order in the city at a considerable cost in human life.

Kucherenko had read the report on the Leipzig crisis. He was appalled. Kucherenko was no bleeding heart, nor was he particularly sympathetic to the Germans. He had grown up on a steady diet of Russian propaganda about the German horrors against the Russian people in World War II. But he was a skilled professional soldier and did not approve of actions that threatened to bring on an unwanted conflict with NATO. Kucherenko was fond of military history, and the recent incidents reminded him of historical examples of the failure of colonial regimes. He didn't like to think of Soviet involvement in Central Europe as a colonial relationship, but he was hardheaded enough to admit that it was. To secure a stronghold in a colony, acquiescence of the local population was a cheaper route to control than purely military actions that aroused the locals. Recent Soviet actions in East Germany had enraged the populace and were rapidly turning their grudging acceptance of Soviet control into stubborn and irrational resistance.

What ignited the troubles with NATO was the Kremlin decision to restrict travel into West Berlin. Significant segments of the political leadership in Moscow were convinced, against the evidence, that the West Germans were provoking the disturbances. It was a comfortable myth to explain why East Germany had so suddenly turned violent. West German television was doing nothing to calm the situation. A television documentary in late July on Soviet brutality during the 1945 fighting in Germany was particularly shocking to the Russians. Two other matters triggered the action. Many in the Kremlin were convinced that West Berlin was serving as a staging area for NKFD terrorist actions. The Soviets were convinced of West German complicity in the recent bombings and assassinations of Soviet officers. Furthermore, the city was serving as a magnet for fleeing East Germans. As a gesture of goodwill in the early 1990s, the Soviets had acquiesced to reducing the barriers along the border. East Germans were taking advantage of gaps in the barriers to flee into West Berlin. The local GSFG officers were demanding permission to beef up border security using army forces. But a special Central Committee delegation that had visited East Berlin in late July urged caution. East Berlin was a powder keg of frustrations. The delegation members had been brusquely informed by East German party officials that Soviet military action in Berlin could result in outbreaks far worse than those in Leipzig.

The restrictions in transit consisted initially of rigorous searches of automobiles and trucks using the roads leading into Berlin. The Soviets also threatened to block air routes into Berlin unless some form of Soviet or East German "customs" inspection of incoming flights was instituted. The action was intended as a calculated overreaction to the developments in East Germany. The Kremlin, with little subtlety, passed the word to West German leaders, as well as the U.S. and other NATO states, that the action was intended mainly to coax some reaction from the West German government to help dampen the situation. The Kremlin hoped for some restrictions of German television broadcasting, as well as more vigorous efforts to hunt down NKFD terrorists on West German soil.

## The West German Response

The West German reaction was not what the Soviets had hoped for. The Germans did not consider the Soviet actions to be a simple gesture of concern, but further evidence of Soviet ham-fisted and brutal occupation policy. The German public was horrified by the brutality of Soviet troops in suppressing the disturbances in East Germany, and no German politician could argue for conciliation. The Bundestag (West German parliament), under considerable public pressure, mobilized two divisions and moved them up to the border opposite the two main roads into East Germany. At the same time, Bundestag representatives tried to make clear to Soviet officials at the embassy in Bonn that this should not be construed as a military threat, merely a substantive action showing how concerned the Federal Republic was about the deteriorating situation in East Germany.

August was a nightmare in East Germany. Rather than the disturbances subsiding, they continued. The Soviet forces began to slowly disarm the East German forces. Tanks and other equipment were called in for special overhaul, only to have certain vital parts become suddenly "unavailable." East German Army units were put through particularly vigorous training, using up what small inventories of live ammunition were on hand. But Soviet officers were shocked at the level of pilferage from stockpiles and were fearful of how much equipment had been squirreled away by dissident troops. During the second week of August, they would discover just how large this cache had become.

On 7 August, Berlin witnessed a large demonstration, ostensibly to show solidarity with the victims of the Leipzig catastrophe. The Soviets decided that the Germans would not be reliable enough to control the uprising, and used their own security forces. The problem was much the same as in Leipzig. The Soviet Interior Army forces troops were young recruits, many from Central Asia and the Caucasus. They were not well equipped to handle crowds, and were poorly trained. When confronted by large crowds, they panicked and began using their weapons. Although the German marchers were mainly from church groups, several clandestine resistance groups, army deserters, and NKFD terrorists were also in the city. When the Soviets tried using weapons to break up the demonstrations, they came under fire themselves. This led to a bloody melee, with the Soviets firing at the innocent crowds, not able to discern the riflemen in buildings nearby.

Although the kasernes for the German 1st Motor Rifle Division[5] nearby were given close scrutiny by Soviet forces, no one expected any kind of concerted anti-Soviet action from them. The Soviets trusted that their informers would warn them well in advance of any likely disturbances. Unbeknownst to them, the division was a hotbed of anti-Soviet sentiment. The German political officers who normally acted as the main conduits for internal control were in fact some of the main instigators of clandestine anti-Soviet agitation. The informer network had been turned on the Soviets. The Soviets were told that the situation in the division was calm, and that the units were still loyal. On the surface, this appeared to be the case. But a clandestine organization had been building up since late July, with plans to attack the cordon around West Berlin and permit a massive escape of East German troops into the western part of the city. The group did not have sufficient arms to directly confront the Soviets

---

5. The Warsaw Pact term "motor rifle" is applied to military units that NATO usually calls "mechanized infantry."

on the battlefield, but felt they were armed well enough to get through the border defenses. They even had some armored vehicles ready to go.

When fighting broke out in the city on 7 August, and news of the massacres began to filter back to the kasernes, the 1st Motor Rifle Division insurgents modified their plans. They decided to open a breach on the southwestern edge of the inner-city barrier near Treptow Park, and keep it open by force if necessary to help in the escape of any civilians who could manage to reach the site.

## The Treptow Park Incident

The border breach by the German troops took place on Saturday night, 9 August. The Soviet officers were getting plastered, as is the Soviet Army tradition for Saturday nights, and in violation of the usual rules, enlisted personnel also had been provided with alcohol to keep up morale after the most recent Berlin troubles. German soldiers, dressed in Soviet officers' uniforms with faked passes, were able to move about 1,200 troops out of their kasernes, drive into the city past Schonefeld airport, and deploy opposite the inner-city barrier by about 0100 early Sunday morning. Soviet troops were either lured away or killed, and the engineers set about clearing a path through the minefields and barriers. A defensive perimeter was set up covering about eight city blocks. The leaders of the insurgency had already contacted other underground leaders and told them to prepare a demonstration for the following morning at the Soviet Memorial in Treptow Park. The underground leaders had no idea what the soldiers were planning. The troops also managed to set up an improvised radio station, which would be used to broadcast to the city at large once the action had begun.

The West German border police knew what was happening before the Soviets did. In the early morning hours, a small team of East German Army insurgents sneaked across the border and made contact with German border police. The police informed Bonn of the action, but it took some hours before the Federal Republic officials began to comprehend what was happening. Many West German officials felt it was a Soviet provocation. This action was bound to drag the Federal Republic into the East German crisis, but the results could not be predicted with any certainty.

On the morning of Sunday, 9 August, a rather large demonstration began. Soviet troops moved into the area with plans to disperse the group as soon as it was convenient. Special KGB Border Guards[6] units had been brought in to replace the hopeless Interior Army forces. Soviet officers watching the disturbance were flabbergasted when they heard demonstration leaders announce over bullhorns that a breach had been made in the wall on the opposite street, and that people interested in doing so could flee into West Berlin without hindrance. The crowd itself was quite shaken by the news, but soon there was a rush, mainly by young people, down the streets toward the wall.

The demonstration turned into pandemonium. The Soviets began firing into the area, then tried to press their way into the crowd in an attempt to reach the wall. East German soldiers had set up cordons to prevent this. The Soviet troops were in fact outnumbered by the Germans, and when fighting broke out, the Soviets hastily withdrew. It took nearly two hours for the Soviets to regroup and move up reinforcements. Regular army units and tanks were then brought up, and the Soviets became aware that the West Germans were moving their own troops and police to areas opposite the breach in the wall. News of the action had reached people all over town, and it was proving nearly impossible to move troops through the city due to the enormous crowds in the streets.

The local commander, Col. Yuriy Shevchenko, had about a regiment of motor rifle troops and KGB Border Guards, and about twelve tanks. He was ordered to seal the breach at all costs. His units fought rear guards from the insurgents for nearly two hours, without being able to make much headway. The Germans were obviously well entrenched and well positioned, and Shevchenko simply didn't have the force needed to overcome them. More and more army units were brought up as the day dragged on, but some units were hit by sniper fire, and others were simply bogged down inside massive crowds, which showed little willingness to disperse. Some Soviet commanders were reluctant to use gunfire for fear of provoking more action, but other units were not so squeamish.

By Monday morning, Soviet units had managed to approach the breach on both sides and were firing their tanks into the no-man's-land. The fire was striking buildings on the West German side, which NATO officers had warned Soviet liaison officers in West Berlin would not be tolerated. On the West German side, huge crowds had gathered to see what

---

6. The KGB Border Guards are a paramilitary force used to patrol the Soviet Border. They are equipped like light infantry, and are considered more politically reliable than average military units.

was happening and to voice their support of their German compatriots from the other side of the wall.

Around 1100, the unexpected happened again. During a lull in the fighting, when West German and Soviet military officers were trying to negotiate a cease-fire, the West German crowds managed to surge forward into the barrier area, forming a human wall to protect fleeing East German civilians. A local Soviet officer, confused as to the identity of the civilians in the barrier zone, ordered his troops to open fire on them. West German police and soldiers, aghast at what was happening, returned fire against the Soviet troops.

For about two hours, there was sporadic firing across the barrier strip until the last elements of the East German Army insurgents began withdrawing. The Soviets tried to chase the fleeing troops across the barrier, only to encounter fire from West German police and soldiers on the opposite side. A cease-fire was arranged later in the afternoon as cooler heads prevailed.

## The Berlin Blockade

The Kremlin was outraged by the West German role in the latest riots. Hard-liners insisted that all roads leading into Berlin be closed, and air routes suspended. Others pointed out that this was not simply an infringement on German sovereignty, but that it violated Soviet understandings with the U.S., Britain, and France. It was pointed out that the U.S. had tried to distance itself from West German actions, and had tried to cool down the situation. This was read by the hard-liners as an American unwillingness to back the more strident German demands for Soviet troop withdrawals to defuse the continuing unrest. The hard-liners believed that the U.S. wanted to continue its gradual troop withdrawals begun in 1991 under the MBFR (Mutual Balanced Force Reduction) treaty. In the end, this line of reasoning prevailed, and the blockade was announced, beginning 15 August.

The Germans responded by threatening to challenge the air blockade. On the first day of the blockade, the Germans did indeed send in two military transport aircraft with fighter escort. The last flight was attacked by Soviet fighters, and the transport was lost. The Bundeswehr was mobilized and units began moving out of their kasernes toward the inter-German frontier. The Germans began to concentrate their forces opposite the two main roads into Berlin. They felt that their response would force NATO, and especially the U.S., to take a stronger line against Soviet actions, but the United States was extremely critical of the German move. Surprisingly, France backed Germany. Europeans were outraged by Soviet brutality in East Germany, and only fear of another European war led to restraint.

Although the U.S. refused to back the German actions, there was considerable fear in NATO that war was possible. The Soviets seemed unable to control the German situation. Demonstrations had begun in Poland and Czechoslovakia. Soviet control over the vital three Northern Tier Warsaw Pact states was being seriously questioned. The U.S. and NATO leadership was split on how to respond to threats of unilateral West German military action. It was unthinkable that the Germans could engage in military operations in East Germany without dragging in NATO. The Bundeswehr, although a very capable force, was significantly inferior in size and strength to Soviet forces in East Germany, to say nothing of reinforcements. The U.S. hard-liners argued that it was time to back the Germans and try to extract concession out of the Soviets as the price for forcing the Germans back away from the brink. A UN peacekeeping force in East Germany was suggested as an alternative to heavy infusion of more Soviet forces.

The battle for the Berlin air corridor began in earnest on 27 August, when the Germans resumed air flights due to food shortages in the embattled city. A Soviet attempt to shoot down two more transports was met by heavy German fighter activity and the loss of several Soviet fighter aircraft. One of the transports was shot down on the outskirts of Berlin by a surface-to-air missile (SAM). The Germans responded by bombing the SAM site, as well as several others that had been firing. Air battles continued for four days. On 1 September, a German Hawk missile battery shot down a Soviet MiG-29 Fulcrum fighter that had followed a flight of returning German fighters into West German airspace. The Soviets responded by sending a squadron of Su-24 Fencers strike aircraft to attack the Hawk site. They mistook an American Hawk site for the nearby German site. The forces of U.S. Army-Europe were put on war alert. France announced that it would abide by its NATO obligations, and in the spirit of the 1991 Franco-German military pact, would begin moving its forces forward into the Federal Republic.

The critical issue for the Kremlin leadership was the attitude of the U.S. The Americans were discouraged by the German crisis, especially in the wake of improving USSR-USA relations following the MBFR treaty in 1991. But the new Democratic U.S. president was an unknown quantity. The Soviet ambassador in Washington requested an urgent meeting in the last days of August. The Soviets came back from the meeting deeply troubled and uncertain of U.S. intentions. The president had spent much of the meeting in monologues about how a new treaty was needed to prevent the use of tactical nuclear arms or chemical weapons in a European context. The Soviets had expected a certain amount of discussion about this, due to the current treaty negotiations on these issues. And they knew that these subjects were a personal hobbyhorse of the new president since the election. But they were bothered by the amount of attention given them. They were concerned that this indicated that the Americans viewed the war as being inevitable, and that the Americans were hinting that they would not go nuclear if the Soviets did not.

This is not what the U.S. government had intended to say, but the new president, not at all experienced in international diplomacy, had conveyed the wrong impression. State Department officials visited the embassy the following day in the hope of clarifying the U.S. position. But by this time, a special Kremlin adviser was on his way back to the USSR with a firsthand report for the General Secretary. He was not optimistic. The American position was that the Soviet Union should withdraw all but four divisions from East Germany in return for U.S. withdrawal of all its ground forces from continental Europe.

## War Council in the Kremlin

The Kremlin meeting of 9 September brought together the top party and military leadership. The situation in Germany had not improved, and the Polish situation continued to deteriorate. The Polish Army was nearly useless, and the Czechoslovak Army was little better. There was considerable concern on the part of the top military leadership that NATO planned to exploit the Warsaw Pact dissension in an operation aimed at severing East Germany from Soviet control. The U.S. proposal about joint U.S.-Soviet troop reductions was taken as a sly American attempt to further weaken Soviet control in East Germany and to pave the way for a German reunification.

Although the U.S. had not yet mobilized, most European NATO states were either at or near war alert. Furthermore, the KGB indicated that the U.S. was beginning clandestine efforts to recall American-owned merchant shipping under flags of convenience, and reestablish them under U.S. control. Most American warships were behaving as though it were peacetime, but there seemed to be an attempt to get a large number of ships to sea. The Americans were making very conspicuous efforts to keep their strategic forces at low readiness levels, and were curtailing their bomber flights. Some of the more astute Communist party officials became concerned that the KGB was "cooking" the intelligence to suit the biases of hard-liners in the KGB leadership.

Another European war seemed quite possible. What concerned the Kremlin leadership was that NATO was growing in strength while the USSR was weakening. Warsaw Pact strength continued to drain away in the infuriating string of disturbances, hooliganism, and anti-Soviet actions of the Germans and Poles. The Soviet Army had never placed great reliance on the Warsaw Pact armies. But Soviet logistics lines ran through Poland and Germany, and the growth of Central European anti-Soviet terrorist groups threatened these vital links.

The Soviet Defense Minister was instructed to present a list of military options. The suggestion that Berlin be seized was dismissed. Such an action would certainly lead to U.S. mobilization and increase the likelihood of a European war with NATO at full strength. Regional options were discussed, but were discarded as being too byzantine and inconclusive. Marshal Ogarkov finally described the most obvious choice: a conventional attack aimed at seizing West Germany before NATO was fully mobilized. The Soviet General Staff expressed their measured belief that the Soviet forces now available in Germany and Czechoslovakia could push to the Franco-German border in seven days. The war would inevitably lead to involvement of American, British, and French troops.

The plan lacked any real strategic rationale. The main impetus was concern over NATO mobilization and the growing pessimism of the Soviet leadership over whether there could be any solution to the current crisis short of war. The gradual U.S. withdrawal from leadership in NATO over the past few years, while long sought by the USSR, was now seen as a major problem. The Europeans, and especially the new Franco-German coalition, was pushing for pan-European goals at the expense of both the U.S. and the USSR. If the Soviet Union hesitated while NATO gradually mobilized its strength, by early winter NATO might have enough force to seize East Germany. A lightning war before NATO was fully prepared seemed like a lesser evil than waiting until NATO inevitably struck across the German border.

This viewpoint was far from being unanimously held by the Kremlin leadership. Many Ministry of Foreign Affairs officials felt that the hardliners were exaggerating NATO cohesiveness in this matter. But Mikhail Gorbachev had given over control of the Foreign Ministry to a new generation of nationalistic Russian conservatives as the price for support of his domestic programs. The KGB and the Soviet Army would not trust the Foreign Ministry in matters of arms control and arms reduction unless they were securely in the hands of officials sympathetic to their viewpoints. And the military was certainly not going to accept further cuts in its forces unless there were assurances that arms control treaties would not include concessions like those found in the INF (Intermediate Nuclear Forces) and MBFR treaties. The Foreign Ministry was now populated by officials who tended to have an instinctive distrust of the U.S., and who viewed American actions as a smoke screen for NATO preparations. Their biases tended to warp their interpretation and reporting of discussions with the U.S. government and cast a decidedly pessimistic view of U.S. intentions in the crisis.

The Soviet Army leadership was not happy about the prospects for war. They were aware, more than any element of the Soviet government, of the weaknesses in the Soviet armed forces. But they were deeply dismayed at what was taking place in Germany. And they were terrified by the prospect of trying to fight a conventional war against a NATO that had had months to mobilize. They warily leaned toward the notion of a preemptive strike against NATO. Soviet operational doctrine favored offensive actions, and the General Staff still thought the Soviet Army had some distinctive advantages.

The KGB was likewise divided about future plans of action; they were not worried so much about the military threat as the domestic political repercussions of the German crisis. Gorbachev's policies of domestic reform had led to a steady increase in consumer goods, personal liberties, and other benefits for the average Soviet citizen. The problem was that this had nurtured a real sense of growing expectations. The average Soviet worker was coming to expect the situation to continue to improve, even though work discipline was as bad as ever, and productivity had stagnated. The strikes in the Baltic had occurred not only in the Latvian and Estonian areas; the shipyards in Leningrad were just as worrisome, and the strikes were now spreading south to auto factories in the Urals and to the industries along the Black Sea. The KGB was troubled by the curbs that Gorbachev had put on their internal activity, and were convinced that further internal disintegration was inevitable. War would not cure these problems, but would create conditions under which the national consciousness could be refocused back to national concerns and away from the lassitude and decadence of the past few years. Thus the KGB officials tended to support the plan to preempt NATO.

The mood at the Kremlin conference was somber. There was an underlying anxiety about the survivability of the Communist system when faced by the rigors of war. The more perceptive party and army leaders wondered to themselves which was the more appropriate historical model for the current crisis. Were they facing another 1914? Was the Soviet Army merely an immense, rotted anachronism about to be shattered by the professional armies of NATO? Would the Soviet Army suffer the fate of the Tsarist army in World War I, precipitating a revolution that would over-throw the regime? Or was the Soviet Union embarking upon another Great Patriotic War as in 1941–45? Such a war would be a horrible experience to be sure, but one that would cement the nation together and demonstrate the vitality of the Soviet system in the face of dire adversity. Certainly most leaders looked back on the Great Patriotic War as one of the few bright spots in Soviet history. The melancholy nostalgia engendered by the legends of that war was one of the few consolations for the Soviet leaders when facing the grim realities of another European war.

By the end of the three-day conference, the Kremlin leadership had convinced itself that the army's plan, code-named Operation Buran (*buran* meaning "blizzard"), would preempt a likely NATO attempt to seize East Germany. There was no longer any discussion of whether NATO actually planned such an operation. It was taken for granted as the con-sensus view of the leadership. The only issue now was when to attack, and how to restrict the war to the conventional phase. The army urged that Operation Buran be launched as soon as possible, preferably by the end of September.

## Moscow Staff Briefing

Colonel Kucherenko reached the meeting room and found the staff officers of the Southwestern Front already seated and anxious. The upper elements of the armed forces knew that something was about to happen, and greeted the occasion with a mixture of apprehension and professional excitement. Soviet tactical commanders may not compare well to their NATO counterparts, but the higher staff officers were a different story. They were intelligent, widely read, and well educated. Their training and approach were based on the pattern of the much-touted German staff system from earlier in the century. They knew that much was expected of them.

Operation Buran was familiar to them, since it was simply a variation on a well-rehearsed war plan code-named Burya (storm). The older Burya plan was typical of the elegant operational plans of the Soviet General Staff. It offered an elaborate set of preconditions for the war and a subtle attempt to place the NATO opponent in the weakest possible position.

The original Burya plan was based on a complex coordination between the Ministry of Defense and the Foreign Ministry in the months preceding a planned attack against NATO. The plan suggested that a major objective of Soviet foreign policy would be to keep the NATO forces at a low state of readiness. This could not be easily accomplished using traditional *maskirovka* (deception and concealment) techniques such as camouflage of troop transports, false radio traffic, and the like. In the modern age of satellite surveillance, it was very hard to mask large troop movements. Instead of trying to mask the buildup itself, the plan was to mask Soviet intentions. The USSR would stage a provocation that would lead to the partial mobilization of Soviet and NATO forces. The war plan left the matter of the provocation open, since it presumed that initiation of the plan had been provoked by some specific crisis. Ironically, the usual provocation used in most staff war games concerned Berlin or the inter-German border. In the wake of the provocation, the Foreign Ministry would make concessions to NATO that would restore calm between NATO and the Warsaw Pact. In a few months, the USSR would find something else to take offense at, leading to another partial mobilization, probably followed by NATO counteractions. This cat-and-mouse game would continue for six months to a year. Characterized by rising and falling tensions, and a string of minor crises, it was aimed to lull NATO into a sort of complacency. The final crisis and troop mobilization would be the real one. By this time, NATO would probably be tired of the incessant games, and regard the latest Soviet mobilization as mere bluster. NATO would be conned away from mobilizing its own forces, viewing evidence of Soviet mobilization as just another futile gesture connected with a new phase of belligerent Soviet foreign policy.

The Burya plan had three variants, called Red Burya, Yellow Burya, and Blue Burya. The variants had different presumptions about Soviet forces and NATO readiness. Red Burya presumed that Soviet forces would

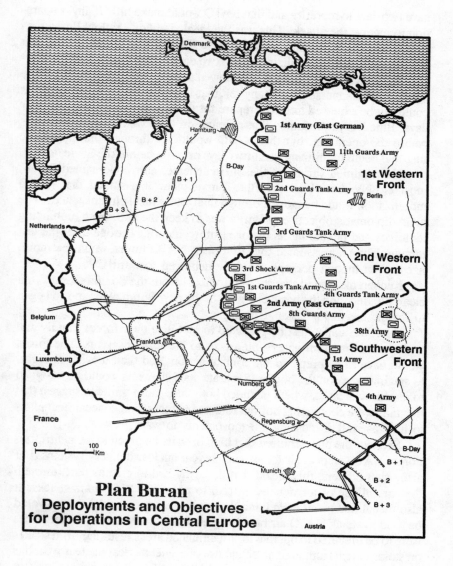

**Plan Buran**
**Deployments and Objectives**
**for Operations in Central Europe**

have two days to mobilize and that NATO would make little if any preparation to receive the attack. This was the ideal situation. Yellow Burya presumed that the Soviet forces would have four days to mobilize, and that NATO would begin mobilizing one to two days before the start of the Warsaw Pact attack. This situation was viewed as being more realistic by many Soviet staff planners, since many felt that the GSFG with reinforcements could not be expected to fully prepare for war operations in less than four days. Blue Burya presumed that preparation time would begin four days before the operation, but that NATO would see through the diplomatic ruse and begin mobilizing itself two days or more before the Soviet attack.

The modified variant of the Burya scheme, now code-named Buran, most closely resembled the Blue Burya plan. It assumed that NATO mobilization would be more thorough than under ideal circumstances. The main diplomatic objective of Buran was to keep the U.S. from mobilizing its forces and beginning its major reinforcement of Europe until the last minute. The plan assumed that European NATO forces would be mobilized, even though perhaps not fully deployed forward.

Kucherenko found that the staff officers from the Southwestern Front clearly understood the basic elements of the new Buran plan, and so began to review the major tasks at hand.

First, the staffs must be prepared to mobilize their forces rapidly and with the minimum of observable traces to Western observers. The forces would have to be prepared for combat action, and then moved, at night, to staging areas on the border. Separate staff elements would be assigned to maskirovka tasks, which included both false radio traffic to suggest that the units were conducting normal routine business, and concealment plans to hide as well as possible all movements forward.

Second, the plan required that high priority be given to the neutralization of NATO tactical air forces and tactical nuclear delivery systems. For army staff officers, this meant that the army had to play its part, through the careful use of air defense forces, to blunt any NATO air attacks. It also meant that army rocket and artillery assets and special forces would be used to attack NATO air bases and nuclear storage areas. Soviet forces were to be prepared to operate in contaminated areas resulting from strikes on storage areas, although no actual use of Soviet tactical nuclear weapons was presumed. Possible Soviet use of chemical weapons should be kept in mind, and troops would be issued stern warnings about remaining prepared for the use of chemical weapons.

Third, the foremost objective of the army forces would be the neutralization of NATO tactical defenses by skillful use of fire and maneuver by Soviet armed forces. This would be accomplished at the following norms. The initial NATO defenses would be overwhelmed and breached in two to three days of fighting at depths of fifty kilometers. It was presumed that divisional forward detachments, such as independent tank regiments, would be committed on B+2 or B+3 to begin the exploitation of breaches in NATO forward defenses. By B+3, the Soviet Armies would begin to commit their Operational Maneuver Groups (OMGs), in the form of reserve tank divisions, to further exploit any successful penetrations by divisional forward detachments. Front OMGs, in the form of Unified Army Corps (UACs), would be committed at the discretion of front commanders when the forward detachments and OMGs had successfully ruptured the NATO defenses. The OMGs and UACs would be the shock forces that would spearhead the Soviet forces' deep penetration, followed by additional Soviet units for the encirclement and destruction of NATO armies.

The Southwestern Front would launch its attack out of assembly areas in the Bohemian Forest in western Czechoslovakia, into Bavaria. The first echelon would consist of 1st Army and 4th Army, each with two motor rifle divisions and one tank division. Each army had about 1,000 tanks, and more than 1,500 other armored vehicles of various types. Front reserves, or second echelon, would be the 38th Army, which would be in place by B+2 with three more divisions. Additional reinforcements would be available under some circumstances. These nine Soviet divisions would face from five to six partially mobilized NATO divisions—the U.S. 1st Armored Division, the German 4th Panzergrenadier, the 1st Mountain and 10th Panzer Divisions, and the French 3d and 5th Armored Divisions.

The 4th Army, the southernmost of the attacking armies, would drive toward Munich with the Alps on its left flank and the Danube River on its right. Operations from Czechoslovakia into Austria would be conducted by a separate Czech-Soviet Army. The objective of the 4th Army would be to defeat the German 4th Panzergrenadier and 1st Mountain Division in the initial defensive positions. The French 3d Armored Division could be expected to be encountered defending the approaches to Stuttgart and would probably be dealt with by a left hook by the neighboring 1st Army on B+3. The largest city in the area, Munich, would be dealt with by B+3.

The 1st Army would advance on either side of the Schabische Alps. Its right boundary with the neighboring 8th Guards Army was a line run-

# Southwestern Front

**Unified Army Corps**
**Artillery Division**
Heavy Artillery Brigade
Scud Missile Brigade
Air Defense Missile Brigade (SA-12)
Airmobile Assault Brigade
Spetsnaz Brigade
Helicopter Transport Regiment
**Chemical Defense Brigade**
**Engineer Brigade**
**Fuel Pipeline Brigade**
**Motor Transport Brigade**
2 Pontoon Bridge Regiments
2 Assault Crossing Battalions
**Signal Brigade**
Intelligence Regiment
Radio Interception Regiment
Radio/Radar Interception Regiment
Radio Jamming Regiment
Air Defense Jamming Regiment
Radio Relay Battalion

| 1st Army | 4th Army | 38th Army |
|---|---|---|
| Tank Division | Tank Division | Tank Division |
| Motor Rifle Division | Motor Rifle Division | Motor Rifle Division |
| Motor Rifle Division | Motor Rifle Division | Motor Rifle Division |
| Air Defense Brigade (SA-11) | Air Defense Brigade (SA-11) | Air Defense Brigade (SA-11) |
| Ballistic Missile Brigade (SS-21) | Ballistic Missile Brigade (SS-21) | Ballistic Missile Brigade (SS-21) |
| Attack Helicopter Regiment | Attack Helicopter Regiment | Attack Helicopter Regiment |
| Engineer Brigade | Engineer Brigade | Engineer Brigade |
| Signals Regiment | Signals Regiment | Signals Regiment |
| Motor Transport Regiment | Motor Transport Regiment | Motor Transport Regiment |
| Pontoon Bridge Regiment | Pontoon Bridge Regiment | Pontoon Bridge Regiment |
| Assault Crossing Battalion | Assault Crossing Battalion | Assault Crossing Battalion |
| Chemical Defense Battalion | Chemical Defense Battalion | Chemical Defense Battalion |
| Intelligence Battalion | Intelligence Battalion | Intelligence Battalion |
| Radio/Radar Interception Battalion | Radio/Radar Interception Battalion | Radio/Radar Interception Battalion |
| Radio Interception Battalion | Radio Interception Battalion | Radio Interception Battalion |
| Early Warning Battalion | Early Warning Battalion | Early Warning Battalion |
| Radio Relay Battalion | Radio Relay Battalion | Radio Relay Battalion |
| Long Range Recon Company | Long Range Recon Company | Long Range Recon Company |
| Spetsnaz Company | Spetsnaz Company | Spetsnaz Company |
| Helicopter Liaison Squadron | Helicopter Liaison Squadron | Helicopter Liaison Squadron |

ning roughly through Nurnberg to Stuttgart and then Karlsruhe on the Franco-German frontier. On B+4, in conjunction with an influx of reserves from the 38th Army second echelon, the 1st Army would swing southward into the Wurtemberg region, cutting off any retreating NATO forces from the 4th Army attacks and securing the entire Franco-German frontier in the operations zone of the Southwestern Front. Elements of the U.S. 1st Armored Division could be expected to be encountered around Nurnberg. But the main opposition was expected to come from the 10th Panzer Division and the French 3d and 5th Armored Divisions.

The staffs from the Southwestern Front were handed envelopes containing more explicit details of the operation. B-Day was scheduled to be 30 September, only a week off. The basic concepts were pretty well understood from previous staff war games using the earlier Burya plans. The attack on this front was clearly not the main one, given the relatively modest forces involved. This was in large measure due to the terrain. The main Soviet blow would come up north in the Fulda Gap region in the 2d Western Front zone of operations. But the fighting on this front would be quite intense, given the fact that German divisions would be in the initial defensive positions.

The terrain was not the easiest for mechanized operations. The initial attack would be launched out of a hilly region across an area that was heavily forested. More to the point, there were very few major east-west roads. What roads existed were likely to have heavy concentrations of trucks and logistics support equipment on them, which would make ripe targets for attacking NATO aircraft. If the Germans prepared their defenses well, infantry forces with antitank missiles could substantially delay any force moving through this region. It was also a major headache to plan logistical links across the Sudeten Mountains into Czech Bohemia. The handful of mountain roads would funnel most of the supply trucks into congested arteries that would make juicy targets for NATO fighter-bombers. The staff would have to put special emphasis on providing heavy air defense coverage in the mountains to keep out the NATO aircraft.

The aim of the first day's operation would be to clear the hilly and forested areas along the border. A difficult area would be the Rachel National Park in the 4th Army sector. Beautiful scenery, lousy battlefield! The second day's operation would be to reach the eastern bank of the Danube River in the 4th Army sector by afternoon, in anticipation of a major river crossing operation that evening. The 1st Army would reach the Danube the following day. The Danube was a significant natural obstacle, and defenses along the river could be expected to be substantial. Breaching the Danube would be the most significant single event of the offensive. If the river could not be breached in enough depth, the attack on this front would be seriously compromised. Some of the staff recalled problems they had encountered in previous war games. In several recent war games, the 4th Army had failed to penetrate the initial border area for more than two days, and had serious problems with supply routes.

One of the officers expressed surprise that so little use was being made of other Warsaw Pact armies. Kucherenko related a popular joke to underline his lack of confidence in the use of the Warsaw Pact forces. "A Polish soldier stumbles across a magic lantern by the shores of the Vistula and the genie grants him three wishes. 'For my first wish,' says the soldier, 'I want the Chinese Army to invade Poland!' The genie complies. Months later, the invasion over, the genie asks the soldier for his second wish. He says again that he wishes the Chinese Army to invade Poland. The genie, a bit bewildered, complies with his wish. Several months later, the genie returns and asks the soldier for his third wish. The soldier asks again that the Chinese Army invade Poland. The genie, unable to restrain his curiosity any further, asks the Pole why he wished the Chinese to invade his country. 'Ah, but don't you see,' he said, 'for the Chinese to invade Poland three times, their army would have to pass through Russia six times!'"

It was a well-known tale, but the officers laughed anyway. The Poles and Czechs were being used in the overall operation, but in less critical areas, such as Denmark and Austria.

The meeting broke up into small groups as each front, army, and divisional staff group huddled together to discuss the plans and to prepare questions for Colonel Kucherenko. The briefing packet was not very explicit about the current disposition of NATO forces, but Kucherenko explained that additional details would become available over the next few days.

As the meeting broke up late in the afternoon, Kucherenko and his colleague, Colonel Burlatskiy, finally had a chance to chat. Burlatskiy would be with the staff of 1st Army in its attacks toward Nurnberg. Kucherenko asked Burlatskiy's opinion about the likely course of the war in his sector.

"So, Stepan Romanovich," Burlatskiy replied, "I see you've favored our 4th Army with a real plum assignment." It was all too obvious that Yevgeniy Burlatskiy was being sarcastic.

"Yevgeniy, you know that we don't have any additional forces ready for you since the bosses cut our forces in Czechoslovakia two years ago. I know the terrain is bad. But you people will have much more artillery than average, and more air support."

Burlatskiy was not satisfied. "Stepan, I do not mean to be rude. But you STAVKA boys with all your computer models of our Great Patriotic War battles forget one thing. It's not the 1940s. It's the 1990s. Your expectations for our advance through Germany are grossly unrealistic. We'll be lucky to fight our way out of those forests in a week."

Stepan Kucherenko was disturbed by his friend's pessimism, all the more so because he respected his judgment. Burlatskiy was no hack or careerist. He came from a long line of military officers and took great pride in his profession. Like many staff officers, Burlatskiy was an avid student of military history. His particular interest was the impact of technology on modern warfare. It was Burlatskiy's conviction that the general Soviet view of modern warfare was too heavily flavored by its Great Patriotic War experiences. There was too much of a tendency to regard the current battlefield as a repeat of the 1943–45 battlefield, just with more firepower.

Burlatskiy explained to Kucherenko that his opinion was quite different. He believed that the heavy diffusion of antiarmor weapons to the infantry and the artillery raised the specter of World War I rather than World War II. Artillery in World War I was the primary killing arm, and coupled with the machine gun, dominated the battlefield. The tank came along and eventually changed the balance on the battlefield. The tank could not be easily stopped by machine guns or artillery. The balance of power on the battlefield shifted from weapons like artillery and machine guns, which favored the defense, to mobile weapons like the tank, which favored maneuver and the offensive. This became very evident in World War II. But since then, the infantry had become very heavily armed with potent antitank weapons, especially guided antitank missiles. In World War II, artillery was almost useless against tanks in the traditional indirect fire mode. But now, with submunition ammunition and guided artillery rounds, the artillery also weighed in against the tank. The tank was far more threatened than in the past war. And if the tank and its other armored offspring were threatened, offensives were threatened. Burlatskiy suggested that the new NATO technologies might favor the tactical defender and drain much of the mobility and maneuver out of the vaunted Soviet tank armies. His opinions would prove to be all too accurate, much to the consternation of the Soviet Army.

## Analysis

Under what circumstances would the Soviet Union attack NATO forces in Central Europe? As this fictional account suggests, the most likely cause would be a global situation that posed a direct threat to the USSR. A collapse of the Central European buffer states, especially East Germany, is one of the more plausible possibilities. The Soviets would fear that the collapse of East Germany could cause a domino effect in the other Northern Tier Warsaw Pact countries (East Germany, Poland, and Czechoslovakia). The scenario also suggests that other forces could be at work in precipitating a Soviet decision. War is not always a rational affair. Distortions in intelligence, misperceptions about U.S. and NATO intentions, and internal troubles could bias Kremlin decision-makers into favoring war as a political option.

The decision to initiate a war with NATO would not be taken lightly. The Soviets would have to consider the very real likelihood that the war would spill over into unacceptable areas. Certainly, the possibility of the war escalating into a strategic nuclear exchange with the U.S. is a real impediment to any Soviet consideration of using conventional forces in Europe. But there are other concerns as well. How would British or French leaders respond to Soviet air attacks on their countries? Would they contemplate using nuclear weapons if their countries were threatened by invasion? Would the U.S. use its tactical nuclear weapons if the collapse of West Germany seemed imminent? What would the limits of a "conventional" war be? Would the war spread to a confrontation between U.S. and Soviet naval forces in the Pacific? Would the Soviet Union confront NATO conventional forces in the Balkans, or in Turkey? Is a regional war in Europe possible without the great risk of a global war like World War II?

Another source of anxiety for Soviet war planners is China. There is an old Russian joke from the 1970s: What two languages are taught in Soviet schools? Why Hebrew and Chinese, of course. Hebrew for those who are leaving, and Chinese for those who are staying. It must seem absurd to most Americans or Europeans that the Russians are fearful of Chinese ambitions against them. Yet concern over the Chinese threat has remained a staple of Soviet strategic thinking since the 1960s. The Russians regard the Chinese in much the same way that Americans regard the Russians—that is, a more primitive society, and therefore one more likely to resort to war since they have less to lose.

This thinking has a direct impact on any Soviet war plans for a confrontation with NATO. The enormous Soviet force structure is based on the notion that it should be adequate to deal with any combination of enemies. That is, it should be able to handle both China and NATO simultaneously. The Soviet Union has about eighty divisions in war-ready condition, and a further one hundred thirty divisions that could be brought up to strength in about a month. In contrast, the U.S. has eighteen war-ready divisions, and about ten divisions that could be brought up to strength in a relatively short period. The twenty-eight U.S. divisions have more troops than average Soviet divisions, but not that much more combat power.

In a confrontation with NATO, a substantial portion of the Soviet armed forces would remain in Asia, opposite the Chinese frontier, to deter any Chinese attack. To Americans or Europeans this may seem a bit imprudent. Why maintain a large force opposite the quiet Chinese frontier, when they could be used in an actual war? Yet the Soviets did precisely that in World War II. A surprisingly large portion of the Soviet Army remained stationed in the Far East, to counter any actions by the Japanese. Even in the grim days of 1941–42, the Soviets left 2,000 to 3,000 precious tanks in the Far East. Soviet perceptions of the threat against their country are very different from U.S. or European assessments.

## Why Is the Soviet Army So Large?

From a Western point of view, the very large size of the Soviet Ground Forces, more than two hundred divisions, seems excessive for legitimate needs. The Soviet Union alone has about 53,000 tanks. This compares to about 15,000 for the U.S. The disparity in forces between the USSR and NATO leads many to conclude that the Soviet Union plans to use these forces in an offensive fashion against NATO.

Yet in the forty-some years since World War II, there have been very few threats of the use of Soviet conventional forces against Europe. Through all the years of cold war, NATO forces have been badly outnumbered and badly outgunned. Although NATO may feel that Soviet advantages in the total number of most conventional weapons lead to the temptation to use them, Soviet perceptions on the issue differ. For staff planners like the fictional Colonel Kucherenko, these perceptions reside in the back of his mind, shaping the way he plans for the confrontation with NATO.

NATO forces in Central Europe have about 13,000 tanks, and about thirty tank and mechanized divisions. With reinforcements, that could be brought up to more than 15,000 tanks in a month. The Soviet Union and the Northern Tier Warsaw Pact states have about 17,000 tanks in place, and fifty-five tank and mechanized divisions. This is not substantially more than NATO at full mobilization. However, the Soviets also have well over 23,000 more tanks in European Russia and in nearby areas that could be brought to bear in a confrontation with NATO. This works out to a 1:2.6 ratio in favor of the USSR.

There is little debate that the Soviets have more tanks than NATO, more artillery, more troops, and a general numerical superiority. The so-called "bean count" favors the USSR and the Warsaw Pact. But do these disparities really matter? A historical example might help explain Soviet perceptions of this situation. In 1941, when the Germans invaded the USSR, they used about 3,000 tanks. The Soviets had more than 25,000 tanks and armored vehicles. Many of the Soviet tanks were old, but then too, so were many of the German tanks. Although grossly outnumbered, the German panzer divisions smashed their far larger opponent. By the end of 1941, the Soviets had fewer than 3,000 tanks facing the Germans in European Russia, and the Germans had more than 2,000. The Soviets saw an enormous inventory of modern weapons swept away at very modest losses for the Nazi invader.

This historical example is not given to suggest that numbers do not matter, or that 1991 is the same as 1941. Numbers can matter, but they should not be seen as a clear, reliable indicator of combat power. In the victorious years of 1944–1945, the Red Army had more tanks than the Germans, but the disparity was nowhere as great as in 1941. They then had about a three-to-one advantage rather than the eight-to-one advantage of 1941. But the Soviets marched to victory in 1945 as they had failed to do in 1941. The crucial difference between 1941 and 1945 was that the Soviets had learned how to employ their tanks. Still, it took a significant numerical advantage to overcome the highly skilled Germans.

A similar picture could be portrayed in regard to other key types of weapons: aircraft, artillery, and antitank weapons. These historical patterns of Soviet inferiority in the tactical use of modern weapons are a contributory factor in the bloated size of the Soviet armed forces. What to a NATO observer seems an unnecessarily large number of weapons, to a Soviet military planner seems like a prudent total to balance a traditional Western advantage in the employment of high-technology weapons. Do these Western advantages still exist? Is the disparity as great as in 1941, or is it more similar to 1945? Has the modern Soviet Army managed to narrow the gap? Or indeed, is there no qualitative gap at all? The following chapters will examine how the Soviet armed forces are likely to perform against NATO at a tactical level with these quantity-versus-quality issues in mind.

In spite of poor tactical performance against Germany in World War II, the Soviet Union eventually prevailed. Why was this so? German apologists have long suggested that it was simply a matter of mass: The Russians had more troops, more tanks, more airplanes. The Germans claim to have been outnumbered but not outfought. There is a measure of truth to this. The Soviets certainly did enjoy significant numerical advantages. But there are some subtle issues that are important to understanding the way the Soviets fight wars.

To begin with, the argument that the Soviets won because of superiority in the numbers of weapons seems a bit disingenuous to anyone familiar with the USSR during World War II. It is usually assumed that the Soviet Union was an economic powerhouse like the U.S. or Germany. It was not. It had to import most of its advanced machine tools from the West. Its military trucks were little more than old license-produced Ford Model AAs with a coat of green paint. Not only was the Soviet military economy heavily dependent on the West for technology, but the Germans managed to gut most of the major industrial facilities. Soviet military industries were located mainly in areas of European Russia that the Germans managed to capture in 1941. The Soviet Union evacuated much of the factory equipment, but they were forced to reassemble the machinery in the Ural Mountains, often without adequate buildings.

In spite of these horrendous problems, the Soviets were able to outproduce the Germans in many key weapons categories, such as tanks and artillery. They carefully shepherded what modest industrial resources they had. They stopped or greatly curtailed production of locomotives, warships, automobiles, tractors, and many other types of equipment in favor of the raw essentials of war: tanks, artillery, small arms, aircraft, and ammunition. There is an old military adage that tactics are the realm of the armchair general and logistics the realm of the professional soldier. The Russians demonstrated a greater appreciation of the industrial underpinnings of modern war than the Germans, and this contributed greatly to their eventual victory. In contrast, German war industries were poorly directed, and suffered the additional disadvantage of a concentrated Anglo-American bombing campaign.

But piles of weapons do little good if poorly used, as the 1941 debacle revealed. It took the Soviets three years of bloody fighting to learn the tactics of modern mechanized warfare. The fighting in 1944–45 showed that the Soviets had learned these lessons well. It has long been assumed that the victories of 1944–45 were attributable to sheer brute force, of masses of men and machines overcoming the small, emaciated skeleton of the German Army. But over the past decade, military historians in the West have finally begun to pay closer attention to how and why the Soviets managed to develop an effective fighting machine from the wreckage of 1941. The German-inspired myths of the 1950s have gradually given way to a more sophisticated understanding of the roots of the Soviet victory. The conclusion of this new generation of historians is that the Soviets, although less skilled than the Germans at the tactical level, became proficient masters of the operational arts. It was this skill, as much as advantages in equipment, that gave the Soviets victory in 1945.

*Tactics* refer to the war-fighting techniques of small units, running the gamut from an infantry squad of a dozen men to a tank division of 10,000. The Germans were masters of these skills, arguably finer than most other Western armies, including the American and British. *Operational art* refers to the war-fighting techniques of large formations, from armies (two or three divisions) to fronts (two or three armies). Operational art is the bridge between tactics—the way that armies fight—and strategy—the aims for which armies fight. The Russians perfected their skills in the operational art in the later years of the Great Patriotic War, and were able to circumvent their shortcomings in the tactical skills.

The Soviets became masters of operational techniques ignored or poorly used by the Germans. For example, recent studies on Soviet operational art point to Soviet interest in maskirovka (deception) as an essential war-fighting skill. Soviet front commanders would cleverly hide real units and create fictitious phantom divisions. These deceptions would confuse the Germans as to the real situation confronting them. Expecting an attack by the phantom divisions, they would move their own forces to repel an attack in the wrong sector. In the "quiet" sector, where there appeared to be few forces, the attack would develop. German forces would be hit by massively superior Soviet forces, outnumbering them eight to one or ten to one. At these ratios, superior German tactical skills didn't really matter.

It was not that the Soviets actually enjoyed an eight-to-one or ten-to-one advantage over the whole front, but their skills in the operational arts permitted the Red Army to mass and employ its mediocre units with overwhelming force and with the greatest possible effectiveness.

The great debacle of the German Army Group Center in Byelorussia in the summer of 1944 is a classic case. Although little known in the West, this was one of the greatest defeats of the German Army in World War II. The Soviets managed to convince the Germans that the offensive would come in the Ukraine. It did not. It came in the poorly prepared Byelorussian region, leading to a massive loss of troops and equipment.

Among students of Soviet military affairs, it is now even becoming a cliché that the Soviets are masters of operational art. There is still a feeling that their tactical skills may not compare to those of their NATO counterparts, but that at higher leadership levels, the Soviets are likely to excel. What does this imply for Soviet operations in Central Europe against NATO?

The Soviets have obvious advantages over NATO in several key areas. The Soviets enjoy a unified command system: What the Soviet Union wishes, the rest of the Warsaw Pact does. NATO is a voluntary alliance of bickering democratic states. Although the U.S. has often dominated NATO, in the past decade, European countries, especially Germany, have begun to increase their role in NATO leadership. But NATO actions still require a consensus. In times of peril, issues such as mobilization of the NATO armies can ill be afforded lengthy debates or dissension. But debate and dissension are likely.

NATO strategy, or operational doctrine, is subject to the internal needs of host countries, especially Germany, and not to actual military requirements. NATO's forward defense policy is largely a result of German unwillingness to voluntarily sacrifice any of its population and terrain at the outset of a war. To make matters worse, the Germans are not keen on the establishment of border defensive works or minefields to slow a Soviet advance due to a deep-seated aversion to actions that suggest that the separation of the two Germanies will continue. And the disposition of NATO forces, and particularly the weaknesses of the Northern Army Group with its heavy concentration of the more poorly equipped NATO forces, is due more to historical peculiarities of occupation policy in the late 1940s than to any coherent military strategy.

Yet Soviet operational skills cannot be taken for granted. The Russians did display considerable capability in high command during the later years of World War II. But it took two costly years of fighting for the Soviet commanders to acquire these skills. Will Soviet military commanders, unbloodied for forty years in a conventional land war, display the same skills as combat veterans from a half-century ago? Will staff officers and military leaders, like the fictional Colonel Kucherenko, be able to translate the academic skills of the staff academy into real war-fighting abilities?

This is a very difficult question to answer. The evidence is contradictory. The picture presented in some writings by Soviet émigrés suggests that many Soviet officers suffer from the same kind of careerist malaise that is widely criticized in NATO armies. Perhaps it is even worse than in the NATO armies. In the Soviet Union, the armed forces are a good career. They mean prestige, a decent salary, and more importantly, access to critical goods in a society bereft of even the most basic consumer goods. The Soviet Union is a superpower that cannot manage to provide its citizens with a reliable supply of toilet paper. But a Soviet officer can count on adequate housing, and his family will have access to restricted army food stores. The housing may not be the best by Western standards, nor the food as palatable, but by Soviet standards, it is a comfortable life. The emphasis then is on what can be extracted from a military career, not what skills will make the officer a more proficient warrior. Soviet émigré writing is very critical of the decay of professional interest in Soviet military officers. All of the well-managed staff academies and war games will do no good if the officers are more concerned with the trappings of the office than with the skills required to engage in combat on the modern battlefield.

## War by the Numbers

One is also inclined to wonder if the Soviet military is able to manage a war any better than the Soviets manage (or mismanage) their economy. Soviet military art has some of the same underpinnings as Soviet economic management. Marxism-Leninism leads to an infatuation with "scientific" rules and norms for human activities that are often more complex and subtle than the academic tools used to study them. To their credit, the Soviets have engaged in extensive historical operations research to determine issues such as the number of rounds of artillery ammunition needed to destroy a partially entrenched infantry company in a defensive position. The reduction of the uncertainties of the battlefield to a set of simplified numerical norms may be useful to logistical planners needing to know how much ammunition to prepare for war. But how useful are they to real war fighting? Will they lead officers to place undue influence on stagnant rules and guidelines and discourage personal observation and judgment? And can they respond to changing technology and the changing pace of modern warfare? One is tempted to conclude that the Soviet military leadership is not dissimilar to other elements of the Soviet bureaucracy, and with similar tendencies toward institutional thinking that does not respond quickly to a changing environment.

In many respects, the Soviet infatuation with the use of military history, and in particular the lessons of the Great Patriotic War, reinforces the usual tendency of military bureaucracies to fight the last war. The modern Soviet Army is the ideal blitzkrieg army of 1945. Its shape and composition represent the perfection of World War II–style mechanized combat.

As a result, the Soviets have been slow to adjust to a changing battlefield in a number of areas. For example, Soviet planners have noted the high attrition of tanks and other weapons in modern wars, like those fought in the Mideast in 1967 and 1973. This has reinforced the Soviet preconceptions stemming from the World War II experience that overwhelming reserves of equipment are needed. Yet the lesson drawn by the Israelis is not that more reserves of equipment are needed, since that equipment is often miles away and not accessible to the field commander. Rather, their conclusion has been that combat support has to be enhanced, since many tank casualties can be dealt with if adequate recovery and repair equipment is handy. The Israelis were losing up to 75 percent of their tanks in the first eighteen hours of fighting in 1973. Yet they found that about 70 percent of these losses were due to mechanical failures or minor battle damage that could have been repaired relatively quickly, and the tank returned to combat. The Israelis responded to the growing lethality of antiarmor weapons on the battlefield by enhancing combat support. The Soviets have not followed suit, and Soviet divisional combat support remains weak. The Soviets have less than half the number of armored recovery and repair vehicles per tank than comparable NATO armies, and the systems tend to be less capable. Although the Soviets have paid considerable attention to tank recovery, the emphasis has been on correcting the errors of the World War II experience, and not on examining whether a far more fundamental change in attitude toward divisional combat support is required by the changing realities of modern warfare.

Combat support is not the only area where Soviet thinking has changed very slowly. The Soviet incorporation of novel technologies is another example. Helicopters add considerably to the combat power of land forces. They are useful for scouting, the transport of raiding parties, rapid resupply of forward units, and antitank fighting. The Soviets have recognized the usefulness of helicopters, especially after the experience of Afghanistan. Yet they have been slow to integrate helicopters into their tank and motor rifle divisions. Divisions are supposed to have a helicopter unit, but over the past few years, the Soviets have been tending to pull the helicopters out of divisions and consolidate them in special helicopter units at the call of army and front commanders. Undoubtedly, army and front commanders can put helicopters to good use, but so can divisional commanders. A divisional helicopter reconnaissance unit can fulfill a vital role in a fast-paced battle. The Soviets still rely on ground vehicles for this role, whereas their American counterparts have an extensive assortment of helicopters, which is much more effective.

To some extent, these shortcomings are not purely an issue of doctrine. The Soviets have real economic constraints on the type and quantity of equipment they can incorporate into their divisions. When you have two hundred ten divisions, even a small program such as adding another two dozen recovery vehicles to the divisional tables of equipment becomes a major, and expensive, program. The Soviets would probably like to add squadrons of helicopters to their divisions. But building up an inventory of helicopters large enough to satisfy the requirements of a large force structure takes years to accomplish. For example, at the current rate of acquisition, it takes the Soviet Union more than two decades to replace all of its tanks with new models. Any major change in doctrine that requires the adoption of new equipment takes decades to accomplish, even given the prodigious production rate of the USSR's massive military industries. The Soviets may excel in novel tactical concepts, but it is often difficult to translate these into practice due to the sheer size of the Soviet military establishment.

## Current Soviet Operational Plans

The operational plan depicted in the fictional scenario illustrates current tendencies in Soviet operational planning. Needless to say, the Soviets don't publish their actual plans for operations in Central Europe. But careful reading of open-source Soviet military literature can provide a close approximation of Soviet plans. The scenario is based on an unclassified study prepared by the U.S. Army's Soviet Army Studies Office, based on open Soviet sources.[7]

The plan depends on mass and speed to overcome the NATO defenses. Students of World War II military history will not find it terribly different from campaigns of 1944–45, even though the tools of the trade have changed in fifty years. An important ingredient in the plan is an attempt to mask Soviet formations, so that opposing NATO forces are uncertain of how large a force they face, and where it is concentrated.

The Soviets' plan would be to concentrate three or more divisions against a single NATO division. Once a breach in the NATO defenses is secured, a mobile force would be inserted into the breach to exploit it before NATO could react. Soviet operational plans stress the use of fire and maneuver. Artillery, air attacks, and direct mechanized attack shatter the defender with fire. Once the fire has sufficiently weakened the opponent, or should the opponent leave a position weakly defended, the highly mechanized Soviet forces would use their mobility to pour into the breach. *Fire* acts to shatter the enemy where he is; *maneuver* aims to exploit the points where the enemy no longer is, or no longer is strong.

Modern defensive doctrine aims to minimize the damage caused by the breach by having mobile forces available to counterattack the rupture. The Soviet forces must not only be able to defeat the initial forward defenses of NATO, but to shatter any defenses erected behind the initial defensive positions.

For this reason, the Soviets place great stress on forces used to exploit the breach and fend off counterattacks. In recent years, this type of force has come to be called an operational maneuver group, or OMG. The OMGs are not a specific type of unit, such as a tank division or motor rifle regiment. Rather, they are forces used for the exploitation role at different levels of tactical combat. For example, when a Soviet motor rifle division confronts a NATO unit, it might use an independent tank regiment as its maneuver force. In the case of an army, the OMG might be a tank division or an independent tank regiment reinforced with other units. At the level of a front, the OMG might be a formation tailored to front exploitation, like one of the new Unified Army Corps.

---

7. This scenario is heavily based on the study "The Soviet Conduct of War," prepared by the Soviet Army Studies Office of the U.S. Army Combined Arms Center, Fort Leavenworth, KS, in March 1987. The study's principal author is Col. David Glantz.

## Plan Buran and Perestroika

In the era of *glasnost* and *perestroika*,[8] Plan Buran may seem to some readers to be a throwback to the neolithic age of the cold war. Surely, Soviet pronouncements of a new defensive doctrine have heralded an end to the sort of offensive operational planning illustrated by Plan Buran?

At the time this book was written, the effects of perestroika have been very modest. The Soviets have indeed proclaimed an interest in a new defensive doctrine. However, the Soviets have publicly announced a defensive doctrine for decades, while the Soviet military has continued basing its strategy and operational art around offensive operational planning and tactics. "Defensive doctrine" seems to be a case of political semantics, not military policy.

Soviet claims about a defensive restructuring lack credibility because the Soviets have not provided any evidence of what type of actions they are undertaking under the rubric of perestroika. For example, they have not provided copies of current staff training, showing a new defensive orientation compared to past training. They have provided no indications that they plan to trim back the production of weapons such as tanks and self-propelled artillery. There is no evidence that the tank and motor rifle divisions are being reorganized to make them more "defensive."

There have been cosmetic changes, which sometimes can create a false impression of real change. The Soviets' pathological obsession with military secrecy appears to be slowly easing. They are allowing Western observers to visit Warsaw Pact exercises, and to inspect new weapons to a degree that would have been unheard-of five years ago. But at the same time, Soviet censorship of their military press has not changed at all in regard to issues of military strength, unit organization, and military technology. The Soviets still do not publish an accurate military budget, and have admitted as much. They have never made any serious effort to publicly describe the size or composition of their armed forces. Military censorship is still so extreme that the designation of old weapons is secret and unprintable, even thought they are known in the West. A recent Soviet book on tank technology skipped all mention of the T-64 tank, first in

---

8. *Glasnost* is the Russian word for openness, and is commonly associated with Gorbachev's attempts to open Soviet society to a more candid view of itself. *Perestroika* is the Russian word for restructuring and refers to Gorbachev's program for national renewal.

service in the mid 1960s, to say nothing of more recent tanks such as the T-80. The Soviet military remains one of the most secret organizations in the world today. Military subjects that are considered routine and openly published in the West are forbidden subjects in the USSR. Soviet military secrecy breeds mistrust and is a major complicating factor in arms control agreements.

This is not to totally discount the effects of perestroika on the Soviet armed forces. For the Gorbachev economic reforms to succeed, it will be necessary to trim back extravagant Soviet military spending. The Soviet Union currently spends in excess of 15 percent, and perhaps as much as 21 percent, of its gross national product on defense. In contrast, the U.S. spends about 7 percent, and most European countries spend around 3 to 4 percent. Gorbachev undoubtedly seeks to channel some of this funding back into the ailing civilian economy.

The cuts announced by Gorbachev in December 1988 are the first steps to accomplish this task. Plans were to remove 10,000 tanks from the force structure (about 20 percent), and about 500,000 troops (about 10 percent of the current force). Furthermore, Gorbachev promised the reduction of six divisions from East Germany, Czechoslovakia, and Hungary. The reduction in tanks will probably involve thirty-year-old T-54s and T-55s, not new tanks. Nevertheless, reducing the Soviet inventory of tanks by 20 percent implies reducing the number of Soviet tank and motor rifle divisions by comparable amounts. Even with these changes, the Soviet Army will remain a massive force with substantial numerical advantages over NATO. An operation such as the fictional Buran would still be possible even after the 1988 cuts come into effect.

Further cuts, which would be sufficient to dampen Soviet offensive capabilities, will probably await a NATO/Warsaw Pact conventional arms control agreement. The Soviet military does not appear happy about the cuts promised by Gorbachev in 1988. Dissension with the Gorbachev plan probably accounts for the dismissal of the head of the Soviet General Staff, Marshal Akhromeyev, in December 1988, although the Soviet press claimed that Akhromeyev retired due to his health.

There is reason to suspect that perestroika will eventually lead to even greater changes in the Soviet military, the sheer size of which, even after the promised cuts, demands an exhausting share of the Soviet national effort. Soviet officials, in private, have suggested to Western officials that the USSR may be reconsidering the traditional notion that the armed forces must be configured to resist all possible combinations of enemies.

This could foreshadow an eventual reduction in the number of divisions, and in the amount of equipment acquired for the Soviet Army.

Such changes will probably take a decade. Nikita Khrushchev attempted to make sweeping changes in the Soviet military in the early 1960s, alienating the military leadership. This was a contributory factor in his eventual ouster. Gorbachev has most likely learned a lesson from this, and reform will come more slowly. For the more perceptive military leaders in the Soviet Union, reform is welcome. There is concern that the Soviet Army is falling behind NATO in technology. Some military leaders appreciate that a sound economy is the basis for a sound defense. For these leaders, perestroika is seen not as an attempt to diminish the military, but to strengthen its vital economic and technological roots.

It is unlikely that the Soviet Army of the mid-1990s will be so radically different that an operation such as Plan Buran will be impossible. Even with force reductions, the Soviets are likely to maintain a substantial conventional force in Central Europe. What will prevent Plan Buran from ever happening is the Soviet conviction that it will not succeed. As is suggested in the following chapters, the Soviet armed forces, for all their power, cannot be certain that their elegant operational plans will function properly in the turmoil of a real war.

# CHAPTER 2

# Motor Rifle Attack:
# The Skirmish in the Hofzell Woods

**1400, 30 September, Bavarian Forest**

Nineteen years old, eighteen months in the army, and off to war. Sergeant Stanislav Demchenko sat, crunched up and uncomfortable, inside his squad's BMP-2 Yozh infantry fighting vehicle.[1] Well, it wasn't exactly "his" squad. It was the squad of Lt. Ivan Bobrov, the platoon commander. But when it came time to dismount and fight on foot, he would be in charge of the squad in the field.

Demchenko, better known to his buddies in the squad as Stashu, was the assistant squad leader. He was the son of farmers from a small *kolkhoz* (state-owned collective farm) east of the Lvov. Like many western Ukrainians, his family was Ukrainian Catholic, even though this church was suppressed by the state. Stashu was not particularly religious, but his family's background did little to help his career in Soviet society. One of his uncles had been an anti-Soviet Ukrainian insurgent in the late 1940s, a fact duly noted in his dossier. On the positive side, he had proved to be an able student at his polytechnic school, and was active in a local DOSAAF[2] motorbike club. His enthusiasm for cross-country motorbikes had

---

1. The BMP-2 Yozh is a lightly armored infantry transporter, comparable to the American M2 Bradley IFV. *Yozh* means "hedgehog" in Russian and refers to the fact that the infantry squad inside can poke their guns out and fire from the inside.

2. DOSAAF is the Russian acronym for the Voluntary Society for Cooperation with the Army, Air Force and Fleet. It sponsors many athletic and sports clubs; its role is further explained later in the chapter.

attracted the attention of the local DOSAAF military representative. He was impressed with Stashu's enthusiasm and skill, and when draft time came, he recommended that Demchenko be sent to an NCO (non-commissioned officer) academy after basic training. Demchenko's family background ruled out a posting to an officers' school or to any of the prestige services such as the Strategic Missile Force or Air Force. But he wasn't so suspect as to be dumped into a construction battalion. Demchenko's skill with motorbikes and other mechanical equipment led the ground forces selection board to post him to a BMP-2 motor rifle unit. The BMP-2 requires a good deal more care to operate than other infantry vehicles, and the ground forces were chronically short of technically skilled recruits.

The NCO academy in Sverdlovsk had not been particularly challenging for Demchenko. He was a very bright student and had no problems learning the elementary combat skills taught to new NCO candidates. Life in the academy was better than that in a regular unit. All of the candidates in his class were new recruits, so there wasn't the usual abuse and hazing from senior soldiers in the unit. There was enough abuse from the officers! After six months of training, Demchenko was posted to a motor rifle battalion of the 18th Guards Motor Rifle Division in Czechoslovakia. As a new junior sergeant, he was assigned to the BMP-2 of a platoon commander, Lt. Ivan Bobrov.

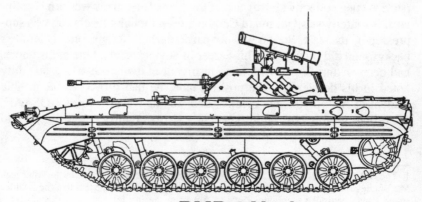

## BMP-2 Yozh
## Infantry Combat Vehicle

A Soviet motor rifle platoon consists of three BMP-2 armored infantry vehicles. One BMP is commanded by the platoon leader, a young lieutenant; the other two are commanded by sergeants. The BMP armored infantry vehicles had a squat, menacing look. Demchenko's company had started the war with a full complement of the newer BMP-2 Yozh. The Yozh had a 30mm autocannon, which spit out half-pound, armor-piercing shells at a rate of about two hundred fifty a minute. The troops called it the "woodpecker" due to its staccato sound. The woodpecker could penetrate light armored vehicles such as troop carriers. And, if you were lucky, it might penetrate the thin rear armor of a main battle tank. But it could not penetrate the thick frontal armor. To defeat tanks, it had a Konkurs[3] antitank missile launcher mounted on the roof. This could burn out any of the older NATO tanks, such as the American M-60 or the German M48A5. But it wasn't powerful enough to deal with tanks with Chobham armor, such as the newer German Leopard 2 or the American M1 Abrams.

Each BMP contains an infantry squad. The BMP-2 carries nine soldiers. There are two crewmen, a driver, and a vehicle gunner who handles the woodpecker. The squad leader sits in the turret with the gunner to direct his troops. In the alleyway to the left of the turret and behind the driver is a seat for the squad sniper with an SVD sniper rifle. At the rear of the BMP-2 is seating for six soldiers—two bench seats, holding three soldiers each. Two of the soldiers are regular riflemen, armed with AKS-74 assault rifles. There is also an assistant squad leader (such as Demchenko) with an AKS-74 assault rifle, a grenadier with an RPG-16 antitank rocket launcher, and a squad machine gunner with a PKM light machine gun.

Demchenko's squad was typical of Soviet Ground Forces units. Over the past few years, more and more ethnic minorities were being drafted into combat units. In the old days, combat units were predominantly Slavic: Russian, Byelorussian, or Ukrainian, with a smattering of ethnic minorities. Most of the minority draftees were dumped into paramilitary construction battalions for the duration of their two years of duty. They would see a rifle for the first and last time while swearing their military oath. After that, all they'd see would be shovels and wheelbarrows. But

---

3. *Konkurs* is the Russian word for "contest." It is the code name for a medium antitank missile that NATO calls the AT-5 Spandrel. It is wire guided and has a range of about 3,000 meters. Its closest NATO counterparts are the American TOW and the Franco-German HOT missiles.

these days, in the early 1990s, there just weren't enough Slavs to go around anymore. The minorities had to make up the slack.

Demchenko's squad was a good example of this. The platoon commander, Lieutenant Bobrov, the squad machine gunner, Pvt. Nikolai Grachev, and the RPG-16 grenadier, Pvt. Fyodor Ignatov, were all Russians. The latter two were off collective farms and were not exactly university material. The BMP-2 driver, Pvt. Kurbanbay Irisbekov, was a Turkmen from Soviet Central Asia. His understanding of Russian was poor, and Demchenko had no idea why they had trained him as a driver.[4] Admittedly, driving a BMP-2 was a good deal easier than driving a tank, but the driver was expected to assist in maintaining the vehicle. Irisbekov tried hard, but he just wasn't clever when it came to hardware. Demchenko was luckier with the vehicle gunner. He was a young Latvian,

## BMP-2 Yozh Squad

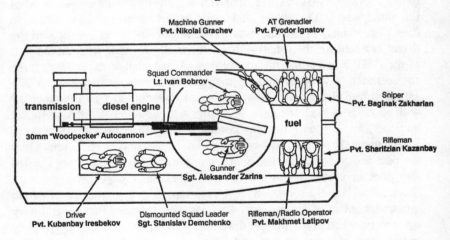

----

4. This is not as implausible as it seems. In 1988, a T-80 tank driven by a Kazakh was accidently steered onto the train tracks on the Leipzig-Berlin line in East Germany. It stalled, and in the ensuing crash six Germans were killed and thirty injured. The Soviet investigating team found that the driver could not read Russian warning signs at the crossing, didn't understand his commander's instructions in Russian, and hadn't figured out how to use the tank's night vision devices.

Aleksander Zarins, a very bright kid, active in the Latvian DOSAAF rally car clubs. Like many Latvians, he was a bit standoffish from the Russians. But he and Stashu Demchenko got along well and kept the vehicle in shape. They usually assigned Irisbekov the simple tasks and the dirty jobs. He had little choice in the matter.

The squad's sniper was a young Armenian, Baginak Zakharian. He was an excellent rifleman, which was surprising since he came from the city of Yerevan. But coming from a major city, Zakharian had received a good education and spoke Russian reasonably well. The two squad riflemen were also from Central Asia—Sharifzian Kazanbayev, a Tatar, and Makhmet Latipov, a Beshari from Kazakhstan. Both spoke acceptable Russian, or at least knew enough to get along. It was Soviet policy to mix the different ethnic groups because the army did not want ethnic cliques to form. They assumed that mixing the groups would force soldiers to speak Russian with one another. This worked to a point, but in the garrison, troops from similar backgrounds did hang around together whenever they had the chance. It was a relief to speak one's native tongue and reminisce about "the good old days" before army life.

And here they all were, bouncing down a forest road in West Germany, a polyglot Eurasian squad, off to do battle with NATO. Stashu Demchenko had managed to change the normal seating arrangement in the BMP. He preferred to sit in the forward seat behind the driver. At least this gave him some forward vision. When they dismounted, it was important for him to know the situation confronting them. From the back seats, it was difficult to get any sense of the battlefield.

His unit was riding down route E53 near Zweisel. The area was mountainous and wooded. Coming from the hill country near Lvov, Demchenko felt at home. The scenery was picturesque. But the rest of the squad was uneasy. To the young men from Central Asia, the forests seemed gloomy and foreboding. The damp, foggy weather combined with the terrain created an especially claustrophobic aura. On either side of the road were dark pine forests, the tops of the trees grazed by the low-hanging fog. The three Russians in the squad, all from the wide open steppes, found the countryside here particularly unappealing. The night before, the squad had spent time bragging of their martial skills and the fate of any German luckless enough to encounter this dangerous bunch. By morning, however, the cheap heroism had evaporated. Anxiety and uneasiness had taken its place.

Riding the BMP-2 into combat is no joy. The vehicle is very cramped inside, and its torsion bar suspension is stiff. When traveling over rough ground, you feel every bump and ditch. The fact that there is little padding on the seats doesn't help matters. And unless you are a dwarf, your head touches the roof. If the vehicle starts bouncing around during cross-country travel, your head will get slammed back and forth against the roof. Infantry helmets give damn little protection against this kind of abuse. Riding in BMPs is not for the squeamish or those prone to claustrophobia. Not only are you crammed in shoulder to shoulder with the rest of the squad, but you can't see anything. The vehicle is very dark inside, with only a halfhearted attempt at interior illumination. And in combat, gear and stowage piles up, and pretty soon the small electric lights are completely covered. Each rifleman has a small periscope to view the outside. But the periscope opening is only about two inches by four inches. If you try to look through it while the vehicle is in motion, you're inviting a bad case of motion sickness. You have to bend over to use the periscope, which makes you even more vulnerable to the pummeling from vehicle motion. Your head keeps bobbing up and down from the herky-jerky ride of the BMP, and the view outside seems to have the same sickening up-and-down motion. Riflemen soon learn to curb their curiosity and just sit back.

An even more disagreeable experience occurs when the squad tries to fire its weapons from the inside of the BMP. Demchenko and the 1st Squad had done this often enough on qualification training. Each rifleman has a small firing port in front of his seat. The AKS-74 assault rifle, the current version of the Kalashnikov AK-47, is designed to fit into this socket. So you fold up the stock on the rifle, and push the barrel into the plug. Actually firing the rifle requires some interesting contortions. You're supposed to aim the rifle using the periscope, but the receiver of the rifle is stuck into your chest, so it's hard to bend forward to peer through the periscope. The best way to do this is to let the gun rest under your armpit, but then it's hard to move the gun to either side. The worst moment comes when everybody fires. The noise of an AKS-74 is bad enough on the outside. From the inside, the noise is deafening. The rifles spew out cordite fumes, and the air becomes very difficult to breathe. You can't aim after a few bursts, because your eyes are watering from the fumes, and the sights are becoming fogged up from all the smoke. And try changing a rifle magazine while your gun is plugged into the socket!

As uncomfortable as the ride was, the squad's soldiers had other things on their minds. Like all soldiers in combat for the first time, they wondered what battle would be like. They worried about how they would act.

They wondered where the enemy was. When would the Germans start firing at them? Would some German tank come swinging out of the woods and blast their little BMP to bits? When would the fighting start? The claustrophobia of the dank interior of the BMP, combined with fears and anxieties about battle, made the riflemen of 1st Squad wish they could get out of the BMP and fight on foot. Then at least they could see their enemy.

The morning had been uneventful. The regiment had crossed the Czech-German border at 0600, after having heard thirty minutes of heavy artillery fire. Demchenko left his hatch open for the first part of the ride. The terrain reminded him of his native region near Lvov. Then Lieutenant Bobrov told him to shut the hatch. It was against regulations to travel in combat areas with the hatch open, and Bobrov treated the rules very solemnly. They were several kilometers to the rear of the divisional vanguards. The roads through the forest were narrow, and the columns were warned not to bunch up. The first sounds of fighting came around 1000, when lead elements of the division ran into the first German prepared positions about ten kilometers over the border. The Bavarian forest was ill suited for any large-scale fighting with armored vehicles. Any fighting in the woods would have to be done on foot. Work for the infantry!

The first signs of combat came an hour later, when the squad drove past the site of the fighting they had heard earlier. Traffic had slowed due to rubbernecking by the later columns. On the right side of the road, Soviet riflemen guarded three or four NATO soldiers. They wore the old pattern U.S.-style steel helmet. From their gray-green uniform, Demchenko recognized them as German troops. They were a bit older than he expected, maybe reserve troops. On the left side of the road was a burned-out BRM. The BRM was a lot like a BMP-2, but had a different gun and was usually used for scouting. Something, probably a missile, had hit it on the turret front, and the left side of the turret was caved in. It also must have burned and suffered an internal explosion, since the hull was rent open at the seams. Farther over in the clearing were at least two burned-out BMP-2s and a burned-out T-80 tank. Apparently this was an advance guard that was ambushed by German antitank missile teams. A little LuAZ-967M ambulance was carrying away two badly burned tankers on stretchers.

There were other signs of war as well. Not all the civilians fleeing the area had escaped, and the artillery bombardment had killed soldiers and civilians indiscriminately. A small village farther down the road had been the scene of some fighting. Civilian vehicles were strewn around the burned-out buildings, some with dead passengers. Livestock was running free, and many cows were lying dead or wounded in the fields. There were few signs of German military vehicles, but several dead soldiers lay near the ruins.

Around noon, the 2d Battalion of the 55th Guards Motor Rifle Regiment (MRR) was called forward to deal with German defenses. This was the battalion to which Demchenko's squad was attached. Stashu could hear Bobrov over the vehicle radio speaking with the battalion commander. The platoon was to move down the road about a kilometer, where it would be directed to its objective.

The platoon's assignment was straightforward. The road along which the 55th Guards MRR had to pass went through a large clearing. Some German troops were positioned in a small clump of buildings about 2,000 meters to the right of the road. The Germans had several Milan antitank missile launchers,[5] and were firing on the columns from the 55th Guards MRR as they passed. The Germans had managed to sneak one missile team forward, and it had hit a few armored command vehicles, which were still burning. Gunfire from a BMP-2 had eliminated this team, but the regimental commander feared that his units would continue to be subjected to missile attack unless the German position was cleared. The regiment's 3d Company/2d Battalion, to which Bobrov's platoon belonged, was being

# BMP Platoon

(3rd Platoon, 3rd Company, 2nd Battalion, 55th Guards Motor Rifle Regiment of the 18th Guards Motor Rifle Division)

| **1st Squad** | **2nd Squad** | **3rd Squad** |
|---|---|---|
| Platoon Leader | Squad Leader | Squad Leader |
| Lt. Ivan Bobrov | Sr.Sgt. Fastov | Sr.Sgt. Yermakov |

---

5. The Milan is a Franco-German medium antitank missile, common in NATO. The U.S. equivalent is the Dragon and the Soviet equivalent is the AT-4 Spigot. It is operated by a two-man crew and is man-portable.

assigned to eliminate the German missile positions in the buildings and deal with any other German forces in the clearing.

Normally, an attack like this would be supported by tanks. But since none were immediately available, and there was some urgency to overwhelm the enemy positions, the attack would be carried out by the BMP company alone. The company was to deploy at the edge of the road and dismount troops 1,500 meters from the building. The idea was to leave the BMP-2s back beyond missile range, but close enough to provide fire support from their 30mm autocannons. The Milan missiles would easily blow apart a BMP-2. The only additional fire support the company would have was a single 30mm AGS-17 Plamya grenade launcher, which would have to be carried forward into range by its crew.

The BMP company had three platoons, of which Lieutenant Bobrov's was one. Bobrov's platoon would be on the left flank of the attack, and the other two platoons to the right. In all, there would be ten BMPs in the attack: three in each of the three platoons, and the company commander's to the rear watching over the action. Lieutenant Bobrov instructed Private Irisbekov to place his BMP in the center, between Sergeant Fastov's BMP on the left and Sergeant Yermakov's on the right. Once the BMPs had been moved into position off the road, Lieutenant Bobrov called the neighboring two BMPs and explained the mission. Bobrov, Demchenko, and the squad leaders and assistant squad leaders of the two neighboring BMPs gathered behind Bobrov's BMP to get instructions.

"This will be a standard dismounted attack," explained Bobrov. "The enemy troops in those buildings in front of us are armed with antitank missiles. Our objective is to capture and hold those buildings and clear out any German troops in the area. On the radio, we will call the objective 'Oreshnik' [Hazel]. We will advance in the BMPs to 1,500 meters from the objective. The squads will then dismount. Sergeants Fastov and Yermakov, you will stay with your vehicles and direct fire support. The assistant squad leaders will take the squads into action. You will advance at a walk to 300 meters. The platoon to our right has a Plamya grenade launcher and it will provide fire support on any observed enemy positions. Cover the last 100 meters in a run. We will give you fire from the 30mm guns. It is important for the squads to stay in radio contact with the BMP. Identify targets for us. Is everything clear?"

"Yes exactly so, Comrade Lieutenant," came the reply. It sounded like a school cheer, more appropriate to a playing field than a battlefield. But routine procedures like this distracted the soldiers from their anxieties,

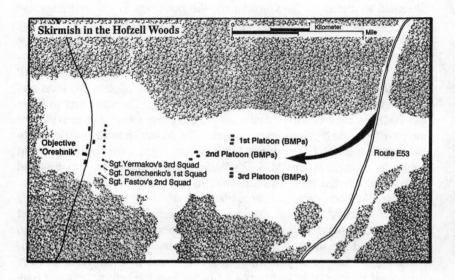

and made the battlefield seem a little more familiar. The platoon sergeants crawled back into the BMPs and awaited the company commander's signal.

At 1245, the company commander fired off a green flare. The engines of the ten BMPs were already warmed up, and the BMPs began their charge toward Objective Oreshnik. The BMPs were stretched out for half a kilometer, with about fifty meters of space between them. The Germans did not begin firing during the approach. The squads sat in the back of the BMPs, mute and anxious. Everyone took the opportunity to check his kit.

The equipment of the Soviet soldier is less elaborate than that of the average NATO soldier. The web gear is very simple, usually just a belt and a harness, which doubles as suspenders. On the soldier's right hip is an ammunition pouch, containing two additional banana magazines for the AKS-74 assault rifle. Each magazine holds thirty rounds, for a total of about ninety rounds of ammunition. Soldiers can be issued grenades, which are carried in the pockets of their uniform or in the gas mask bag on their left hip. On the back of their belt is a water canteen and an entrenching shovel, the most troublesome items. Soldiers can't wear the canteen or shovel while they're riding in the BMP, because they get in the way of sitting down. So they are either attached after dismounting from the vehicle, or left in the vehicle.

When the BMPs came to a halt a couple of minutes after the start signal, the squad commanders sounded a small klaxon as a signal to dismount. The two rear doors of the BMPs were thrown open and the squad piled out. Half the squad peeled to the left, the other half to the right. They formed a skirmish line in front of the vehicle. Demchenko was the last to leave the BMP, and he kept an eye out for any gear left behind. To keep in touch with Lieutenant Bobrov and the BMP, he had an R-126 radio. It was cumbersome, so he assigned Makhmet Latipov, one of the riflemen, to carry it for him. He signaled to Latipov to follow him. Demchenko formed up the squad in the usual skirmish line, with Latipov and him in the center. To their right was Nikolai Grachev, with the squad's PKM machine gun. To their left was Fyodor Ignatov, the squad grenadier, with his RPG-16 rocket launcher. At the extreme left was Baginak Zakharian with his SVD sniper rifle. Sergeant Fastov's squad was on their left, and Sergeant Yermakov's on their right. Although Stashu Demchenko was not the senior sergeant of the dismounted group, he took charge, since he led Lieutenant Bobrov's squad. Demchenko shouted, "To battle. Move forward," and the three dismounted squads of 3d Platoon began advancing.

At first, it seemed like a parade ground. No fire came from Objective Oreshnik. Every soldier in the squad hoped that the Germans had fled! The objective was slightly uphill from their positions, and there was precious little cover between the squad and the buildings. There was no sign of movement from the German positions. It took about six minutes for the squad to cover the first 500 meters. The walk seemed interminable, with every soldier anxiously awaiting the sound of the first volley.

Makhmet Latipov halted for a second and listened intently to the radio. Demchenko walked over to him. "Comrade Sergeant, Lieutenant Bobrov wants to speak to you." Demchenko took the headset.

"Listen, Stashu," said Bobrov. "The company commander has changed his plans. He thinks the *nyemtsi*[6] have abandoned the objective. He wants the 2d Platoon to mount back up and push forward to the objective. You keep moving forward on foot. Over."

---

6. *Nyemtsi* is Russian for "Germans."

Stashu replied, "Understood, over."

The BMPs to the right began moving forward and the squads got back aboard. In seconds they began racing toward the farm buildings. Demchenko looked to both sides, and said in a loud voice, "We're continuing on foot. Everybody keep an eye on the buildings."

Fyodor Ignatov chimed in, "Lucky slobs, they get to ride all the way."

Ignatov had hardly finished griping when from a small gully on the east side of the farm, there was a little flash of light. From their vantage point, they could barely see the slight flickers of rocket exhaust as a Milan antitank missile began bearing down on the BMPs from 2d Platoon. The BMPs obviously did not see this. Their advance had brought them into range of the enemy missiles.

Demchenko raced over to Latipov and grabbed the headset to the R-126 radio. "Lieutenant Bobrov, to the right of the buildings. Enemy PTURS."[7]

There was no time for Bobrov to react. The first Milan struck the BMP on the right side. It exploded and the BMP came to a halt. The missile hit the front compartment, ripping into the diesel engine and splashing burning fuel all over the front of the vehicle. The rear doors swung open and the squad began to hurriedly dismount. As they were doing so, the ammunition in the BMP began cooking off. The fire quickly spread to the stored Konkurs missiles. The heat ignited their propellant, giving off a hellish whoosh as the fuel flashed and burned for a brief moment. A second Milan missile was launched from the opposite side of the farm seconds after the first. It struck the BMP to the left, on the bow. The engine of the BMP absorbed most of the blast, and the crew was able to get out. This BMP did not suffer the horrible fire that had engulfed the other vehicle. The gunner or commander stayed with the vehicle, valiantly trying to seek out the missile team that had hit their vehicle.

The ground to the left of the farm buildings danced as the autocannons knocked big clumps of earth into the air. However, the BMP gunner had misjudged the location, and a second missile flew out. By now, Private Zarins, the gunner in Lieutenant Bobrov's BMP, had spotted the Milan team and began hammering away at it. Zarins fired high-explosive rounds, which hit the ground near the Milan team with fiery smacks. His aim was

---

7. PTURS is the Russian acronym for an antitank missile. It is usually pronounced "pee-turs."

good. The missile lost guidance and plowed into the ground some distance from the BMPs. The 1st Platoon had brought the other Milan team under fire. The crew from the damaged BMP finally abandoned their vehicle as the fire worsened, and it too blew up when its ammunition cooked off. What remained of the 2d Platoon was a single BMP-2. Its commander had found a small gully, and the BMP rested there while awaiting further orders.

The two squads from the destroyed BMPs were pretty shaken up. They lay on the ground some distance from the burning vehicles. As Demchenko and the 3d Platoon moved abreast of them, Stashu and the other squad leaders motioned to them to advance. One of the squads moved forward. But the squad from the first BMP had lost both its commander and assistant squad leader. They stayed where they were, ignoring the signals from the neighboring platoons, content to hug the earth.

After losing two BMPs to the defenders, the company commander decided to engage in a little preventative fire support. The two remaining platoons of BMPs opened fire on the farm buildings. For the advancing squads, it should have been comforting to see the enemy positions hit by fire. But some of the squads were startled by the sound of the autocannon and machine gun rounds whizzing so close over their heads. Two of the squads instinctively hit the ground. The advancing line of riflemen became more ragged as squads dropped down.

It took Demchenko's squad nearly fifteen minutes from the time of dismounting to reach a point about 300 meters from the farm. So far the enemy had held back firing on the squads, for fear of attracting the unwanted attention of the BMPs. In the tradition of Russian infantry since the days of Marshal Suvorov and Napoleon, Demchenko shouted *"Urra!"* His squad joined in the battle cry and began charging the enemy positions at a slow run. Neighboring squads followed suit. The Germans began opening fire on the charging Soviet soldiers.

So far, the range was too great for accuracy on either side. The BMPs responded to any sign of German small arms fire. The most effective fire support came from the sole surviving BMP of 2d Platoon. Not only was it closer than the other seven BMPs, but there was a big gap in the infantry in front of it due to the losses the 2d Platoon had suffered. It was easier to fire at the Germans without hitting any of the advancing Soviet riflemen.

As the squads advanced, they fired their AKS-74 assault rifles from the hip, as they had seen in Soviet training films. Unfortunately, it takes only a few seconds of firing to empty a thirty-round magazine and many of the charging soldiers ran out of ammunition before they were close to the German positions. Excited from the run, they didn't stop to reload but charged forward anyway. The Germans returned fire, but it wasn't very heavy. The 1st Platoon on the far right of the charge took several well-aimed bursts. Demchenko and his platoon were spared the worst of it.

One of the Milan teams popped up again; it had survived the attempts of the BMPs to gun it down. The surviving BMP from the 2d Platoon tried to bring it under fire, but the gunner, concentrating on hitting the Milan team before it fired, failed to notice Sergeant Yermakov's squad. The hammering of the BMP's woodpecker autocannon began. Demchenko watched in horror as the tracer sprayed into the midst of Yermakov's squad, hitting several soldiers in the upper chest. The effect of a 30mm slug on a human is gruesome. The survivors in Yermakov's squad threw themselves to the ground and refused to move forward.

Before the other two squads of 3d Platoon got within grenade range, Sergeant Fastov's squad on the left began to take heavy fire from a small gully. Several German infantrymen were well dug in, and shielded by a small hill from BMP fire. They hit Sergeant Fastov and most of his men in a succession of quick volleys of rifle fire. Then they turned their attention to Demchenko's squad.

Demchenko shouted to his men to halt and hit the ground. Private Zakharian, the sniper, was the squad member nearest the Germans, and he was hit in the leg. The round had hit the bone itself, crumpling Zakharian. In extreme pain, he cried out for help. The other squad members ignored him, trying to bring the Germans under fire. Demchenko and his radioman hid behind a slight rise in the ground. He looked around for Nikolai Grachev, with the squad machine gun. Grachev was huddled behind a tree stump some distance away, seemingly frozen in place. The other rifleman, Kazanbayev, was out of ammunition and was furiously trying to reload. The RPG gunner, Fyodor Ignatov, was trying to free himself of the backpack with spare rockets. These projected over his head, and if hit by rifle fire would explode, and him with them. Demchenko began firing at the Germans, but his single assault rifle alone was not enough. He was soon out of ammunition. To make matters worse, some other German infantry had noticed the plight of the 3d Platoon and seemed to be making their way toward them to finish them off. By now, the Soviet and German troops were in too close a proximity for the BMPs to offer much covering fire.

Demchenko shouted to Kazanbayev to throw him a banana magazine of ammunition. The little Tatar stared back at him, stupefied. In all the noise and excitement, Kazanbayev had forgotten what little Russian he knew. The source of the problem finally occurred to Demchenko, and he pointed to the open feed on his assault rifle, shouting "Hungry, hungry!" The two words that every Soviet soldier knows are "hungry" and "tired." Kazanbayev threw over a magazine, which struck Demchenko's helmet.

Demchenko ordered his radioman, Makhmet Latipov, to drop the radio and fetch the PKM machine gun. Latipov nodded and ran at a crouch over to Grachev's little haven behind the tree stump. Grachev had not frozen. He had been hit in the chest by rifle fire and was in shock. Latipov cocked the PKM and from a prone position began firing into the German position. Ignatov finally had managed to free himself of the harness, and aimed the RPG-16 rocket launcher at the Germans. To his horror, Demchenko noticed that the back end of the RPG was pointed at him. He managed to roll clear before Ignatov fired. Excited by the fighting, Ignatov had not realized that the end of the rocket launcher was perilously close to his own right leg. When he fired, he badly scorched the back of his leg. But the rocket grenade did the trick. The machine gun fire had killed two or three Germans, and the rocket grenade broke the nerve of the few other German infantrymen. Two or three Germans tried to make their way back toward the farm building.

Another group of Germans had worked its way into an irrigation ditch between Demchenko's squad and the survivors of Sergeant Yermakov's squad to the right. Yermakov's squad was having a hard time of it. Yermakov had been one of the soldiers inadvertently hit by BMP fire. The squad had repulsed an earlier German attack, but in the process had exhausted most of its ammunition. Like many inexperienced troops, the men had little fire discipline, and were prone to fire off long bursts. It didn't take long to exhaust three magazines. The squad PKM was already out of ammunition. The men were using grenades to fend off the Germans. They tried to radio for help, with no luck.

Demchenko could see the problem, and after collecting Latipov and Kazanbayev, began cautiously moving toward the Germans. Intent on wiping out Yermakov's squad, the Germans did not notice the approach of Demchenko and his riflemen. At a range of about thirty meters, Demchenko and the remnants of 3d Platoon began hitting the Germans from the side. Of the four of them, two were hit by a quick burst from the PKM, another was hit by Kazanbayev's rifle fire, and the fourth tried to run but Demchenko caught him with a single burst. The squad began to cautiously move forward toward the farm buildings.

There seemed to be little fire coming from the farm buildings, which were small and made of orange brick. The faces of the buildings were badly gouged by cannon fire from the BMPs. Big chunks had been blown away by high-explosive rounds, and the armor-piercing rounds had made holes straight through the walls. The German infantry had abandoned the farmhouse when the roof had caught fire. The Milan team lay sprawled near their missile launcher, their bodies roughly mangled by the 30mm cannon fire from the BMP. Two or three German riflemen remained behind a stone wall at the rear of the farm. Demchenko, his two men, and the remnants of Yermakov's squad carefully made their way through the farmyard. The Germans opened fire as Latipov came around the corner of an outbuilding. Luckily, he was not hit. He fell backward on his rump, which knocked the wind out of him. Kazanbayev had picked up an AKS-74 with a BG-15 grenade launcher on it from a dead rifleman of the 3d Squad. He aimed it carefully at the wall, hitting it squarely with a 30mm grenade. The grenade shattered the wall, spraying the Germans behind it with sharp shards of fieldstone. With three out of four wounded, the Germans surrendered.

Demchenko and his men carefully inspected the remaining buildings for other German troops. It was done in the usual fashion: A grenade goes in first, then a stream of rifle fire. They found a few dead German soldiers, probably killed earlier in the battle. Some Soviet riflemen from the 1st Platoon could be seen on the other end of the farm, making their way through a stone barn. They seemed to have overcome the resistance there as well. By now, a BMP-2 from 2d Platoon had made its way to the outer entrance of the farm. It seemed sure that the farm was securely in Soviet hands.

The cost had been high. The company had lost two BMPs to missile fire. The dismounted infantry had suffered the worst. Of the fifty-four men who had begun the assault, nine had been killed and twenty-one wounded or injured. The Germans had lost two Milan launchers and about eighteen men. Four German soldiers had been captured.

Aleksander Zarins, the gunner on Bobrov's BMP, spoke a bit of German. He was sent forward for a quick interrogation. After a rough frisking, Zarins questioned the German prisoners. Not regulars, but reservists from a territorial brigade, they were unwilling to say how many other troops from their unit were in the area. In fact, they were quite obstinate, and Zarins could get little out of them even after a few smacks in the face with a gun butt. Bobrov radioed to battalion headquarters to send a jeep to pick them up for a proper questioning by the regimental staff.

Demchenko left the farmyard and returned to the spot where his men had been hit. Ignatov was sitting on the ground with his right trouser leg torn away. He had a nasty-looking burn on the back of his right leg and was trying to apply a cloth bandage. Private Zakharian was flat on his back, with a pool of blood under his shattered leg. Ignatov had already applied a tourniquet to stanch the bleeding. Both Ignatov and Zakharian would live. Nikolai Grachev was another matter. He had been hit twice in the upper chest. One rifle bullet had shattered his left shoulder; the other had smashed into his left lung. The power of modern assault rifle ammunition was appalling. Grachev was ashen and having difficulty breathing. Demchenko tried to get the attention of the company medic, but there were plenty of other wounded from the other squads. With the help of a soldier from Yermakov's squad, Demchenko brought Grachev to a BMP being used as a temporary aid station. After leaving word with the medic about Zakharian and Ignatov, Demchenko returned to his platoon. The Germans might counterattack, and they would have to be ready.

## Analysis

The average Soviet infantry squad differs in many respects from NATO infantry, especially from American infantry. The Soviet Army is a conscript force, not a volunteer force like the U.S. Army. But many NATO armies also use the draft, notably the West Germans. The differences are due to other reasons.

To begin with, the Soviet Army is the last of the great European imperial armies. It is made up of many nationalities, speaking many languages. There are well over a hundred different nationalities in the USSR, and more than a dozen major language groups. The Soviet Union is far more diverse than most other countries. Portions of the country, such as the Baltic republics and parts of European Russia, are not that different from Central Europe. Other areas, such as Azerbaijan or Turkestan, have more in common with Iran or Pakistan than with Europe. And in the Far East, the nomadic peoples of Siberia share kinship with the goatherders of Mongolia or the Eskimos of Alaska. The training and recruitment policies of the Soviet Army have more in common with the other old imperial armies, such as that of the Austro-Hungarian Army of World War I. Imagine, for a moment, if the United States conquered Mexico and Canada, and drafted Mexicans and French Canadians in large numbers into the army. This does not even begin to compare to the Soviet predicament, since the recruits speak dozens of alien languages.

Ironically, the Tsarist army did not have the recruitment problems faced by the modern Soviet Army. The Tsarist army recruited mainly from the major Slavic ethnic groups: the Russians, the Ukrainians, and the Byelorussians, which make up about 70 percent of the population. They didn't bother to recruit heavily from the Muslim peoples of Central Asia, nor from the nomadic tribes of the Far East. The languages spoken by the Ukrainians and Byelorussians are not identical to Russian, but they share the same roots. The other Slavic groups were culturally similar to the Russians. Most belonged to the Orthodox church, and most came from similar peasant backgrounds.

The Soviet Union has a different rationale for military recruitment. To begin with, it no longer has the luxury of exempting the ethnic minorities from military service. The large size of the Soviet armed forces demands a large annual intake of new recruits. But also, the Soviets view military service as a national duty, in the broad sense of the term. Army duty is intended to homogenize this polyglot and diverse country. Recruits are forced to use Russian. They are subjected to vigorous political indoctrination. And they learn very quickly who is boss in the USSR.

## The Language Problem

In spite of all the efforts at Russification, and education and political indoctrination in secondary schools, many recruits are barely literate in Russian. Many are barely literate in any language. And there are substantial cultural differences. Muslims now make up more than 25 percent of the annual intake of draftees, and the percentage is rising. The Soviet Army accepts its role in Russification to a point. It is not organizationally prepared for extensive language training. Recruits least able to get along in Russian are siphoned off into paramilitary construction battalions, since the army combat branches really don't want to bother with them.

There is a distinct pecking order among the five arms of the Soviet armed forces. Highest priority goes to the Strategic Missile Force, which controls Soviet intercontinental ballistic missiles. Draftees are expected to be fluent in Russian. This is not the only criterion. The Strategic Missile Force also favors draftees with clean political records, since loyalty to the

Soviet state is viewed as essential to this most sensitive service. The Strategic Missile Force tends to recruit out of the Slavic regions. Minorities are least common in this branch. Three other services are also technically demanding: the Air Defense Force, the Navy, and the Air Force. These forces also have a certain amount of priority in the recruitment of technically adept young men, and they also favor Slavs.

The Ground Forces, the largest element of the Soviet armed forces, tends to receive the highest number of recruits. On average, they are of mediocre quality compared to the other services. The reasons are quite simple. It is the assumption of the military leadership that motor rifle troops, and to a lesser extent tank, artillery, and other specialized troops, need not be as able as the troops going to the other more intellectually demanding services. Soviet Ground Forces training and weapon design are based on the assumption that the enlisted troops in its units will not be capable of sophisticated training or sophisticated maintenance. There is an old saying: "If a weapon is stupid, and it works, it isn't stupid." Soviet weapons have to be simple enough to be handled by troops who do not speak the native language of Russia, and whose grasp of technology may be closer to the seventeenth century than the twentieth century.

## The Militarization of Soviet Society

Recruitment and training are helped along by the pervasive militarization of Soviet society. The average Soviet citizen has more knowledge of the military than his American, or even European, counterpart. As Soviet children pass through the school system, they are encouraged to join state-sponsored youth groups. The state youth groups somewhat resemble Western organizations such as the Boy Scouts and Girl Scouts, but with a heavier dose of political indoctrination. At the age of nine, youth can join the Young Pioneers, which tries to instill a sense of pride in the Soviet armed forces through films, comic books, and lectures. Heroic tales of the Great Patriotic War are a staple of this indoctrination. Memorialization of Russian sacrifices during the war is another example of the ties that are formed between youth groups and the military. Young Pioneers are selected to perform honorary guard duty at local war memorials, each youth in uniform and armed with an (unloaded) assault rifle. Although much of this can be dismissed as ordinary patriotic education, aspects of Young Pioneer activities are blatantly military. Summer youth camps frequently include junior league war games, in which the young boys are allowed to play alongside armored troop carriers, and inspect standard Soviet weapons.

The militarization of Soviet society is also rooted in the considerable pride that the country takes in its performance in World War II. The Communist party likes to boast about its considerable achievements in the economy, education, and health care. These boasts ring hollow in the ears of most Soviet citizens facing the daily reality of food and medical shortages. However, few will deny the accomplishments of the military, especially during the war. Military affairs is the only aspect of modern Soviet society where the USSR stands as an equal with the West.

At the age of fourteen, when teenagers are likely to enter secondary school, they can transition to the Komsomol. Like the Young Pioneers, the Komsomol has its paramilitary aspects; there are war games at summer camp, and heavy doses of political and promilitary propaganda. But Komsomol is more than a youth group. It is the first step toward Communist party membership, which is encouraged by school and community leaders for the most able students, gifted sportsmen, musicians, and other student leaders. Komsomol membership helps at recruitment time; members are more likely to be chosen for prestige services, for officer or NCO school, or for plum assignments. Komsomol membership is a sign of loyalty to the regime. Ambitious students flock to the Komsomol naturally; less enthusiastic students are subjected to a bit of societal pressure by school and community leaders. A teenager such as the fictional Demchenko is unlikely to be a Komsomol member because of his family background, but his commander, Lieutenant Bobrov, almost certainly would be in the Komsomol. The majority of young Soviet officers also belong to the organization.

By the time they reach secondary school, most Soviet students are becoming a bit cynical about the military. After years of indoctrination, the tales of heroism and valor begin to wear thin. Teenage rebellion is becoming as much a part of Soviet life as in the West. It's not that Soviet teenagers are unpatriotic. American teenagers become cynical toward television commercials without rejecting the nature of a consumer society. Soviet teenagers become cynical of the messages of the party, without rejecting allegiance to the society.

Although the Komsomol plays a role in preparing exceptional students for leadership in the army, the DOSAAF has a significant role in preparing the average Soviet student for the military. DOSAAF is a military-sponsored organization designed to drum up support for the armed forces outside the normal party or school system. In a totalitarian society like the USSR, there are no private sports or recreation groups. If you want to play on the local soccer team, you play on a DOSAAF-sponsored team. If you want to build model airplanes, you join a local DOSAAF hobby club. If you want to ride a motorbike, you join a DOSAAF motorbike club.

DOSAAF is sponsored by the military for a variety of reasons. In a country like the USSR where few people own private cars, the Army encourages young men to learn how to drive, and how to repair automobiles and trucks. It is better to train young men in basic automotive skills before they enter the military rather than during the two years they are under the colors. The other advantage DOSAAF enjoys is that it controls a lot of precious resources in a consumer-poor economy. This not only affects cars and motorbikes, but sporting and hobby equipment as well. In the USSR, you can't simply visit a local shop to buy a snorkel or a tennis racket. DOSAAF has an extensive flying club network to teach basic aviation, and sponsors skydiving clubs as well. The DOSAAF leadership is made up mainly of retired military officers, and the training frequently has a military flavor to it. Boys not only learn how to drive Lada sedans, but ZiL-130 trucks (as used by the army), and even BTR-70 armored infantry transporters.

## Preinduction Training

Since the mid-1960s, mandatory military training has been extended to secondary schools. And this applies to girls as well as boys. By the time they leave secondary school, Soviet girls as well as boys will know how to fieldstrip and use an assault rifle. The aim is to have the boys familiar with the basics of military service before they enter. This includes basic weapons training, basic drill, and familiarity with the organization of the armed forces. There is some difference in the training that young women receive. For example, there is more emphasis on medical training than on small arms, due in no small measure to the fact that women are not drafted, and very few women serve in the Soviet armed forces. But young Soviet women will be able to administer basic medical care in the event of chemical or nuclear contamination.

The Soviet Union may be a centrally planned, totalitarian society, but the quality of social services and government programs differs enormously across the vast country. The extent of preinduction training varies as well. Teenagers in the European regions of the USSR have a much greater chance of belonging to the more interesting DOSAAF clubs such as flying clubs or rally car clubs. The quality of secondary school military training is also better in these areas. Many schools in rural Central Asia have poor facilities, if any, for military training. And in some Muslim areas schools have even had to recruit women teachers for military training, which goes against the grain of these traditional societies. As a result, teenagers from European regions of the USSR enter the armed forces with distinct advantages over their Central Asian counterparts. They are more likely to speak Russian, to have had better preinduction training, and probably to have a usable skill that will steer them to the more desirable postings.

The draft inducts eighteen year olds in two waves. The first induction takes place in April and May, and the second in October and November, after the harvest. The Soviet Union is still an agricultural society, and the rhythms of the army have to give way to the rhythms of nature. About 75 percent of all eighteen year olds are inducted in any given year. Deferments come in three categories: education, family hardship, and health. A certain percentage of teenagers is exempted as physically or mentally unfit, and in rare circumstances, young men may be deferred due to family hardships. Educational deferments are not exemptions. In most cases, the student will be obliged to perform military duty after university. Only 12 percent of young men manage to escape military duty altogether. So for the vast majority of Soviet young men, army service is a normal aspect of growing up.

During the induction process, the recruits are assigned their combat unit or training unit. The complicated network of DOSAAF clubs, schools, and party organizations like the Komsomol has some impact on this process. Young men with a good record at a DOSAAF skydiving club have a better chance of entering the elite VDV Air Assault Force. A Russian student with good science grades, a clean political record, and Komsomol membership has a good chance of entering a prestige service such as the Strategic Missile Force. On the other hand, a young Azeri from a rural area of Azerbaijan, with a spotty record of school attendance and a poor grasp of Russian, will probably end up in a construction battalion for his two years of service.

For the average young Soviet citizen, chances are better than even that he will end up in the Ground Forces. Basic training is brief—usually four weeks. The texture of training differs considerably from the experience of most NATO soldiers, and more closely resembles that of a soldier from decades (if not a century) ago. Basic military skills are taught, including the wearing of and care for the uniform, saluting officers, and basic marching drills. Basic training also includes medical examinations and treatment. The USSR is so vast, and its health care system so spotty, that the army is obliged to pay careful attention to communicable diseases. The soldier receives a standard assortment of vaccines. Treatment, when needed, is brief and to the point. If problems are found during dental examinations, for example, the teeth are simply pulled (often without a painkiller!) to prevent further problems with them during the tour of duty.

## Squad Leader

One of the fundamental differences between the Soviet Ground Forces and most NATO armies is the hierarchy of command. The Soviet Army mirrors Soviet society. The Soviet style of command emphasizes rigid control from above. Orders to lower levels of command are in detail and give the subordinate officers less freedom in the way they execute the order. Lower layers of command have less autonomy than in NATO armies.

In the infantry, one of the more interesting structural differences between NATO and the Soviet Army is the matter of sergeants, better known in army parlance as noncommissioned officers (NCOs). In NATO armies, there is the traditional divide between officers and enlisted men. To bridge that gap, the NATO armies have an extensive professional NCO class. The NCOs are not simply technicians. They are leaders in their own right, entrusted with considerable responsibility by the officers to lead the men in their units. In the Soviet Army, there are sergeants, but they do not play the same role as in most NATO armies. The sergeants are not professional soldiers, simply draftees with more technical training. Soviet sergeants are not long-term professionals, and have little more experience in the army than the average draftee. The Soviets have done little to encourage a professional NCO class, and as a result, officers have to do many of the tasks that NCOs would perform in NATO armies.

The reasons for this situation are difficult to trace. The old prerevolutionary Tsarist army had an active and effective NCO class. It earned the resentment of many common soldiers and so was abolished. The Red Army also abolished many traditional aspects of officer distinctions, such as rank insignia and command prerogatives. But traditional officer practices returned in World War II to make the Red Army more combat effective. It is taking much longer to reconstitute the role of NCOs in the army.

The reasons why few soldiers remain in the Soviet Army as NCOs is simpler to explain: The pay is miserable and the life-style is grim. The pay is enough to buy cigarettes and snacks from the local canteen; it is not enough to support a family. There are no provisions for family housing for NCOs; there are simply no provisions for having a family. Life in the army is often brutal, the food is bad, and leave is infrequent. Until the 1970s, there was a single encouragement to stay in the army—the internal passport. All Soviet citizens must carry an identity card, which lists their hometown or city, and they are not allowed to travel freely about the country without an internal passport. Under the old system, a soldier was returned to his city of origin after army service. As a modest enticement to stay in the army for an additional three-year tour, sergeants received an internal passport, which allowed them to resettle away from their original homes. This may not seem like much, but for a farm boy from the rural regions of the USSR, this internal passport was a ticket to the big city, where industrial wages are far better than wages on a collective farm. An extra three years of drudgery in the army seemed like a reasonable price to many young soldiers. Only about 5 percent of the NCOs were long-term sergeants. This career was especially popular with rural Ukrainians, leading to the popular stereotype of the brutal Ukrainian sergeant major.

Since the war in Afghanistan, the NCO policy has been changing. The Soviet internal passport regulations were liberalized in the late 1970s to take into account the more mobile work force of the modern USSR. This reduced the main incentive for long-term sergeants. Afghanistan is probably the single greatest incentive within the military itself for change. The fighting there, even though on a much smaller scale than the U.S. commitment in Vietnam, revealed serious shortcomings in the command structure. It became clear that Soviet training and squad leadership was unsuitable to real combat conditions. The Soviet officer cannot handle all the assorted tasks that must be carried out on the modern battlefield. Some responsibility has to be given the NCOs.

The need for better-trained NCOs has also been prompted by changes in the technological level of equipment used by the modern Soviet Army. The situation faced by our fictional Sergeant Demchenko is a good example. Sergeants like Demchenko receive a special course, lasting about six months. At the end of it, they are given the rank of sergeant and posted to their unit. The course is more elaborate than that of the average recruit, and focuses on the typical tasks the sergeant will be expected to perform.

In contrast, the platoon officer, a lieutenant, receives about four years of training.

In the past, this system worked, because the lieutenant would always be around to direct his troops. But with new weapons like the BMP-2, this is no longer practical. The BMP-2 is complicated enough that the most senior member of the squad has to stay with it to direct its fire. The assistant squad leader, a man like Demchenko, is expected to lead the dismounted squad into battle. The experience in Afghanistan has shown that junior sergeants just do not have the experience or training for this demanding role.

The problem with draftee sergeants is that they have no military experience before they become sergeants. In NATO armies, sergeants generally rise through the ranks. They are given promotions on the basis of proven leadership abilities or other skills. By the time they reach the rank of sergeant, they have a clear understanding of the basic skills of soldiering. More importantly, they have a clear sense of what will be expected of them as leaders. Most Soviet draftee sergeants have no proven leadership skills beyond those judged by the draft board. Worst of all, they have no experience in the nature of army life. The Soviets have a system of rewarding outstanding enlisted men by giving them a rise in grade, but the majority of the sergeants remain one-term, draftee NCOs.

Furthermore, the Soviet Army is plagued with a tradition of hazing. Soldiers with two years of service bully soldiers with one and a half years, who bully those with only one year, and so on. Senior soldiers have the new recruits do the dirtiest jobs, and may even openly steal from them. This further dilutes the leadership role of sergeants. New sergeants are bullied by soldiers of lower rank who happen to have more service time. These hazing practices have been widely criticized in the Soviet press due to Gorbachev's policy of glasnost, but it will take years to end this tradition.

In a platoon like the one described in the fictional scenario, there is only a single professional soldier, the lieutenant. All of the sergeants are draftees. At the most, they will have almost two years of military service. In contrast, in a NATO platoon, several of the sergeants are likely to be long-term, professional soldiers. Because these sergeants have had experience and have shown proven leadership skills, the officers can entrust them with responsibilities far beyond those to which a Soviet sergeant would be assigned.

For example, in carrying out missions, Soviet combat leaders are much more explicit in their instructions than in NATO. The soldiers, including the NCOs, are expected to follow prescribed battle drill unless instructed otherwise. Soviet training does not encourage initiative on their part. In American and Western European society, there is an attitude that any actions not expressly forbidden are permissible. In Soviet society, due to the effects of Stalinism and police repression, the opposite is the case. What is not expressly permitted is forbidden. American society tends to be anarchic, with individuals taking it upon themselves to decide how they should act. Indeed, after World War II, a captured German officer is reported to have said: "War is chaos. Americans are good at war since they practice chaos every day." Traditional Russian communalism, combined with the lingering effects of Stalinist repression, leads to more cautious behavior. There is an old Russian expression, "The nail that sticks out will be hammered down." Soviet soldiers do not stick their necks out. They follow orders but go no further. If they lose their officers or leaders, or if an unusual situation crops up unexpectedly, they tend to lose momentum and wait for further instructions.

## Battle Drill

These traditions and attitudes lead to rigid command and control practices in the squad. For an NCO to pass his examinations, he has "tickets" to punch. These are tactical field exercises to determine whether the soldier has learned the basic NCO skills. The tests are very predictable, and the NCO cadet knows that many of the responses will be by rote learning. For example, one of the standard elements of the test is entitled "The Squad in the Offensive." There is a prescribed set of commands for the NCO to follow. These include the phrases "Squad, to the vehicle," "To your places," "Prepare for battle," "Start the engine," and "Move forward." This may seem remarkably elementary to most NATO soldiers. But to the Soviet Army, these basic drills are essential. It must be remembered that the cadet sergeant will probably be commanding a polyglot squad, several of whose members do not understand Russian very well. A limited number of key commands becomes familiar to the squad members, and they are expected to respond in a fashion every bit as rigid as the syllabus for cadet NCOs.

This is fine for a peacetime army. Everybody punches their tickets and displays the capability to perform their prescribed tasks. But real combat is chaos, and not reducible to simple training standards. Take, for example, fire discipline. Soviet troops are taught to fire their assault rifles from the hip during assaults. But the assaults in peacetime training cannot include the effects of fear and confusion on the part of the soldiers. As depicted in the scenario, the squads are likely to follow the training "by the book," with the result that by the end of the charge, they are running perilously low on ammunition without having really accomplished much by its expenditure. Soviet training norms assume that certain quantities of ammunition will be expended to eliminate certain types of targets, such as entrenched antitank missile launchers. But many of these norms are ridiculously low. The average Soviet soldier carries a very modest amount of ammunition. The tendency to follow rigid training procedures, combined with the uncertainties of real combat, can lead to disaster. This happened repeatedly in Afghanistan. There are numerous accounts in the Soviet press of squads being cornered by the *mujihadeen* after running low on, or running out of, ammunition and being forced to heroic extremes to escape.

The scenario depicted here presents the fictional Soviet squads with a straightforward objective. This is a "best-case" scenario. The Soviets considerably outnumber the Germans, and by sheer mass and firepower, they overcome the enemy. The young assistant squad leader is a competent individual with a certain amount of initiative. His troops perform well in their first battle in spite of their lack of experience. They run low on ammunition, but have enough to accomplish their task.

But this scenario could have been written in a very different fashion. Suppose the Germans had used light machine guns instead of assault rifles. How would a standard Soviet infantry attack hold up against that? Soviet training does not include realistic interplay between attackers and defenders. The standard training presumes that the infantry attack overruns the enemy positions without preparing the squad leaders for the possibility that they will endure such high losses that the mission will fail.

## The Soviet Rifle Squad

The configuration of Soviet infantry teams is also a bit odd. For example, the inclusion of a sniper in each platoon is curious. The sniper is a lingering aftereffect of Soviet experiences in World War II. The bulk of Soviet combat actions in this war were defensive, static holding actions. Snipers played an important role, since Soviet rifle training was often inadequate. The Soviets favored massed fire from submachine guns, which had considerable shock value and didn't require much marksmanship. This mentality still prevails. At long ranges, during static defensive operations, the snipers could provide much needed long-range firepower. But on a mechanized battlefield, it is hard to see how a sniper will fit in. The SVD sniper rifle does not have the rate of fire of the assault rifle, and the sniper seldom has a specialized role in assault tactics. The size of Soviet rifle squads continues to diminish, and the sniper seems to add less firepower to the platoon than an ordinary rifleman in many tactical settings.

Other Soviet infantry equipment is also curious. One of the most awkward examples is the matter of fire support from the BMP-2 infantry fighting vehicle. The BMP-2 is extremely low to the ground, so low, in fact, that the gun is not much higher than the height of an average soldier. This means there is a considerable risk that troops advancing in front of the BMP-2 can be hit by friendly fire unless the gunner is extremely careful; this was suggested in the unfortunate fate of Sergeant Yermakov's squad in the fictional account. This problem has led to peculiar Soviet infantry tactics that stress keeping open an avenue of fire for the BMP-2. This works well on training grounds where the targets can be carefully positioned, but on a fluid battlefield, this is likely to be a significant hindrance. Ironically, the American equivalent of the BMP, the M2 Bradley IFV, has been roundly criticized in the U.S. press for being too high! The press has never bothered to consider the effects of having an infantry vehicle with a gun positioned so low that it threatens its own dismounted troops.

## The Likelihood of Reform

The Afghanistan experience has forced Soviet tacticians out of their complacency. The Soviet Ground Forces are now beginning to examine what changes will be necessary to correct deficiencies found in the fighting. There has been considerable criticism of the fact that units, which passed their peacetime training exercises with flying colors, performed miserably in combat. There have been two tentative steps in reform over the past few years—more realistic training and more capable NCOs. The Soviets are experimenting with a less rigid and predictable training syllabus in an attempt to make training more realistic. It is unclear if these attempts can overcome deeply ingrained traits of Soviet military culture. The current system has been configured over the years to favor a sort of "grade inflation." There is little risk that a unit will fail its major tests unless the squad, platoon, company, or battalion commanders are monumentally incompetent. Scoring is predicated on the assumption that the majority of units *should* pass. This complacent attitude to training is probably most strongly rooted in the desire of the officers to avoid embarrassing failures.

The Soviet military officer class is much like the rest of Soviet society. It is a bureaucratic institution, with a rigidly equalitarian frame of mind. There is little attempt to foster a competitive spirit among officers. The military culture fosters an amiable degree of complacent mediocrity. Difficult training tests for the troops carry the risk that an officer's performance will be called into question. It is more comfortable for all concerned to have a lax training norm so that most units will pass. War seems unlikely, so peacetime garrison duty may as well not be career threatening. This kind of corruption and decay is common in many peacetime armies. But it was found to be deeply wanting in Afghanistan.

Many of the new-generation Soviet Army leaders, such as Marshal Nikolai Ogarkov and Marshal Dmitri Yazov, have decried these tendencies. Yazov made his reputation within the Ground Forces by introducing novel training techniques. Ogarkov made his reputation by insisting that the Soviet Army try to match the qualitative advantages of NATO. It has yet to be seen whether the criticisms of sloppy training that have become commonplace in Soviet military journals will actually result in fundamental changes in the nature of Soviet garrison life.

The same applies to the matter of improved sergeants. The real problem with the existing system is that sergeants remain in the Soviet armed forces for too short a period to develop any expertise. Unless the army plans to introduce radical reforms in matters such as pay and family support for NCOs, it is doubtful that the exhortations about improving NCO training will matter that much. The Soviet Army has begun tentative steps to address the problem through a program of warrant officers (*praporshchik*). But this is halfhearted at best, and not radical enough to provide sufficient qualified combat leaders. The creation of a large, skilled NCO class is unlikely for a variety of reasons. It would require a major infusion of rubles to pay for new base housing for professional NCOs and their families. It would place a large drain on the state defense budget, since it would require a major increase in pay for the professional NCOs. And it would deprive the civilian work force of a significant body of able men with leadership abilities.

So long as the Soviet armed forces maintain their bloated force structure, it will be difficult to enact substantial reforms of the command structure. The current effort appears to be aimed at giving sergeants greater responsibility and autonomy, but without a commensurate increase in pay or other inducements. It is the cheap approach to reform, expecting productivity growth without capital investment. And its chances for success are very limited.

The issues of infantry squad command are typical of the quality-versus-quantity debate in the Soviet Army, which tends to favor quantity over quality as compared to NATO armies. Even though squad for squad, the Soviet forces may be somewhat inferior, two or three Soviet squads will confront every single NATO squad.

## Soviet Infantry Vehicles

This dilemma of quantity versus quality also affects infantry mechanization. The fictional account of the skirmish of Demchenko's platoon was a best-case scenario with a well-equipped unit. Not all Soviet motor rifle units are lucky enough to be equipped with the BMP-2 Yozh. The majority of units are equipped with the older BMP-1, or with wheeled infantry transporters such as the BTR-60, BTR-70, or BTR-80.

The BMP-1 has nearly the same chassis as the BMP-2, but has a different turret and one or two more squad members. The BMP-1 Korshun turret uses a 73mm low-pressure gun instead of the 30mm autocannon of the BMP-2. This is a peculiar hybrid system, designed mainly to fight tanks. These days, however, the warhead is too small to be very effective against tanks. The real problem is that the system has a very poor effective range (700 meters), less than a common NATO antitank missile such as the Milan, which is effective to about 1,500 meters. In the scenario, the BMP-2s were able to sit back, beyond Milan range, and provide fire support, since their 30mm autocannons were effective to about 2,000 meters in this role. In the case of the BMP-1, that would be impossible. The BMP-1s would have the option of either staying in the rear and not providing fire support, or moving forward behind the infantry and risking destruction by enemy antitank missiles.

The other disadvantage of the BMP-1 is the placement of the squad commander. In the BMP-2, the commander is in the turret next to the gunner. He has access to the powerful sighting equipment in the turret and so he can obtain a very good picture of the battlefield confronting his troops. In the BMP-1, the commander sits in the alleyway behind the driver. He has a simple periscopic sight, and does not have the field of view of a squad leader in a BMP-2. When the squad dismounts, the squad leader is apt to be less prepared than is the case with the BMP-2 squad. These problems stem from the fact that the BMP-1 was designed to fight on a different battlefield than the conventional battlefield depicted in the scenario. The BMP-1 was designed in the late 1950s and early 1960s, when Soviet doctrine presumed that tactical nuclear weapons would be used. It was assumed that infantry would have to fight on radioactively contaminated battlefields, mounted inside the vehicle. This was also in the days before the advent of highly accurate wire antitank guided missiles (ATGMs). It didn't matter that the gun could not outrange ATGMs, because they weren't very common, and it was expected that the infantry would be fighting from inside the vehicle anyway.

In the 1970s, it became apparent that the war might take place under purely conventional conditions. Under these circumstances and in the presence of ATGMs, mounted attack became very risky. Soviet tactical doctrine suggests that in the presence of ATGMs, as in the scenario here, the attack be conducted with the infantry dismounted and fighting on foot. The squad would attack from a mounted position only if the enemy was disorganized or not equipped with antitank weapons.

In spite of its limitations, the BMP-1 is superior to the other alternative, the wheeled armored infantry transporters. The BTRs are all very similar in appearance. They have eight wheels and a sharply angled hull. The wheeled suspension gives them better mobility on roads than BMPs, and they are a good deal faster. They are also less complicated than BMPs and are easy to maintain. But they have many drawbacks. They are more poorly armed than BMPs: Their only armament is a 14.5mm heavy machine gun, which is less destructive than either the 30mm autocannon or the 73mm gun of the BMPs. They are more lightly armored. In Afghanistan, the mujihadeen found that they were vulnerable to close-range heavy machine gun fire against certain parts of the side. They are less mobile in rough country. They tend to get bogged down in deep mud or snow, and have a harder time traversing obstacles than tracked vehicles.

The older vehicles, like BTR-60PBs, were gasoline powered, which made them especially vulnerable to fires. Gasoline propulsion for combat vehicles is a bad idea. Once the fuel starts to burn, there is little chance to save the vehicle. Afghanistan is littered with their burned-out hulls. The BTR-60 was nicknamed the "wheeled coffin" by Soviet troops. The BTR-70 went to diesel fuel, but retained the peculiar two-engine configuration of the BTR-60, which causes a lot of maintenance headaches, since it means there are two transmissions to worry about. The reason for this layout is purely economic. The Soviet Union has a limited supply of large truck engines, and it was cheaper to use two cheap light truck engines than one scarce and expensive truck engine. The BTR-80 finally did away with both of these problems by adopting both a single engine and diesel propulsion.

The oddest feature of the BTRs is their hull shape. Exit and entrance are through side hull doors. It helps if you are an acrobat to get in and out of them. The BTR-60PB is the worst, but the BTR-70 and BTR-80 are only marginally better. This is not very important if the squad dismounts or loads on board outside the range of enemy fire. But it makes the process of exiting and entering the vehicle very dangerous if under enemy fire. The BTR-60 was viewed so skeptically by the Czechoslovak and Polish armies that they decided to develop their own BTR equivalent, the OT-64 SKOT, which has a single diesel engine and spacious rear doors for easy access.

Why is the BTR so bad a design? It has more to do with economics than technology. Soviet armored vehicle designers are talented, but were tightly constrained in the design of the BTRs. The Soviet Army wanted a top-of-the-line infantry vehicle for its forward deployed troops facing NATO. These units got the BMP. But the Soviets could not afford to equip all their divisions with that vehicle. The cost of wheeled infantry vehicles like the BTRs was about one-seventh that of a BMP, and the BTR was designed to be light, simple to manufacture, and cheap to maintain.

The BTR option is an example of the Soviet tendency for a high-low mix. The Soviets cannot afford to equip their whole army up to NATO standards. So they equip part of the army with top-notch hardware like the BMP, and the rest of the army with low-grade equipment like the BTR. This is not unknown in NATO. For example, the British Army has been adopting the Warrior, which is a counterpart to the U.S. Bradley and the Soviet BMP-2. But to flesh out other units, they are also adopting the Saxon, which is worse than the BTR-80 in many respects. But this is less common in NATO than in the Warsaw Pact. The U.S. Army is currently acquiring only the high-tech M2 Bradley, even though the older and simpler M113 APC remains in service as well.

Like the country from which it springs, the Soviet Army is very diverse. The motor rifle divisions in interior military districts such as the Urals are apt to be equipped with troop carriers, artillery, and small arms from the 1960s. They do not necessarily share much in common with the high-grade units in the Group of Soviet Forces-Germany or the Central Group of Forces in Czechoslovakia. As a result, it is easy to misjudge the quality of the Soviet armed forces. An assessment that considers the "average" Soviet unit is apt to underestimate the quality of the Soviet forces opposite NATO. An assessment that acts as though all Soviet units are up to the standards of the units facing NATO can exaggerate the overall quality of Soviet forces. An appreciation for the diversity of the Soviet Army is essential in making a balanced assessment of their effectiveness.

# CHAPTER 3

# Tank Attack: The Charge at Pressbach

0530, 3 October, East of Pressbach, FRG

Captain Pavel Krylov's head slumped forward, colliding with the target designator sight in front. His padded tanker's helmet protected his forehead, but the sudden jolt woke him up. The inside of his T-80M[1] tank was pitch black, and it took him several seconds to remember where he was. Over the earphones in his helmet came the noisy crackle of an incoming message.

"Vorona One, Vorona One, come in please. Sokol Three here, over."[2]

It was the voice of his 3d Company commander, Lt. Vladimir Vasilev. Krylov adjusted the throat mike on his helmet, and turned on the overhead turret light so he could see the adjustment controls on the tank's R-123M radio. The audio level was too low. After three days of fighting, Krylov had suffered some hearing loss from the incessant noise.

"Sokol Three, this is Vorona One, over."

"Vorona One, I've been trying to reach you for two minutes. We have a visitor, near the left clearing. Shall I engage? Over."

Krylov realized he was so exhausted he simply hadn't heard Vasilev's

---

1. T-80M is the term used in this book to refer to the Soviet T-80 main battle tank when fitted with explosive reactive armor. The actual Soviet designation for this version is not known. The T-80M is armed with a 125mm gun and has a three-man crew—a driver, gunner, and tank commander. Unlike most NATO tanks, it has an automatic loader instead of a fourth crewman.

2. The radio call signs for this unit use the names of birds. *Vorona* is Russian for "crow," *Sokol* is Russian for "falcon."

initial radio calls. It wasn't good radio discipline to continue to repeat calls. Vasilev should have sent a runner. Something must be urgent. Krylov got on the tank intercom.

"Pavel, what do you see down by the clearing?"

The tank gunner, Sgt. Pavel Ossopovich, looked through his passive night sight. The vehicle was nearly a kilometer away. The sight depended on moonlight, of which there was precious little that night. It was damn difficult to determine precisely what the vehicle was. Then, for a moment as it moved, it was silhouetted against the skyline. A thin barrel. A scout vehicle, not a tank.

"Comrade Captain, it looks like a scout vehicle of some sort."

"Is it one of ours?"

"Comrade Captain, it does not appear to be ours. It has no night position lights on. Shall I prepared to engage?"

Krylov, still a bit groggy from his interrupted sleep, thought for a moment. He had not been informed of any Soviet scouts being sent out in front of his position. It was not like the regiment not to inform him of activity in his area. Still it could be a straggler. Or a NATO vehicle hunting out the location of his unit for an artillery strike or attack. It would be prudent to eliminate the threat. He switched to the radio.

"Sokol Three, you are closer. Engage the hostile, over." Krylov expected to hear the sharp report of the neighboring tank's gun. There was nothing but silence.

"Vorona One, we have problems, over."

Krylov reacted quickly. He switched from radio to mike. "Pavel, we will engage." Then he switched from the personal to the professional. It

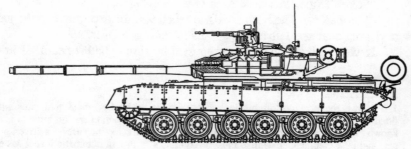

**T-80 Tank with Explosive Reactive Armor**

would be straight battle drill, without pleasant familiarities. "Gunner, hard core . . . target, 850 meters."[3]

Krylov heard the ammunition carousel under their seats make its usual whirring sound. The automatic loader was seeking out an antiarmor projectile from the different types of ammunition available. The steady metallic clanking of the autoloader continued. Instinctively, Krylov moved rightward and pulled his coveralls taut. The autoloader mechanism would sometimes catch on the uniform of the unwary, and slam the hapless crew into the gun breech along with the ammunition. With two hard smacks, the autoloader pushed home the projectile, followed by the propellant casing. The whole operation took about ten seconds. Krylov heard his gunner on the mike.

"Hard core, loaded . . . engaging target."

Krylov braced himself for the blast. The big D-81TM 125mm gun fired, shaking the entire tank. Krylov lost his night vision as the sky in front of the tank filled with the enormous muzzle flash. The huge mass of the gun slammed backward in the tank, spewing out a metal stub casing into the hopper—the tiny remnant of the ammunition.

"Gunner, report."

Ossopovich had closed his eyes as the gun had fired, and now looked into the sight. The target had obviously been hit, since it was burning fiercely. In seconds, the vehicle exploded.

"Target destroyed, Comrade Captain."

Krylov was content that his gunner had hit the target with only a single round. But he was bothered about its identification. No other enemy vehicles seemed present. He decided to walk over to the neighboring tank rather than compromise radio security any further. He radioed the nearby tank.

"Sokol Three, I'm coming over."

"Vorona One, understood, out."

Krylov climbed out of his T-80M. It was still dark outside, but there

---

3. There are two standard choices of ammunition for the 125mm gun on the T-80, a high-explosive round for engaging lightly armored or unarmored targets, and a high-velocity antiarmor round. The Soviets usually call this latter round a "hard-core" round, whereas the usual U.S. name is "sabot" or APFSDS (armor-piercing fin-stabilized discarding sabot). The T-80 does not usually carry a high-explosive antitank (HEAT) round. However, some T-80s can fire a guided antitank missile through the tube in lieu of conventional ammunition.

was enough moonlight to make out the dark shape of the neighboring tank. Lieutenant Vladimir Vasilev was already out of the tank and standing by the side.

"Vladimir Sergeivich, what was the problem?"

"Captain, it was the ammunition. As it was going into the breech, I noticed the propellant casing was smeared with oil. It could have misfired in the gun. We'll have to clean it out."[4]

"I'm glad you caught it. Look, we'll have to send someone down to that vehicle once the fire has lessened. Let's find out what it was. Send one of your tanks, and tell them to be careful near the tree line."

As they were speaking, a UAZ-469 jeep pulled out of the woods behind them with its faint night driving lights on. As it approached, Krylov recognized it as one from Yastreb (hawk), the code name for the 65th Guards Tank Regiment, to which Krylov's 18th Guards Independent Tank Battalion was attached for this operation. Krylov's battalion had been kept in reserve by the commander of the 18th Guards Motor Rifle Division[5] for use at an opportune moment. Apparently that moment had come.

The damp October weather, the jarring ride of the past three days of hard road marches, and the stress of command had taken their toll on Pavel Krylov. He was thirty-four years old and had been a captain for three years.[6] His career was unexceptional. He had come from a traditional Russian military family. His father, a tanker like himself, had served in the final year of the Great Patriotic War. Krylov's unit had been stationed in Czechoslovakia before the war. It did not have the newest equipment,

---

4. The ammunition for the Soviet 125mm gun (and also the German and U.S. 120mm gun) uses semiconsumable propellant casing instead of the traditional brass or aluminum casings. This type of casing is now popular, since it burns up when the gun is fired, and so the interior of the tank doesn't fill up with spent metal casings. However, these casings, if contaminated by oil or other substances, can burn erratically, or the case can rupture. Soviet tankers are trained not to fire damaged ammunition.

5. Soviet motor rifle divisions have one tank regiment and two motor rifle regiments. Some divisions, like the one depicted here, have an additional complement of tanks in the form of an independent tank battalion. Krylov's unit is one of these. This unit is intended to act as a forward detachment, or to exploit breakthroughs won by the larger regiments.

6. Although one might expect a battalion commander to be a major by NATO standards, Soviet units are often led by more junior officers than their NATO counterparts. Indeed, Soviet battalions are sometimes commanded by senior lieutenants.

neither the T-72MS nor the T-84A. But the T-80M was a good tank. Its turbine engine gave it a great deal of power, and its armor was relatively effective in stopping NATO antitank missiles.

His battalion was typical of most Ground Forces units in the Central Group of Forces. About 60 percent of the unit was Slavic—mainly Russian, but a significant number of Ukrainians and Byelorussians. These troops usually caused the least problem. At least they could speak decent Russian! They were not the brightest he had ever known; the "prestige" services usually siphoned off the bright ones for technical services and the star athletes for special forces. Krylov's battalion was left with the average and below average. Their training was adequate by Soviet standards. His deputy, Sr. Lt. Nikolai Gorin, had made certain they had passed the mandatory field trials. Maybe they had cut a few corners in training, but then everybody did.

Krylov's battalion had been moved to the vanguard yesterday afternoon, the third day of the war. It had been three grim days of waiting. The division had moved across the Czech-German frontier near Klatovy in the early morning of 30 September. The terrain of the Bavarian woods favored the defenders. Their main opponent was supposed to be the 4th Panzergrenadier Division (the German equivalent of a Soviet motor rifle division). But the encounters were so sporadic and vicious, it was very difficult to tell exactly who their opponents were. Most of the captured prisoners were from reserve territorial brigades, not from the regular Bundeswehr. They were not especially well equipped, having mostly old M113 troop carriers and old model Leopard 1 tanks. But they did have the deadly little Milan antitank missiles.

The forest was too thick in most places for tank traffic, and most of the traffic was canalized down forest roads. As a result, it was fairly easy for the Germans to set up ambushes. The worst were the hidden missile squads. They were like lice. You just couldn't lose them.

A Soviet column would move down a forest road. Sometimes the lead vehicle would be hit by missile fire. Other times, the Germans would wait until the column had passed and would open fire with Milan missiles from the rear. The division had tried everything. Heavy artillery bombardment was futile. The forest deadened any artillery fire, and the Germans were usually dug in. The motor rifle division dismounted their infantry from their BMP-2 infantry vehicles and sent them forward along the edge of the forest, with the vehicles farther to the rear. This lead to heavy firefights with German infantry, from prepared positions in the woods. While the

Germans were usually overcome, the process was long and costly. The division was far behind its schedule.

The 18th Guards Motor Rifle Division was supposed to reach the Danube River south of Regensburg by the end of the second day of fighting. An advance element of the division had in fact reached the river late the previous night. But it would take at least another day to bring up the divisional bridging equipment, which was strung out back to the Czech frontier. The 65th Guards Tank Regiment (GTR), to which Krylov's battalion was now attached, had been sent down the main road to Deggendorf in an attempt to seize bridges over the river. The divisional commander hoped that a plunge southward might save him the time and cost of a risky river crossing operation. But the divisional commander expected heavy fighting for Deggendorf. So he planned to send Krylov's battalion on a parallel course through some small roads east of Hunderdorf to try to reach the Danube in a less conspicuous location. If the main assault failed, or if the Germans blew the bridges, he would have an alternative location to launch a river crossing operation.

For the first two days of the war, Krylov's battalion had seen little fighting. The battalion was held in divisional reserve, and moved forward in march formation behind the advancing units. In a way, it was a more demoralizing experience than actually being in combat. The roads were littered with the debris of war. Most sickening of all, it was mostly Soviet equipment—burned and shattered BMPs, tanks, and trucks. Sometimes, the medical units had already cleaned up the area before his tanks rolled past. But often, Krylov's tanks rolled past the scene of fighting that had concluded less than an hour before. The sights and smells of the burned wreckage and mutilated bodies were numbing.

Krylov's battalion had first seen combat on the night of 1 October, two days before. The battalion was used to support an attack by the 65th GTR near a small town. The terrain was finally opening up a bit, although it was still forested, and rather hilly. The Germans were equipped with Leopard 1 tanks. Although it was pitch black, the Leopards had begun firing at Krylov's battalion from their positions near a small copse. Obviously, they had passive night vision sights, since there was no evidence of infrared searchlights. His T-80M tanks had passive sights as well, but it was difficult to pick out targets against the dark tree line. His tanks were crossing a field, and the contrast was enough to enable the Germans to see his unit. He instructed his unit to use their infrared searchlights in white light mode, switching to infrared. The sudden glare of the searchlights temporarily blinded the Germans' passive night sights, and the infrared searchlights made the task of locating the Germans all the easier. The searchlights also made the Soviet tanks very obvious, but they heavily outnumbered the German tanks. After about a half hour of fighting, the Germans withdrew, leaving behind four Leopard 1 tanks in flames. Krylov's unit had lost three tanks and suffered damage on one more.

The third day was tense and uneventful at first. The 65th GTR moved forward, and Krylov's 18th GITB (Guards Independent Tank Battalion) remained in reserve awaiting further instructions. The day was spent putting the tanks in order and helping the divisional recovery teams with 65th GTR tanks disabled in the previous night's fighting. In the late afternoon, the battalion was ordered forward to assist in another night attack. Only two companies were involved, since the terrain didn't favor the commitment of all five of the battalion's companies.

The fighting that night went very badly for Krylov's unit. He had committed the 5th Tank Company, commanded by Yuriy Dmitryev, and the 1st Company of Nurken Abdirov. Dmitryev's company stumbled into a position defended by an enemy tank platoon. The Germans had opened fire at 2,000 meters, well outside the normal visual range for passive night sights. Dmitryev had tried the same trick as the night before, illuminating his opponents with the tank's searchlights in the hopes of temporarily blinding their night sights. By the time they recovered, his company should have covered half the distance to their objective. Unfortunately, the enemy tanks were not using passive night sights, but thermal imaging sights. They were not blinded; to the contrary, the sudden use of searchlights only made Dmitryev's tanks more obvious. In short order, all ten tanks from the company had been hit. Abdirov's company attempted to respond, but began being hit by guided antitank missiles.

The T-80M is fitted with reactive armor, and the initial strikes by the missiles harmlessly exploded the reactive armor.[7] But Abdirov's crews had never seen reactive armor go off at night. The effect was spectacular. The bricks on the turret front exploded from the impact of the missile, but

---

7. Explosive reactive armor (ERA) consists of small metal boxes filled with high explosive. When the shaped charge (chemical energy) high-explosive warhead of an antitank missile strikes the box, the box explodes and propels a metal plate at the missile warhead. This reaction blunts the penetration of the missile warhead. Reactive armor is designed mainly to stop shaped charge warheads, like those fitted to infantry antitank rockets and guided antitank missiles. It has no substantial effect on the standard types of tank ammunition used in tank combat, such as the APFSDS (kinetic energy) projectile.

the explosion deflected the missile blast, preventing the missile warhead from penetrating the tank. The blast rocked the tanks, which startled several crew members, who thought their tanks had been mortally wounded. The crews were edgy, since survivors from the 65th GTR had warned them that they had only a few seconds to abandon a tank once it was penetrated. It had become painfully obvious that Soviet tanks blew up rather easily. Actually, Abdirov's tanks had not been penetrated, but the flash, noise, and lack of experience led to panic. Three tanks that had been hit were abandoned by their crews. Two more tanks were hit and halted. The remaining tanks moved forward, but in the confusion could not find Dmitryev's wounded company. The fighting ended around 2000, with the enemy withdrawing.

Krylov's battalion was ordered to halt for the night and await orders. Krylov drove up to the clearing where Dmitryev's company had been hit. Of the ten tanks in the attack, four had received solid turret hits, which had resulted in internal explosions. All the crew had been killed almost instantly. Three tanks had suffered hull penetrations, but at least part of the crews had been able to abandon the tanks. Two tanks had received hits in the engine compartment and suffered mild fire damage. One had been hit in the track and was immobilized. There was nothing Krylov could do to recover the damaged tanks. He supervised the surviving company members as they tried to locate the wounded and the survivors. His deputy battalion commander and political officer, Sr. Lt. Nikolai Gorin, cleared up the situation with the badly shaken 1st Tank Company. The 1st Company commander, Nurken Abdirov, was the only Kazakh officer in the battalion. Gorin did not have a high regard for him, although his men found him to be a competent and tough officer.

Krylov ordered the companies to adopt a nighttime defensive position in the hilly area near the site of the earlier skirmish. The tanks were to be kept away from the woods, for fear of German troops sneaking up at night with antitank weapons. They were to position their tanks with clear lines of fire toward the woods, but all were warned to place the tanks in hull-down with only the turret above the hill contours. It was an elementary precaution that the crews should have naturally adopted. But Krylov knew his men were exhausted by the four hours of road march and the unexpected skirmish.

The crews had nearly two hours of preventive maintenance work before they could bed down. Krylov longed for the days with the old T-62s. They were not as complex, and had four-man crews. The daily maintenance chores were simpler and there was an extra man to help out. The T-80s had only a three-man crew. Their autoloader, improved fire controls, and transmission required much more careful maintenance. And, because of the autoloader, there was one less man to do the work. The real problem in the unit was boresighting the guns. The D-81TM 125mm tank gun was an awesome weapon, but a bit big for a forty-two-ton tank. When it fired, the whole tank reeled. The severe recoil knocked around the fire controls, and could bash the gun out of boresight. If not dealt with, the tank gun lost accuracy at longer ranges.

Some of the battalion had managed to boresight their guns the previous morning after the first skirmish. But not all. And now the 1st Company had been involved in the night's fighting, maybe knocking their guns around a bit. At night, it was too awkward to try to do any boresighting, so Krylov just tried to put the issue aside. The 1st Company had not used much ammunition, but he made certain they filled up their autoloaders for the next day's likely encounters. As a last measure, Krylov checked to be sure that the companies put out sentries. Each tank was expected to keep one of its crewmen awake for guard duty on hour-and-a-half shifts. Every third tank kept one man at the passive night sight, with the tank powered up.

At about 0300, early on the morning of 1 October, Captain Krylov curled up as best he could inside his T-80M tank to try to get some sleep. There were probably another thousand things to check on, but he would need his sleep for the next day's fighting. It was from this sleep that Krylov had been awakened moments before, due to the unexpected enemy patrol. And now there was a visit from the regimental staff to deal with.

The visiting jeep screeched to a halt near the T-80M tank. Krylov recognized the officer as Capt. Maksim Denisov.

"How are things, Pavel Ivanovich?" enquired the captain.

Krylov was surprised he even remembered his name. "A bit tired, Captain Denisov. So what brings you here?"

"We're planning a major attack today, Comrade Captain, and your battalion will be used in full strength. Come on over to my villiys[8] and I'll explain your orders."

---

8. *Villiys* is Russian slang for "jeep." It stems from the fact that the Red Army received large numbers of Willys jeeps during World War II, and the name stuck. In fact, this "jeep" is a UAZ-469, a Soviet-manufactured vehicle more similar in size and weight to civilian jeeps than to the U.S. Army's smaller M151.

Both officers entered the rear seats of the UAZ-469. It was still dark outside, so the staff captain brought out a small flashlight to illuminate the maps.

"We think we finally have the Germans broken in this sector, Captain Krylov. One good push and the road should be free over the Danube at Deggendorf. We should be able to push our reserve motor rifle regiment into the gap, and into the better country beyond. Your assignment is to overwhelm the German positions in the area west of this main approach. At the same time, our regiment will be attacking on a parallel course farther east. When you have secured this ridge line, in Pressbach, your battalion will swing slightly to the right and grab a position astride the river. If we take some bridges at Deggendorf, we won't need to launch a river crossing here. But you never know. This river crossing is vital to the success of our operation."

Captain Denisov handed Krylov a 1:50,000 scale map of the area, and continued his instructions. "The situation is as follows. Your battalion is currently on the fringe of this woods. Beyond the woods is a shallow depression, a bowl if you will, about a kilometer across. Above the valley is a low ridge, about seventy-five meters higher than the depression. There's a small clump of farm buildings there. The ridge continues about two kilometers westward to another rise, where the village of Pressbach is located. We have reason to believe that the village is held by about ten enemy armored vehicles. There are seven or eight tanks, and some infantry transporters. This was the unit your troops encountered last night.

"Colonel Rudnitskiy suggests the following. You are to move your battalion into the depression, which will give your battalion room to spread out and prepare battle formations. There are two roads leading into the depression. You may have to fight for the clearing, but we think the main enemy defense is on the second ridge, where the village is located. You should keep one company in reserve, split up between the farm buildings on your right flank at Hill 320 and the farm buildings at the crest of the first hill in the center of your position. You should probably consolidate your Yashcheritsa[9] missiles with this unit to give you overwatch cover-

---

9. *Yashcheritsa* (Russian for "lizard") is the name used here to refer to a new guided anti-tank missile fired from the 125mm gun. The AT-8 Songster was the first of these missiles. Apparently, however, new types are entering service, using laser guidance rather than radio command guidance.

age. The three remaining companies should be spread out, with one moving out of the depression to the left of the main farm, and the other two moving between the main farm and Hill 320. Move at top speed. Once you have moved out, the enemy will undoubtedly begin firing on you. Keep moving. You have 2,500 to 3,000 meters to cover. Your overwatch company can probably knock out three or four of the enemy tanks. Don't begin slowing down to fire until you are about 1,000 meters from the enemy. And make sure you know where they are before you begin engaging them.

"Once you have overrun their position, police up the area, and move your battalion south to the edge of the river east of Bogen. The attack will start at 0700. You should have your battalion in the clearing by 0630. We will give you a little artillery prep on the village, but frankly, it won't accomplish much. Any questions?"

"No, Comrade Captain, it's quite clear. But let me ask you this. The tanks my companies encountered last night were not the usual Leopard 1s. They seemed to have thermal sights. Are we facing a Leopard 2 unit, or some new tank unit in the sector?"

"Comrade Captain, you forget that the Germans have been modernizing the old Leopard 1s. Some of the rebuilt vehicles do have thermal sights. We have no evidence of any other unit in the sector. But it is possible we will encounter American M1 Abrams a bit farther west beyond Regensburg. Is that all?"

Krylov nodded and crawled out of the back seat of the jeep. He had no time to waste. The regiment obviously expected him to move his battalion through the woods at dark, and into the clearing at just about daybreak. He was not happy with the idea of moving into the woods in the dark. But from the looks of the map, the two roads leading into the woods were very narrow—too narrow for Milan missile teams. The Milans needed a good 350 meters before they could be sure of guidance. Besides, Captain Denisov seemed to know that the Germans had pulled back to the Pressbach Hill. Krylov radioed his four company commanders to meet at his tank promptly. He also instructed them to have their crews off-load any Yashcheritsa missiles from their tanks and pass them over to the tanks of Lieutenant Abdirov's company.

The small group gathered behind Captain Krylov's tank. Lieutenant Abdirov saw the battalion political officer, Senior Lieutenant Gorin, and moved to the other side of the circle. Captain Krylov brought out the area map and hung a small electric lantern on the cradle for the rear fuel drums.

"Comrades, we'll be setting off for our objective by 0600, so we have to make this meeting brief. Our objective is a ridge about four kilometers to the west, just beyond this woods. Regiment informs us that the nyemtsi have pulled back beyond the woods and are occupying the village of Pressbach on the ridge. It's not really a ridge so much as a slight rise. At 0600, we move out from here in two columns. Lieutenant Bogdanov will take the lead with 2d Company through the center part of the woods. The 1st and 3d Companies will follow. Lieutenant Larikov will take 4th Company around the northern end of the woods and move down this path. At 0630, I will give you a radio signal to begin moving into this depression here. It is possible that the enemy has forces in these farm buildings near Hill 320, and over here in the farm at the center of the area. Expect trouble. If we come under fire, the lead elements from 2d and 4th Company will have to deal with it quickly.

"Once we're safely out into the bowl, we will take up battle formation. We are going to attack in a line formation with 2d, 3d, and 4th Company. Nurken Ivanovich, your 1st Company is going to serve as overwatch. When we move out of the bowl, you divide up your company in two, half over here at Hill 320 and half here in the main farm. You keep us covered with missile fire."

Krylov could see that the little Kazakh was upset.

"Comrade Captain, I am very sorry for the shameful performance of my men last night," said Abdirov. "I can assure you that it will not happen

# 18th Guards Independent Tank Battalion

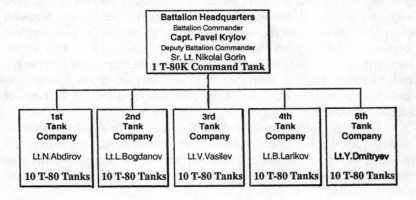

again. You do not have to fear for the valor of my men. We would be pleased to be in the vanguard of the attack."

Krylov realized that the honor of the Kazakh had been offended. "Comrade Lieutenant, I did not select your company to play the overwatch role because of the troubles last night. That kind of action can be expected from inexperienced troops in difficult circumstances. I picked your men because your company has consistently done the best of our battalion in gunnery exercises. As we all know, you have more crew with tank sniper distinctions than any other. We are depending heavily on you for our safety. Regiment insists that we use a fast approach to the objective. Hold the firing until we close to 2,000 meters. We have to get in close and wade into the enemy positions. We cannot afford to engage them in long-range duels from a halt. So in each of your companies, let one platoon halt their fire around 2,000 meters, while the other two platoons continue to close with the enemy at top speed. Don't use smoke unless you really need it. Abdirov, you will be responsible for destroying as many German tanks as possible while we make this approach. Your fire must keep their heads down."

Abdirov was a bit concerned when Captain Krylov mentioned the use of smoke mortars. If any of the tanks did use smoke, it would make his job of providing overwatch much more difficult. The smoke might obscure the target. But Abdirov, never prone to question the instructions of his superiors, was even less so after the embarrassing performance of his company the night before.

Before the meeting had concluded, a tanker from Vasilev's company approached the group.

"Comrade Captain, I wish to report."

"Proceed," replied Krylov.

"Comrade Captain, we attempted to inspect the wreckage of the enemy vehicle. It appears to have been an American vehicle of some sort from the markings on its parts. The damage was too great to tell exactly what it was."

Krylov concluded it was probably an American-built M113, in German service, which they had been encountering for the past few days. (Had he seen the thin barrel, as had his gunner, Ossipovich, he would not have come to this conclusion.[10]) He ended the meeting.

---

10. The vehicle was an American M3 Bradley cavalry scout vehicle. Vehicle recognition is a common problem in both the Warsaw Pact and NATO.

"Is everything about our objectives understood? . . . Fine. . . . Mount up and let's move. The regiment and the division are counting on us to take these positions."

Krylov used the foothold on the right side of his T-80M to lift himself up. The back of the tank was littered with tarps and equipment, so he had to clamber over the reactive armor bricks to get to the turret roof. He tried to be careful not to dislodge any of the bricks. These funny little blocks could save his tank.

The hatch was open, and his gunner nodded when he climbed into the turret. Krylov hadn't realized how bad the inside stank. There was the lingering smell of cordite from the firing earlier, mingled with the smell of sour soup and sweat. He had spilled a ration of soup on the floor, and by now it reeked. He plugged the cord from his helmet into the tank intercom and radioed the driver to start up the tank. The T-80M began with its characteristic whine. Krylov stood up on his seat to see how the rest of the battalion was doing. There was just about enough light to see the dark silhouettes of the tanks. A few hatches were open, and a pale blue light shone out. Most of the tanks had their small formation lights on. The drivers had switched on their infrared driving lights, unseen to the naked eye, to guide themselves through the dark.

The tank column winded its way through the woods, Krylov's tank about five tanks back from the head of the column. As the lead tank approached the opening into the bowl, it halted. Lieutenant Bogdanov got out, as did Krylov, and walked along the woods to the opening. The terrain in front was ploughed farmland. There was considerable evidence of armored vehicle traffic, crisscrossing the fields. To the left, the outline of a large farm could barely be seen in the early morning mist. There was just enough light to see the other, smaller farm at the foot of Hill 320 on the right side. Krylov had a pair of image-intensification night vision binoculars, and used them to survey the high country in front of his tanks. He saw no evidence of enemy forces on the rise in front of him, but then even if they were there, he probably wouldn't be able to see them.

Moving out of the woods would be risky. Krylov told Lieutenant Bogdanov to move out a single platoon of tanks very quickly, and to fire their smoke grenade launchers as soon as they cleared the opening, in order to create a cloud in front of the opening. If they were engaged, they were to eliminate the opposition. At this point the rest of the battalion would exit. Krylov radioed Lieutenant Larikov, whose company would be pushing out of the other road to the right near the foot of Hill 320. He was to follow the same procedure.

At 0630, the two platoons came charging out of the woods, spraying out smoke grenades. There was a slight ground fog, and the flowering smoke grenade cloud blended imperceptibly into it. The action did not seem to elicit any fire from the main farm, but when Lieutenant Larikov's platoon turned around the edge of the woods, a few antitank missiles came in their direction. Two hit, but the reactive armor panels defended the tank against penetration. What was odd is that the missiles struck the roof bricks, not the usual front or side bricks. Larikov had heard of top-attack missiles, but this was the first he had seen of them. Larikov's platoon fired into the farm buildings near Hill 320 with high explosive, and after a dozen rounds, they halted. No more missile fire came from the farm. Larikov radioed to Krylov that his men had spotted two armored vehicles pulling back from the main farm. He said they looked to him like American Bradleys or German Marders, not M113s. Krylov thought for a moment, worrying that the unit they faced might be a fresh American or German armored unit, and not the remnants of the roughed-up German territorial brigade they had been fighting. He hoped this wasn't the case.

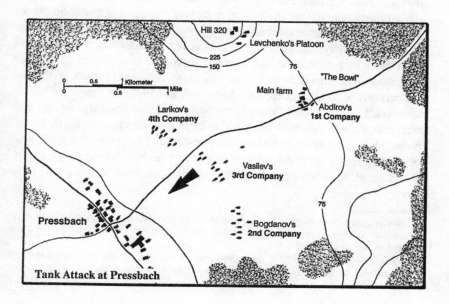

**Tank Attack at Pressbach**

With the bowl safe, the battalion moved forward. When the war had started, the battalion had numbered fifty-one T-80M tanks.[11] There were ten tanks in each of the five companies, plus Krylov's command tank. Each of the companies had ten tanks—three platoons with three tanks each and the company commander's tank. Three companies in formation would stretch out about a kilometer and a half. The battalion was down to thirty-seven tanks. Ten tanks had been lost when Dmitryev's company had been wiped out the previous evening, and four other tanks had been lost in other fighting or due to mechanical problems.

The usual battle formation was three platoons in line, about fifty meters between each tank. There would be thirty tanks in the initial attack, stretched out over a distance of about one and a half kilometers. The 2d Company, commanded by Sr. Lt. Leonid Bogdanov, was expected to use the gully to the left of the main farm to approach the Pressbach Hill. The 3d and 4th Companies would attack across the main pastures. They would have the toughest time. Krylov would follow these two companies.

At 0700, the tank crews heard the sound of outgoing artillery. It sounded like Grad 122mm rockets[12] rather than tube artillery. The rockets smashed into the village on the rise three kilometers to the west. At this signal, Abdirov's divided tank company moved out in the lead to occupy overwatch positions at the two farms. The remaining three companies followed suit once Abdirov's tanks were about 300 meters in advance.

Abdirov reached the main farm first, and was the first battalion officer to get a clear picture of the battle area. The objective, the village of Pressbach, was clearly visible across the neat farm fields. Abdirov was a bit taken back by how flat the terrain was after all the trouble getting through the woods. The area in front of Pressbach was completely open, with little opportunity for cover except for a few small dips in the ground. The battalion would have a rough time getting across the terrain if the enemy was well entrenched. Abdirov saw little evidence of enemy activity in Pressbach. The rocket barrage had started a few small fires and left a good deal of dust hanging over the village. Abdirov watched his crews skillfully select good sites with clear fields of fire. There was not a lot to hide

---

11. Soviet tank battalions vary in size. The standard tank battalions serving in tank regiments have 31 tanks. Independent tank battalions are larger, having five companies of tanks instead of the usual three.

12. *Grad* (Russian for "hail") is the name given to the BM-21 122mm multiple rocket launcher used by Soviet artillery units. It fires forty 122mm rockets.

behind, except some rubble from the damaged farm buildings. But at 3,000 meters, the enemy would have a hard time hitting his unit's tanks.

The other half of Abdirov's company, commanded by Sr. Sgt. Vasily Levchenko, reached the small farm near Hill 320 at about the same time. They began moving into the wreckage of the farm buildings, but came under missile fire from the neighboring woods. The enemy antitank gunners had not been destroyed, only driven back by Larikov's earlier tank fire. One T-80M was hit in the rear in the engine, and the fuel began burning fiercely. The crew managed to get out, but came under small arms fire from the woods on Hill 320. Levchenko swung his tank toward the woods to face the enemy with the heaviest array of steel and explosive armor. Another missile struck tank 421, but the blast was deflected by the reactive armor. A third missile hit the top of the engine deck of tank 422, setting it on fire. Levchenko, and Sergeant Shmurian in the other surviving tank, opened fire on the woods. The enemy missile teams distracted them from their main mission of providing overwatch coverage for the main attack. But if they abandoned their defensive positions the missile teams might very well catch them exposed and knock them out as well.

No one was paying any attention to the fighting around Hill 320. All eyes were on the main attack toward Pressbach Hill. As Krylov had feared, the unit they faced was not a spent German territorial mechanized infantry brigade, but the lead element of American reinforcements from the 1st Armored Division. The Americans facing them were two platoons of M1A2 Abrams tanks (the improved version of the M1A1, with depleted uranium armor), two M3A2 Bradley cavalry scout vehicles, and a platoon of M2 Bradleys with infantry. The people giving Levchenko's tanks so much trouble were the infantry platoon. The American force was located mainly on the eastern edge of Pressbach. Their tanks had had plenty of time to pick good firing positions, and the higher elevation of the town offered further advantage. The American tankers were outnumbered about four to one, eight tanks to fewer than forty. But their tanks were better, and they held terrain advantages.

The Americans also enjoyed a bit of support. As the 18th Guards Independent Tank Battalion came spilling over the rise and onto the fields in front of Pressbach, the Americans called in artillery. The American commander had surveyed the scene, and had noted the gully to the southeast of his position. He decided to try to block it by requesting some artillery scattered mines. He also requested a lighter concentration immediately in front of his position, to the northeast. If the Soviets noticed the mines, they would tend to move to the center of the town, where the heaviest concentration of American forces was positioned. The artillery dropped a load of FASCAM antitank mines[13] in the two locations in front of Pressbach in the moments following the arrival of the Soviet tanks.

Krylov's battalion saw the overhead airburst of the FASCAM, but, tightly buttoned up in their tanks, had no precise idea of what the airbursts were. The FASCAM strike was followed by some desultory salvoes of ICMs (improved conventional munitions). The ICM submunitions are grenades about the size of a film canister. They contain a small shaped charge that is large enough to punch a hole through the roof armor or engine deck of a tank. A lucky hit can start a fuel fire or break a track. But American troops had grown fond of them since they could be used to strip Soviet tanks of their reactive armor.

Krylov's concentration was upset by the sounds of explosions around him. The enemy's artillery was firing the much detested ICM rounds at them. Krylov saw the explosive panels on several tanks explode, but the tanks continued on, unimpeded. He hoped that no crews would panic like Abdirov's had done the night before.

The ICM attack was not decisive, but it was more than just a nuisance. Two tanks were hit on the fenders, and an ICM explosion shattered a track link. The tanks were moving at about forty miles an hour, so the split track quickly broke loose, embedding one side of the tank in the soft farm field. One other tank suffered a small fuel fire from an ICM hit, and at least three more had some reactive armor panels explode. The exploding panels did not cause the confusion of the night before, if only because in the daytime the crews could more easily see that their tank had not been mortally wounded. Combat in the daytime is far less frightening than at night.

Abdirov's tanks at the farm attempted to provide fire support for their attacking comrades, but the level of dust, smoke, and mist made it difficult, if not impossible, to pick out any targets at first. Abdirov hoped the situation would clear up once the enemy began firing.

The two American tank platoons held their fire as the Soviets charged forward. At about 2,500 meters, the Abrams began probing the Soviets with their laser range finders. Although they could hit tanks at such a

---

13. FASCAM is the acronym for family of scatterable artillery mines. The antiarmor mines are called RAAM (remote antiarmor mine). A 155mm RAAM mine contains three of these mines, which are dispersed at some height over the ground by a proximity fuse.

range, the probability of penetration was reduced. As the Soviet tanks began approaching the 2,000-meter range, the American tanks began firing.

The Americans could clearly see the Soviets, since they were using their thermal sights, even though it was daytime. The turbine engines at full power kicked up an infrared exhaust plume, which silhouetted the tank against it when viewed through a thermal sight. The first salvo of eight 120mm APFSDS (armor-piercing fin-stabilized discarding sabot) rounds struck in rapid succession. There were seven hits of eight shots. Five hits were kills; the victims exploded in oily fireballs. Two other hits stopped the tanks, but failed to ignite internal stowage.

The APFSDS ammunition used by the Americans hits the tanks at a speed of a mile per second. The depleted uranium rod smashes its way through successive layers of steel, ceramic armor, and more steel. The projectile enters the tank hull like a gory sparkler, spewing a supersonic stream of incandescent metal fragments into the interior. The fragments ricochet off the inside armor of the tank, mutilating the crew and igniting flammable material.

The T-80 tank is an explosion waiting to happen. In the bow, there are fuel tanks on either side of the driver. At the rear of the fuel cells are stowage points for some of the spare ammunition. The large carousel in the floor contains the remaining twenty-three rounds of ammunition in two layers, with the propellant on top. Behind the carousel is another fuel cell, and more ammunition. Once the propellant casings are ripped open and begin to burn, the tank is doomed. The propellant is difficult, if not impossible, to extinguish without an automatic fire extinguisher system. The Soviet system is manual. Once one propellant casing begins to explode, nearby casings begin cooking off in rapid succession. The large quantity of combustible materials, and the ferocity of the metal shards from the APFSDS projectile, create a volatile combination in the inside of the tank. A catastrophic explosion often follows after a few seconds of small-scale fires.

Trapped inside the thick shell of armor, the fragile humans are smashed and burned beyond recognition in the first moments of the horror. Such was the fate of the fifteen men in the first wave of tanks to be hit.

Following the first American volley, the M1A2 Abrams tanks fired their smoke grenade launchers. The whole area in front of the town was obscured in a dense cloud of white smoke. The Americans had effectively blinded the Soviet tanks, which did not have thermal sights and could not see through the smoke. The Americans could see through the smoke, and continued to fire.

Krylov's battalion was now down to twenty-one tanks in the attacking waves, and six more back at the farms. He watched in dismay as the enemy blanketed his positions with smoke. By now, the Soviet tanks were less than 2,000 meters from the town. Retreat was unthinkable, since the Americans would probably continue to engage his tanks anyway. The only thing to do was press forward as rapidly as possible, and hope that the smoke would lift.

The American tanks continued firing volleys into the Soviet formation. Krylov was slightly behind both companies and could clearly see the frightful toll the enemy was exacting against his unit. He felt helpless as the attack churned forward. Krylov's forward-looking periscope and little side periscopes gave him a restricted view of the battlefield. He saw one tank from 2d Company in front of him get hit. It exploded almost immediately, the turret being hurled backward and skidding to the ground only a few dozen meters in front of his tank. His tanks pressed on, anxious to get close enough to begin firing. The smoke and dust were still too thick to clearly make out the enemy positions.

By the time the smoke cloud began to dissipate, Krylov's battalion was less than a thousand meters in front of the enemy positions. Since they had first come under fire from the enemy tanks, sixty long seconds had passed. The American tanks could fire at a rate of four to ten rounds per minute. The eight enemy tanks had pumped out a total of thirty rounds at the twenty-one remaining Soviet tanks. In some cases, more than one round hit the same tank. After the second and third American volleys, nine more Soviet tanks were destroyed, and two were damaged. Two more blew up when they ran over FASCAM mines. There were now only nine tanks closing on the American positions at 1,000 meters range.

Krylov's tank was to the rear of the remaining nine tanks. They were badly scattered over a width of a kilometer. The enemy tanks were still not very evident, but Krylov began to spot them as their guns fired. The muzzle flash was quite bright, lasting less than a second, but it kicked up a great deal of dust, which lingered in front of the tank and made it easier to locate. Krylov was concerned that Abdirov's company was providing no fire support.

The Soviet tanks, anxious to revenge the losses around them, had picked out their targets. The T-80s slowed down to get a better aim and fired in rapid succession. Of the first nine rounds fired, four hit American tanks. Their aim was not as good as the Americans' aim, simply because they could see only the enemy's turrets, not the whole tank. Of the four hits, two American tanks were disabled but not penetrated. One tank was hit in the rear turret ammunition bin, and began burning furiously. The other round hit the elevated commander's cupola on one tank, ripping it off and severely injuring the tank commander. The five other shots had impacted in the ground in front of the American positions, or had flown high or wide of the target. The T-80 did not have full three-axis stabilization, and firing on the move was always less accurate than from a stationary position.

At close range, the American tanks began firing at the Soviet tanks with renewed fury. The Americans had a much easier time acquiring targets, not simply because their FLIR (forward looking infrared) sights could see through the smoke and debris, but because the Soviet tanks were out in the field in clear view, silhouetted against the remnants of the white smoke cloud. In rapid succession, six Soviet tanks were smashed by two more American salvos. The American tankers fired a great deal faster than their Soviet opponents, and in a given time could engage more targets. Two of the American tanks fired more smoke grenades, which further blinded the surviving Soviet tanks. The Soviet tank attack collapsed.

Krylov's gunner took aim for a second time, but the tank was jarred by a sudden explosion on the left side. Krylov and the other two crewmen were badly shaken by the blast. The tank careened out of control for a few meters, coming to rest in an irrigation ditch with its barrel jammed into the soil. It took a second or so before Krylov realized that the tank had not been penetrated. He phoned down to the driver.

"Sasha, where were we hit?"

"Comrade Captain, we've lost a track on the left side, maybe a mine! We're stuck, Comrade Captain. I can't move the tank."

Krylov's tank had run over one of the FASCAM mines that had been dropped by artillery fire at the outset of the fighting. The T-80M was sitting only a few hundred meters in front of the American positions. Krylov could see at least one burning American tank, and saw the muzzle flash of another tank uncomfortably close. With the gun disabled and inoperative, Krylov used the intercom to tell his crew to abandon the tank. He grabbed a stubby AKS-74U carbine and flung open his hatch. The sight behind him was appalling—dozens of shattered and burning tanks. In the confusion of the battle, Krylov's crew managed to get free of the tank without being spotted by the Americans. The M1A2 Abrams tanks were preoccupied with the remnants of the Soviet tank battalion that were still in the fight.

It took several minutes for the smoke and dust to settle. The U.S. tank force was down to four tanks, with the other four either damaged or knocked out. But the Soviet battalion had been mauled far more severely. Six tanks from Abdirov's company remained to the rear near the two farm buildings on either side of the field. Of the thirty-one tanks that had charged Pressbach Hill, all but three had been knocked out. These three began to move gingerly back toward the farms. Abdirov's tanks moved forward from the farm, firing at a steady pace. They had little chance of hitting the American tanks, but hoped to distract their attention away from the retreating survivors.

Of the thirty-one tanks, about twenty-four had suffered catastrophic fires or severe battle damage. The other seven had tracks ripped off by mines or had been hit in the engine compartment. One of the retreating tanks stopped long enough to pick up Krylov and his crew. They clambered on board the hot engine deck.

The three surviving tanks were able to escape the carnage in the Pressbach pastures, because the fires and smoke made it difficult for the American tankers to spot them. The American tanks were methodically attempting to pick off tanks that had been disabled but not burned. A few of the T-80s that had been disabled by mines were still firing back at the American tanks, and Abdirov's company continued their vain attempt to hit the Americans at very long range with missiles in spite of the difficulty in seeing them. Krylov arrived back at the farm with two surviving tanks at about 0815. He ordered Abdirov to prepare his tanks for a possible counterattack by the enemy forces.

He looked out over the Pressbach pasture and could hardly comprehend what had happened. His battalion, hours before at near full strength, now lay smashed and burning. Under a miserable gray German sky, the fields were littered with shattered tanks. A dozen oily black fires boiled up a kilometer away, punctuated by an occasional explosion as more ammunition cooked off. Survivors continued to make their way back in small groups through the morning, but Krylov was well aware that most of his men had probably been killed. The final fighting had taken place at such close range that nearly all of the tanks that had been hit had burned. Crews who were unable to escape in the first thirty seconds stood little chance of survival. If the turret was swung at the wrong angle, it could block the escape of the driver. The turret crewmen each had their own hatch, so more of the gunners and commanders escaped than drivers.

Krylov tried to reach the 65th GTR, but was unable to do so. Finally he connected with a divisional radio net. The 65th GTR had been roughly treated as well. Krylov was told to maintain his position and prepare to attack the objective again. He told the divisional staff in no uncertain terms that his unit was unable to do so, and would be hard-pressed to hold the two farms against a NATO counterattack. In the late afternoon, some motor rifle troops in their BMPs arrived to set up defensive positions. It had been a miserable day. Krylov was told again to prepare a counterattack for 1600.

---

## Analysis

Discussions about the conventional balance of power in Europe almost always begin with the issue of Soviet numerical superiority in tanks and other weapons. As this fictional scenario suggests, numbers alone are not a complete indicator of combat power. The quality of the weapon systems is an important factor, as is the situation in which they are used, the training of the crews, and the leadership of the units. The scenario described here—a Soviet tank battalion attacking a prepared defensive position across open terrain—is a situation that favors the NATO defender. But as the fictional account suggests, factors relating to the quality of the opposing weapons had a decisive effect on the outcome. The Soviet tankers were expecting to encounter a force equipped with equivalent or inferior tanks, but in fact faced a force with qualitatively superior tanks.

This raises several questions. How do Warsaw Pact and NATO tanks compare? Do NATO tanks have any decisive advantages over Warsaw Pact tanks? Why do they have these technical differences? This discussion will focus on two specific tanks, the Soviet T-80M and the American M1A2, in an effort to come to grips with these questions.

The most immediate impression one would get from seeing these two tanks side by side is their difference in size. Although both tanks are about the same width and length, the M1A2 is fitted with a massive, boxy turret.

The T-80M is squatter, and its turret is a good deal smaller. The M1A2 tips the scales at more than sixty-five tons. The T-80M is a good deal lighter, weighing in at a bit over forty-five tons.

Why the great difference in weight? There is a popular notion that Soviet designers build their tanks small to make them smaller targets. This seems to make sense, but misses the real reason. As mentioned in the first chapter, the Soviets are intent on maintaining a large armed forces, capable of handling any combination of enemies. A large army inevitably means a need for a great many tanks to equip the two hundred or so Soviet divisions. Indeed, to fully equip its divisions, the Soviet Ground Forces require in excess of 55,000 tanks. And with technology rapidly advancing, tanks have to be replaced every decade or so with new designs incorporating the latest improvements. This costs a lot of rubles.

The larger the tank, the heavier it is. The heavier it is, the larger an engine it must have. The larger an engine, the more fuel it must carry. The more fuel it must carry, the heavier the tank. This is the vicious cycle that drives up the cost of tanks. The bigger, heavier, and more complicated the tank is, the more rubles it costs. The Soviets have attempted to put a ceiling on tank costs by placing tight weight and size constraints on their design; therefore, Soviet tanks have traditionally been smaller and lighter than comparable NATO designs. When NATO tanks were in the fifty-ton range in the 1950s, Soviet tanks were in the thirty-five-ton range. In the 1970s, the Soviet tanks weighed in around forty tons, with NATO tanks around sixty tons. Yet the Soviets are not content simply to have smaller tanks. They also want tanks that are as well armed, as well protected, and as mobile as their NATO counterparts. What kinds of miracles do Soviet designers conjure up to combine good combat qualities with size and cost constraints?

The Soviets have accepted design compromises that would be unacceptable to any NATO army. To begin with, Soviet tanks are incredibly cramped. The U.S. standard is to design vehicles for the "95th percentile" soldier. In other words, tanks have to be big enough to accept 95 percent of today's soldiers, including those a bit over six feet tall. Soviet tanks are so small, they are usually crewed by troops under a height of about five feet six. Our fictional Soviet tankers, Pavel Krylov and his men, would be shorter than average NATO tankers. This might not seem like that much of a sacrifice, but in older tanks, these small tankers were expected to load fifty-five-pound projectiles into the breech of the gun. While this is possible, it is not surprising that the main gun on a Soviet tank is loaded at a slower rate on average than that on a NATO tank, and so it is fired less often. On newer tanks, the T-80M, the loading problem became so serious that an automatic loader was introduced. Indeed, the Soviets are the first to make widespread use of automatic loaders on main battle tanks. The automatic loaders add to the complexity of the tank, but they keep down the size of the tank and indirectly contribute to keeping down its cost.

Other compromises have been more extreme. Soviet tanks store a good deal of their fuel in external fuel cells over the track. Soviet tanks are mostly diesel powered, and diesel fuel is not as flammable as gasoline. But it does burn. The external tanks are protected with only enough armor to prevent penetration by small arms fire. The NATO tanks store all their fuel within the protective main armor of the tank.

The proximity of all this fuel and ammunition also leads to a propensity to serious fires if the Soviet tank is hit. A tank like the T-80 has fuel and ammunition stored in the front of the hull, followed by a large ammunition carousel on the floor, with more fuel and ammunition behind the carousel. The propellant casing for the ammunition is semiconsumable, making it more prone to rupture than the older style brass or aluminum casings. Ammunition propellant is probably the greatest single fire hazard on board the tank. It contains its own chemical oxidant, so that once it ignites, it is difficult, if not impossible, to stop the fire. In contrast, most of the ammunition in the M1 Abrams is stored in a locker at the rear of the turret, separated from the crew by blastproof doors. If the ammunition begins to burn, the fire is contained to the turret rear, away from the crew. The American tank is also fitted with an automatic Halon fire extinguishing system. This elaborate compartmentalization is impossible on Soviet tanks, since every last cubic inch of space must be filled with some bit of machinery or stowage.

Israeli tankers have found from combat experience that Soviet-designed tanks have a greater likelihood of catastrophic fires after being hit than most other tanks. The Israelis have operated American, British, and their own designs, and have singled out the vulnerability of Soviet tanks in this regard. Aside from the immediate effect of leading to heavier tank losses, this vulnerability has long-term effects as well. The Israelis have found that modern tank warfare is enormously destructive of equipment. Of the 450 tanks in service with frontline Israeli tank units at the beginning of the 1973 war, 75 percent were lost in the first eighteen hours. Many of these losses were due to minor damage that could be quickly repaired. But tanks that suffer serious internal fires are less likely to be repairable, and are less likely to be capable of being returned to combat service. For example, in the 1982 war, of the 1,000 Israeli tanks participating, about 300 were knocked out by combat damage; of this number only about 75 were too badly damaged for repair.

The tight cost constraints forced on Soviet designers also affect the durability of their tanks. Soviet tanks (and many other Soviet weapons) are not as durable as their Western counterparts. For example, Soviet tank engines have a much lower life expectancy than American or British engines. Soviet tank gun barrels have about a quarter the life expectancy of American tank gun barrels, about 120 rounds versus 400 rounds. This lack of durability has little effect in wartime, since tanks have a great likelihood of being knocked out long before their parts wear out. But it does have a major impact on Soviet training.

The lack of equipment durability, and the high costs of fuel and ammunition, conspire against rigorous training in Soviet tank units. In peacetime, Soviet tank units do not have all their vehicles operating at one time. There are strict limits set on the number of hours a Soviet tank can be used in order not to prematurely wear it out. So a unit will keep a portion of its tanks in mothballs for part of the year, operating only a fraction of them at any one given time. Then the tanks that had been in use will be put in storage and the other tanks drawn out for several months of use. This means that on a day-to-day basis, Soviet tankers are less likely to get hands-on experience with their vehicles.

Funding constraints also limit the amount of ammunition fired in peacetime training. An American tanker will typically fire more than a hundred rounds of ammunition annually. Soviet tankers, depending on the priority of their unit, will fire as little as a tenth of this amount. The relative lack of training with live ammunition does not foster critical combat skills, such as the need for speed in battle engagements. The usual training standard for Soviet crews is sixty seconds to engage and destroy a target at a range of 2,000 meters. This consists of ten seconds for the commander to identify and designate the target to his gunner; twenty seconds for the gunner to lay the gun on target, perform the necessary gun adjustments, load the gun, and fire the first round; then fifteen seconds each for two more rounds of ammunition to ensure the destruction of the target. The NATO norm is closer to fifteen seconds, about a quarter the time. The reasons for this enormous discrepancy are both better training and better equipment, and more experienced crews.

The NATO crews tend to receive more training than comparable

Soviet crews, as discussed above. The NATO tanks also have decided advantages in equipment. The new generation of fire control equipment is more automated on NATO tanks than Warsaw Pact tanks, making it simpler to use. Where the Soviet fire control system requires multiple manual input to adjust gun elevation, the NATO system, like that on the M1, requires very few. This is evident in the biannual Canadian Army Trophy (CAT) competition held in Germany among NATO tank crews. The tanks are expected to engage a variety of targets, at various ranges, both from a halt and on the move. Over the past decade, scores have continued to rise as the new generation of tanks, such as the Leopard 2, M1 Abrams, and Challenger, have entered service. In the case of the M1 Abrams, crews have consistently scored hits more than 90 percent of the time, firing in less than twelve seconds after the target popped up. Certainly the CAT competition tends to involve specially selected "Olympic" teams, and it might be expected that ordinary teams are a good deal less proficient. Yet NATO has found that the new generation tanks have been so well designed that the disparity in scores between CAT teams and ordinary teams is not that great. While the better CAT teams might engage and destroy targets in less than twelve seconds, normal crews average about fifteen seconds.

Another factor benefiting NATO tank crews compared to their Soviet counterparts is the matter of experience. The Soviet Ground Forces are a conscript force, and unlike NATO armies, the Soviets do not have a professional NCO core in their army. Soviet soldiers serve their two-year hitch and are back to "civvy street." As mentioned in the previous chapter, very few enlisted men remain in service beyond their two-year hitch. As a result, skills built up during this time are lost when the tanker returns to civilian life.

The NATO armies, on the other hand, especially the U.S., German, and British armies, encourage senior enlisted men to remain in service as sergeants. These armies have a tradition of strong NCO roles, with the NCOs performing many functions that in the Soviet Army would be done by low-ranking officers. In a technical field such as tanks, long-term experience has important effects in ensuring continuity and quality in crew performance. Tanks are usually commanded by sergeants, and experienced sergeants will perform better in critical battle skills than inexperienced tankers like the Soviets who, at the most, have been in tanks for eighteen months.

The Soviets are not unaware of this problem. In 1988, Marshal Akhromeyev visited U.S. army bases, including Fort Hood, the largest

American tank base. The American officers who accompanied him were surprised to see that Akhromeyev showed little interest in the equipment, even the spanking new M1 Abrams tanks. What Akhromeyev was curious about was the details of service life for the enlisted men. He seemed surprised to meet sergeants with nineteen years of duty. The Soviets appreciate the limitations of their enlistment system, especially these days when weapons are becoming more and more complex. Akhromeyev's interest was probably sparked by Soviet plans to reinstate the critical institution of professional NCOs.

Although Soviet tanks have a good many technical drawbacks, Soviet armored vehicle designers have been remarkably ingenious over the years. The Soviets were the first army to employ infantry fighting vehicles (the BMP), the first with smooth-bore tank guns (T-62), the first with fin-stabilized armor piercing ammunition, and the first with tank autoloaders. Shortcomings in Soviet tanks are seldom the result of a lack of technological ability; they are more often the result of tight economic restraints. A good example is the matter of thermal imaging sights. As suggested in the fictional scenario, thermal imaging sights can have a dramatic effect on the modern battlefield, especially when one side lacks them.

It is surprising to find that the Soviets do not currently use thermal imaging sights, especially since they pioneered night fighting equipment. The Soviets were the first army to make widespread use of active imaging night searchlights in the 1950s. But by the time the next generation of night fighting equipment came into being, the Soviets were already falling behind. In the late 1960s, the U.S. began fielding the second generation of night fighting equipment, called image intensification, or passive night-scopes. The first generation systems used searchlights with infrared beams, invisible to the human eye. But they were not invisible to simple detection devices. So a tank using an active infrared searchlight was very visible to an enemy tank equipped with an infrared viewer. The second generation passive sights avoided this problem. Instead of relying on a searchlight for illumination, they depended on the faint natural light that exists on all but the darkest nights. By amplifying the slight illumination of the stars and moonlight, they enabled tanks to see at night. They are sometimes called "Starlight" scopes for this reason. With passive sights, the tank didn't give away its position.

The U.S. developed this technology, but eventually Soviet tanks came to be equipped with these sights. Indeed, Soviet tanks to this day rely on passive image intensification sights for night fighting. The T-80M uses a passive night gunner's sight. The main drawback of passive starlight sights is that they do require some ambient natural light. On evenings that are completely overcast, there is often not enough light for these sights to work. And unfortunately in Europe, there are many overcast nights.

In the early 1970s, the U.S. developed the first practical thermal imaging sights. Like starlight scopes, thermal imaging sights are entirely passive and do not require a searchlight. However, the technology is entirely different. Rather than sensing and amplifying natural light, thermal imaging sights pick up natural infrared energy, or heat, and create a video picture from it. Tanks, trucks, and humans all are slightly warmer than the natural background of earth and trees and, through a thermal imaging sight, will tend to stand out in distinct contrast to the background. This makes thermal imagers (also called FLIRs) ideal as tank sights. Not only do they enable tankers to see at night, but they highlight the sort of objects that tankers are most concerned about—other tanks.

The other distinct difference between thermal imaging sights and the two earlier generations of night sights is that thermal imaging sights are also useful during the daytime. Thermal sights can pick out the difference between tanks and background in daytime just as easily as at night. Even though a tank has a perfectly good daytime telescopic sight, in fact this is an enormous advantage. Modern battlefields are smoky, dusty places. Burning vehicles fill the air with thick clouds of oily smoke, hiding many objects from view. Also, modern tank guns, because of the enormous blast of their muzzles, kick up a great deal of dust and debris when firing. A tank with a thermal sight can see through much of the smoke and other obscurants on the modern battlefield.

Thermal imaging sights are a revolutionary development in tank fighting, in much the same way as radars were for aerial combat four decades ago. They make tanks all-weather, day and night weapons. They enable tanks to fight in conditions that would have otherwise been impossible. And they have interesting tactical implications. A force equipped with thermal sights, when encountering a force without such sights, can hide itself using smoke grenade launchers. While the tanks with thermal sights can see through the smoke, the other side cannot. And so the poorly equipped units are especially vulnerable, because they cannot return fire against their smoke-cloaked opponent. This is what occurred in our fictional scenario at Pressbach.

Why don't Soviet tanks have thermal sights? There are two reasons: cost and technology. Thermal sights are extremely expensive. A fire control system incorporating a thermal sight can easily cost a quarter of a million dollars. On a tank like the Abrams, this is about 10 percent of the total tank cost. On the cheaper Soviet tanks, it would be an even greater fraction of the cost. The U.S. is planning on building about 7,000 Abrams tanks over the course of about ten years. The Soviets build that many tanks every two years. Thermal sights on these tanks are a luxury that the Soviet Army has so far not been able to afford. The Soviets are capable of building thermal sights. Indeed, they have such sights on their attack helicopters and thermal pointers on certain fighter aircraft such as the MiG-29 Fulcrum and Su-27 Flanker. But thermal sights require very expensive manufacturing techniques. In the field of electro-optics, the Soviets have had real difficulties in mass producing many of the key high-tech electronic components. As a result, these components go to high-priority weapons like fighters and helicopters before they go to tanks.

The Soviets will probably eventually adopt thermal sights on some of their tanks. But given the sheer number of tanks needed to equip the Soviet Army, it will take the Soviets a much longer time to equip a significant portion of their force with this feature. By then, the U.S. and NATO may be adopting the next generation of multisensor sights with millimeter wave radars. The technological contest will continue. But at the moment, NATO has some important tactical advantages.

# CHAPTER 4

## Spetsnaz in Action:
## Scouting the Danube Bridgehead

0600, 5 October, Chaloupky Airfield, Czechoslovakia

Senior Lieutenant Mikhail Isakov studied the children's drawings on the school wall. The primary school building near the Chaloupky Airfield had been taken over by his company for lack of enough space in the buildings at the base itself. Isakov could not speak Czech very well, but he could roughly make out the writing on the pencil drawings. The company commander, Maj. Nikolai Danilov, entered the classroom along with the company's *zampolit,* [1] Capt. Aleksei Gelman.

"Good morning, Misha. Where are the rest of the troublemakers?"

"Good morning, Comrade Major. The other platoon leaders will be here shortly," replied Isakov. As leader of the company's 1st Air Assault Platoon, Isakov always made sure his platoon came in first. He arrived at company meetings promptly to keep up the good name of the platoon with the company staff. The remaining platoon leaders trudged in a few moments later. At the head of the pack was the leader of the signals platoon, Sr. Lt. Ivan Varepa. He had been a fine sprinter while in the university, and his physique still showed it. The other two platoon leaders, Yegor Kostin of the 2d Air Assault Platoon, and Viktor Baladin of the 3d Platoon, were stockier. They were tough-looking characters, and Baladin had a broken nose from soccer.

---

1. *Zampolit* is the Soviet term for the unit's political officer, called *komissar* in the old days. Political interference in military affairs is no longer as intrusive as in the past, but it is still present. The zampolit also has a more distinct military role. Besides indoctrination, he is also responsible for training and morale.

"All right, you punks, we've got business to do," snapped Captain Gelman.

Obviously, the company political officer was annoyed at having to wait for the rest of the company officers. Two were still missing, Capt. Gennadi Vinik, the transport officer, and Lt. Pyotr Rushin, the company special weapons officer. The meeting began anyway.

Major Danilov began the briefing. "Soldiers, we have a tough assignment. But I am sure that the 404th Spetsnaz Company will make 4th Army proud. As you are aware, the 4th Army decided against using us for rear area raiding at the beginning of the war. The front's *spetsnaz* brigade is being used for this. We were being saved to spearhead a major operation. Today is it. The 4th Army should finally be breaking out of the damn forest by later today or tomorrow. They need a crossing over the Danube River. The northern wing of our army has been the most successful, so they are being assigned the river crossing operation. It will take place here, between Deggendorf and Straubing." Major Danilov pointed to the map, and the lieutenants examined the 1:50,000 scale maps they had been issued.

The crossing was located at a bend of the Danube River. The northern bank was in the final foothills of the border region that 4th Army had been fighting through since the war began. The choice of the site made sense, since the area near the bend appeared to be flat and should prove to be a good staging area for all the equipment that would be needed to make a river assault. The terrain on the far side of the river was flat and open — the kind of terrain the tankers and motor rifle boys had been praying for since the war began! The fighting in the forest had been miserably tough, from all the reports Isakov had heard.

"We will be parachuted over the Danube early tomorrow morning while it is still dark," continued Danilov. "There are three landing zones. Isakov, you and the 1st Platoon will have the one on the right, to the southeast, code-named Afrika. You will be dropped on the southern outskirts of Stephans-posching. Kostin, you will have the center drop area, here on the road between Wischlburg and Makofen, code-named Peru. And Baladin, you will be dropped in the northwest zone, here to the left, near Irlbach, code-named Kanada. We are going to break up the signals platoon to give each of you a squad. Two of the squad members will provide your radio communications, and the remainder can act as runners if you need them. Lieutenant Varepa, you and your senior sergeant will jump with the company headquarters into Landing Zone Peru along with Baladin's platoon. We will set up a company headquarters, probably around Makofen.

The BMP-2 infantry combat vehicle, popularly called the "yozh," or "hedgehog," by Soviet troops, because it bristles with guns. The main armament is a potent 30mm autocannon, supplemented by the Konkurs (AT-5 Spandrel) antitank missile on the roof of the turret. The BMP-2 is as well armed as its American counterpart, the Bradley, but is more thinly armored and lacks the night fighting, and fire-on-the-move features of the Bradley.

The BMP-1, earlier version of the BMP series, is armed with a 73mm low pressure gun instead of the 30mm autocannon of the BMP-2. The 73mm gun was not entirely successful, being too small to cope with tanks, and too slow firing for proper infantry support. The BMP-1 is called the "Korshun," named after a type of bird.

As in the case of tanks, the Soviets manufacture a high-low mix of armored infantry vehicles. The high end is the BMP; the low end is the BTR series of wheeled transporters, like these BTR-70s. The BTR-70 is cheaper to purchase and to operate than the BMP, but is weaker in armor, firepower, and mobility. There is no direct counterpart to the BTR-70 in the US Army, although the Marines operate a somewhat similar vehicle, the LAV-25.

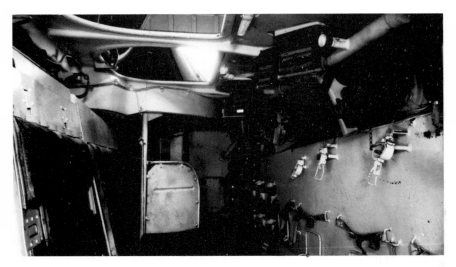

An inside view of a BMP's rear compartment where the infantry squad sits. The seats are in the lower left corner; note the back padding. To the upper right are the periscopes, which enable the riflemen to aim their assault rifles when firing through the ports in the vehicle's side. These vehicles are incredibly cramped, even in peacetime when heavy field gear is not ordinarily carried.

On dismounting from the BMP, the Soviet motor rifle squad usually forms a skirmish line in front of the vehicles. Soviet infantry tactics tend to be more rigid than in most NATO armies due to the language problems, use of conscript troops, and mediocre training. The soldier in the foreground is a squad machine gunner armed with a PKM 7.62mm machine gun. Sovfoto.

A Soviet motor rifle squad deployed in a defensive line. The nearest soldier is armed with an RPG-7, now being replaced with improved antitank rocket grenade launchers. The standard arm of the Soviet infantry is the AK series of Kalashnikov assault rifles, the current type being the 5.45mm AK-74 series. Sovfoto.

*The Bradley fighting vehicle serves in the US Army for both mechanized infantry and armored cavalry and is the closest counterpart to the Soviet BMP. The M2 Bradley is the Army's primary mechanized infantry vehicle and carries an infantry squad in the rear compartment. The nearly identical M3 Bradley is used by mechanized units for reconnaissance, and can carry a few scouts in the rear compartment.* Steven Zaloga.

*The German equivalent of the BMP is the Marder infantry combat vehicle. The Marder is armed with a 20mm autocannon, and also has a remotely controlled machine gun barbette at the rear of the vehicle for further fire support.* Pierre Touzin.

*A T-80 tank with explosive reactive armor during field exercises in 1988. The small explosive bricks can be seen ringing the turret. These explosive bricks prevent the warhead of an antitank missile from penetrating the main steel armor of the T-80 tank.*

*A T-80 tank with explosive reactive armor during a river-crossing exercise in Central Europe in 1988. The Soviet Army pays disporportionate attention to river-crossing operations, realizing that the momentum of mechanized offensives is entirely dependent upon the ability of forward forces to rapidly cross water obstacles.*

*The T-72M1 tank is another contemporary Soviet design widely used in Central Europe. Unlike most NATO armies, the Soviets acquired two different tanks at the same time—the high-cost, high-quality T-80, and the less expensive T-72 as a cost-cutting measure. The T-72M1 has less armor than the T-80, is slower in rough terrain, and is not equipped to fire the AT-8 Songster guided antitank missile. Sovfoto.*

*Soviet tank officers conferring during field maneuvers. The Soviet tanker's uniform is utilitarian: a padded black canvas helmet and black coveralls. The quality of tank officers' clothing is usually better than that of the conscripts. Sovfoto.*

The T-80's American counterpart is the M1A1 Abrams tank. The M1A1 is considerably heavier than the T-80, about 70 tons versus 45 tons combat loaded. The M1A1 has superior armor protection, gun performance, and night-fighting capability, but would probably be significantly outnumbered in any Central European scenario. Pierre Touzin.

The workhorse of Soviet close-air support is the Mi-24 Gorbach ("Hunchback") helicopter, better known in the West by its NATO codename, Hind. The Hind is very large as attack helicopters go, mainly due to the presence of a troop compartment in the center which can carry six to eight men. The Hind D seen here is armed with four multiple rocket pods and four AT-2 Swatter antitank missiles under the center winglets, and a 12.7mm Gatling gun in the nose turret.

"Our mission is to scout this area for an air mobile assault. You will notice that this area has no bridges. There is a rail bridge to the northwest at Bogen, and several bridges to the southeast around Deggendorf. We expect these areas to be heavily protected by the Germans. We expect the drop zones to be largely free of enemy troops. We will spend most of tomorrow scouting the area to check on enemy forces. Our job is to discover the enemy, not engage him. We will report back to the 4th Army staff tomorrow afternoon. If the area looks like we can secure it, they will send in an air assault battalion by choppers in the early evening.

"Now, if they do decide on the air assault, it will be our job to secure the landing zones. Isakov and Baladin will have the tough job: You two will have to secure the roads leading into the area and deal with any enemy vehicles. You will set up ambushes on the roads leading from the west from Straubing, and from the east, around Deggendorf. As soon as the Germans realize we're landing in their rear, they will try to stomp us out. The terrain here is very flat, so they can move their tanks and troop carriers across country if they wish. But they'll probably start by using the roads. It will be dark by then, and they won't want to risk going cross-country. You will hold the roadblocks until relieved by the air assault troops.

"Now, as far as weapons go. Everybody will carry the usual AKS-74s or AKS-74U carbines. But, I'm sure we are going to run into armor. So Pyotr Rushin will be issuing each of your platoons three Metis launchers.[2] You can either give each of your squads one of these, or you can give them all to one squad to form a tank-killer squad. Isakov and Baladin, you had better bunch them up in a special tank-killer squad. You two are the most likely to get hit by enemy tanks. In addition, everybody will be issued at least one RPG-22 antitank rocket.[3] During the airdrop, we will also be dropping two canisters of antitank mines. This isn't an awful lot of mines, so you'll have to be careful where you place them.

"Now, as you can see, you're going to have a lot more hardware than usual. So each of your platoons will get three LuAZ-967 jeeps from the

2. Metis is the Soviet name for the antitank missile system called AT-7 Saxhorn in NATO. It is a small, lightweight system, about the same size as the U.S. Army's Dragon, or the new French Eryx.

3. The RPG-22 is a shoulder-fired, short-range antitank rocket, similar in appearance to the U.S. Army's M72 LAW or AT4 antitank rocket. The rocket is not guided, and is effective only at close range. It cannot penetrate the front armor of main battle tanks, but is effective if fired against the side or rear.

company transport section, each with one driver. One of these should be assigned to your antitank squad, and the other two can be used to bring forward your supplies, mines, and other ammunition. You should not use these for scouting! They are for transport. When you land, keep your eye out for civilian automobiles and trucks. You should take some civilian vehicles. There are fairly good roads in the area, and the civilian vehicles will make you less conspicuous while you are reconnoitering.

"Now, in regard to uniforms. Everybody will wear normal Soviet battle dress. This is not a diversionary mission, it's a scout mission. So let's not play costume ball. I know several of you think you speak pretty good German. But I can assure you that nobody here speaks it well enough to be mistaken for a real German. So don't get cute and try to play 'lost German motorist' on the autobahn. If you can carry out your scouting faster using a car, fine. But don't get caught on the road.

"The Germans will probably have military police roadblocks set up. Deal with them quickly so they don't reveal our operation. Each squad has one SVD sniper rifle, and one night sight. Use them! But remember, we do not want to warn the Germans about our operation. So don't make any rash moves that will alert the German Army to our presence. Make sure you deal with the phone lines in your sector. You're bound to be spotted by German civilians, so make it impossible for them to warn the Army.

"We'll be making the jump at 0300 early tomorrow morning. Our departure time out of the airfield here will be at 0220. We will be jumping low, at 500 meters. Everybody gets one chute, no safeties. You all know that at that altitude, if the first parachute doesn't work, you'll never be able to use a second safety chute. Are there any questions?"

Isakov raised his hand. "Comrade Major, when the air assault troops arrive, what is our mission? Do we stay with them or regroup?"

"A good point, Misha. Look, we do not know how this mission is going to turn out. I think that once the air assault boys land, we will have a hell of a fight on our hands. Deggendorf and Platting are the major concentration points for the Bundeswehr and the U.S. Army in our sector. When they find out an air assault group has landed in their rear, they will try to rub us out before we can link up with our forces on the other side of the Danube. We can expect a heavy attack up Route 8 from the Platting-Deggendorf area. And we might get another attack from Straubing to the west. If the air assault boys can handle it, fine. We'll regroup. I'm sure the 4th Army has other missions for us. But if the fighting gets bad, the air assault battalion is going to need all the help it can get. And I'm sure

# 404th Spetsnaz Company

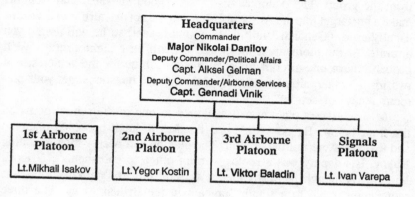

**Headquarters**
Commander
**Major Nikolai Danilov**
Deputy Commander/Political Affairs
**Capt. Alksei Gelman**
Deputy Commander/Airborne Services
**Capt. Gennadi Vinik**

| **1st Airborne Platoon** | **2nd Airborne Platoon** | **3rd Airborne Platoon** | **Signals Platoon** |
|---|---|---|---|
| Lt.Mikhail Isakov | Lt.Yegor Kostin | Lt. Viktor Baladin | Lt. Ivan Varepa |

# Airborne Spetsnaz Platoon

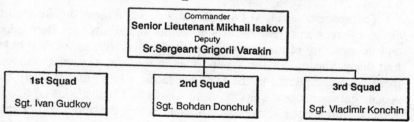

Commander
**Senior Lieutenant Mikhail Isakov**
Deputy
**Sr.Sergeant Grigorii Varakin**

| **1st Squad** | **2nd Squad** | **3rd Squad** |
|---|---|---|
| Sgt. Ivan Gudkov | Sgt. Bohdan Donchuk | Sgt. Vladimir Konchin |

they'll ask the army staff to keep our company under their command until the bridgehead has been achieved."

Lieutenant Varepa raised his hand next. "Comrade Major, what type of aircraft will we be using?"

"We'll be using An-26s," answered Danilov. There was a sigh of relief from the group. The Antonov An-26[4] was good and fast, and wouldn't make a big target like the An-12 or Il-76s that the normal airborne divisions usually used. "Gennadi Vinik will be jumpmaster, so he will assign you aircraft. At the moment, it looks like we will have eight aircraft. We'll probably have one aircraft for each platoon, three for the vehicles, and two for the other supply canisters. If that's it for questions, get your platoons ready for action!"

Misha Isakov's platoon was stationed in one of the schoolrooms on the floor below. By now, they had finished a quick breakfast of bread and tea, and were milling around. The platoon had twenty men including Isakov. His deputy was a senior warrant office (praporshchik), Grigorii Varakin. Although he was called a warrant officer, Varakin's rank was more comparable to a senior sergeant in the British Army. The three squad leaders, Ivan Gudkov, Bohdan Donchuk, and Vladimir Konchin, were also praporshchiks. They were of the new generation of professional NCOs added to the Ground Forces in the late 1980s in the wake of the Gorbachev reforms. Varakin had been in the spetsnaz for six years, while the other squad leaders had each completed four years of duty. Each of the squad leaders had five men under him. These squads were smaller than normal motor rifle or paratrooper squads, but they were better trained.

The spetsnaz received high priority in recruitment, unlike regular Ground Forces branches. Political reliability and loyalty were demanded, and the majority of the troops were Russians or Ukrainians. You didn't find many Muslims or other minorities in the spetsnaz units, although there were exceptions. In the Far East facing China, units usually had Asian contingents, and units opposite Alaska had Inuit (Eskimo) troops. Athletic ability was a prime concern, and many of the troops had promising records in secondary school athletics. The squad leaders were often

---

4. The An-26, code-named Curl by NATO, is a light turboprop transport aircraft. In its Aeroflot passenger version, it carries about fifty passengers. In the paratrooper role, it carries about twenty troops and their kit, or two to three small vehicles.

recruited from the ranks of school captains of soccer and other sports, which provided an indication of leadership skills. Certain spetsnaz units used for diversionary missions had language requirements, but not the army-level companies like the 404th. The 404th Special Operations (Spetsnaz) Company was typical of these units. Its main mission was scouting and raiding. This company often acted as the spearhead for critical missions by army or front airmobile units. Or it could be used for special commando missions against critical NATO objectives.

It would take the company about ten hours to ready itself for the mission. Parachutes would be prepared, and repacked if possible. Weapons would be inspected, and special issue weapons and explosive would be carefully prepared. When jumping into action, Soviet airborne troops carried a much heavier load than the average infantryman. They were the only troops to regularly use rucksacks, since their food and bedding was not carried on vehicles as in the case of the motor rifle infantry. They carried more ammunition into combat, usually 300 rounds versus the usual 90 for motor rifle troops. For missions like this one, where tanks were likely, they carried one or two RPG-22 antitank rockets. Usually one of the six squad members carried an SVD sniper rifle, with an attachable image-intensification night sight. Each paratrooper's weapons were contained in a weapons bag. During the jump, the bag fell on a tethered line below him, hitting the ground first, which prevented the paratrooper from falling on his weapon and damaging it or injuring himself.

Parachute preparation took most of the morning and was done in one of the hangars at the nearby airfield. The An-26 transport aircraft began arriving at about 1100. To the chagrin of Captain Vinik, the jumpmaster, most were regular Aeroflot cargo aircraft without the military cargo handling equipment. For reasons of economy, civilian aircraft were absorbed by the Air Force in time of war. Although inconvenient, these were still usable for dropping the paratroop squads themselves and the weapons canisters. The three militarized An-26s would have to make do for the LuAZ jeeps. The other problem was that the Aeroflot aircraft arrived in Aeroflot livery: white upper fuselages with blue trim and unpainted aluminum wings and lower fuselages. This was completely unacceptable for clandestine operations. After a few hours of searching, Vinik found a supply of flat black paint, and Donchuk's squad was assigned to assist the ground crews in giving the aircraft a hasty paint job. It was done with few of the niceties, and no one had time for the national insignia.

The afternoon was spent preparing the weapons canisters and the load platforms for the LuAZ jeeps. The load platforms usually used retrorocket braking systems to slow the platform at the last moments before impact. But Vinik decided this would be a bad idea for a night drop: The bright blast of the retrorockets would be visible for miles in the flat terrain of the drop zones. Instead, the jeeps would be dropped from higher altitudes with a larger number of chutes. The LuAZ-967 was pretty light anyhow. By late afternoon, in a flurry of activity, the last of the Antonov transport aircraft were loaded and ready for operation.

Isakov brought his platoon together for final instructions. The drop zone was a field about two kilometers on either side, immediately to the south of the small village of Uttenkofen, and north of the hamlet of Freundorf. The airdrop would take place at about 0300, and Isakov estimated the linkup would take only about a half hour, since the whole platoon, plus the added signals team, would drop from a single aircraft. Isakov, on Major Danilov's instructions, assigned Sgt. Vladimir Konchin's 3d Squad the task of linking up with company headquarters to collect the LuAZ jeeps, mines, and other heavy equipment. These would be dropped into LZ Peru to the south of Wischlburg along with WO Yegor Kostin's 2d Platoon. In the meantime, Ivan Gudkov's 1st Squad would begin scouting forward toward the river around Stephans-posching and Uttenkofen, while Bohdan Donchuk's squad would patrol south toward the junction of Route 8 and the A92 autobahn. If the tiny hamlet of Freundorf was abandoned, Isakov decided he would use the buildings to establish the platoon's base of operations.

The platoon received a hearty meal before departure. The political officer, Aleksei Gelman, along with a couple of the members of the company headquarters, had decided to do some improvised "scouting" in the nearby Czech village. They managed to "liberate" about a dozen kilos of good Czech smoked sausages and a jeep full of other sundries, which were served up in one of the hangars where the parachute packing had taken place. The company numbered more than a hundred men, so the food didn't go far. But it was a delightful change from the wartime dry rations.

The aircraft were loaded up with troops at 0130 in the early morning of 6 October. The weather was the usual for this time of year—broken clouds, cold, and damp. As the night went on, the cloud cover broke open, and a crescent moon occasionally broke through. This would make it easier for the company to operate at night, but it would also make their jump more visible. The jump had been coordinated with army artillery, which would lay down artillery fire strikes on German positions around Metten and Bogen to keep them distracted. The An-26s were instructed to make a direct approach to the landing zones down along the Schwarzach Valley, to keep away from the artillery.

Isakov's platoon entered the aircraft from the rear ramp. Counting the added signal troops, there were twenty-five paratroopers in the cargo hold, plus three weapons canisters. The canisters would go out first, followed by Isakov, his deputy platoon leader, and the 1st Squad. The aircraft had elementary folded bench seats, since it was usually used for Aeroflot cargo runs. This was not the best arrangement, but the platoon made do. Isakov made sure that everyone was settled in position and then went up to the cockpit to chat with the crew. There was a crew of four, the pilot, copilot, radio/navigator, and *shturman* (loadmaster). The crew members were all reservists and older than Isakov had expected. The pilot was at least forty-five. They were all Aeroflot personnel in peacetime, but had served in the VTA (Military Transport Aviation) during their service. They had received special training for the past two days in paratroop delivery, and assured Isakov that it would be no more difficult than their usual missions, which involved flying in supplies to arctic teams in northern Russia.

The planes began lifting off at 0215, and when the last of the nine met the formation, they departed to the southwest, in a box formation, three aircraft wide and three deep. The shturman on Isakov's aircraft let him look out the small blister window on the left side of the forward fuselage. His view was a bit obscured by the NKPB-7 sight used to calculate airdrops. At first the scenery was monotonously dark and lifeless. But in a few minutes, the eerie signs of the war became evident on the horizon. The sky in front of the aircraft was lit up by illumination flares, explosions, and fires. From fifteen or twenty kilometers away, nothing was very clear. But obviously, a considerable amount of fighting was going on on the ground below. The shturman told Isakov that the drop would be in five minutes, so he returned to the cargo compartment to prepare his men. He went up to each soldier and checked to see that his parachute harness was snug and his ripcord attached to the static line. He knew that the men had already checked this repeatedly, but it was a good opportunity to show his concern. Isakov took his place toward the rear of the fuselage.

Two minutes before the drop, the rear cargo door was lowered. The An-26 had a system to permit the cargo door to be hinged down below the aircraft to facilitate paratroop drops. The gears and servos whirred away as the door cleared. There was a rush of cold outside air into the compartment, and soon the paratroopers near the rear could see the ground below. Fighting could be seen around the town of Schwarzach. The shturman flicked on the amber warning light, meaning thirty seconds until the drop. At the green signal, Isakov and two of the other men kicked the weapons canisters free. Isakov and his deputy, Warrant Office Varakin, stood at either side of the cargo door and signaled the men to jump in waves of three in quick succession. The jump went without a hitch, and Isakov and Varakin leapt out last.

Isakov was an experienced jumper, but night drops are always frightening. It's very difficult to judge how far you are from the ground as you are falling. There is the overwhelming fear that you may smash into the ground any second. Fortunately, on this jump, there was enough moonlight to see the ground. The view to the north had a strange sort of beauty. There appeared to be tank battles going on in the valley near Schwarzach. The northern landscape was bathed in the unnatural light of artillery illumination rounds. The ground shimmered from the frequent salvos of tank fire. Isakov could see the Danube River about a kilometer to the north. At night, its surface had a metallic sheen against the dark, colorless earth.

Isakov could start to see details on the ground below. Impact any second! He hit the ground hard, but instinctively he rolled. There was little wind, so he had no problem controlling the chute and gathering it up. It was critical that the platoon hide the parachutes, so as not to disclose their presence to the enemy.

Varakin had landed less than a hundred meters away, and was walking toward Isakov with his parachute neatly wrapped in his arms. "Comrade Lieutenant, I would suggest we deposit these in that building to the east."

Isakov agreed. Burying them in a plowed farm field was out of the question. Using a small flashlight, Varakin signaled to the squad leaders to move eastward toward Uttenkofen. The squad leaders reported to Isakov as the platoon coalesced. They had been lucky. No casualties beyond a few sprained ankles and bruises. The bright night had made the jump easier, even if it did expose them to discovery. But judging from the intensity of the fighting to the north, it didn't seem that anyone was paying attention.

At the outskirts of the town was an old garage. Using the night scope on an SVD sniper rifle, Varakin surveyed the edge of the village. There was no evidence of any movement. Varakin and two soldiers from 1st Squad carefully checked out the building. It was abandoned, probably at the outbreak of the war. The same seemed true of the rest of the village.

While the platoon hid their parachutes in the attic of the garage, Ivan Gud-kov led three of his men from 1st Squad through the village looking for signs of life. Several of the houses had their doors open, suggesting they had been abandoned in some haste. They carefully snipped any phone lines they could find, taking trouble to avoid electrical lines. There were only about twenty buildings in the village, and within a half hour, the platoon had searched through them all. From signs, this was the village of Uttenkofen. It was completely abandoned.

Isakov had planned to use one of the villages to the south as a base, but this village would do. He had one of the new radiomen raise Major Danilov. "Aztek, this is Bantu, over."

"Bantu, this is Aztek, over." The radio call signs for the unit were Aztek for the HQ, Inka for the 2d Platoon (LZ Peru), Eskimo for 3d Platoon (LZ Kanada), and Bantu for 1st Platoon (LZ Afrika).

"Aztek, need grid to pick up packages, over."

"Bantu, send hunters to southeast Peru, over."

Isakov told Vladimir Konchin and his 3d Squad to march over to the southeast corner of Landing Zone Peru, near the Stephans-posching rail station. It was a good three kilometers away. Isakov warned them not to

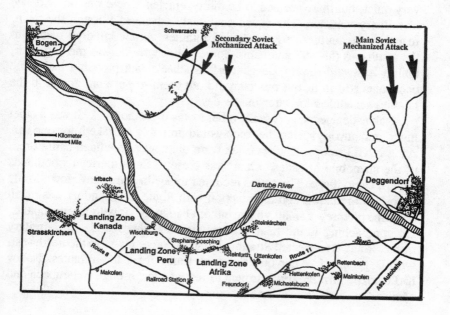

return on the roads, but to go over the fields, which were flat and easy to traverse in a LuAZ jeep. At the same time, he gave orders to Grigorii Varakin, the deputy platoon leader, to take Gudkov's 1st Squad to patrol the town of Stephans-posching itself, as well as Steinfurth. Isakov would lead 2d Squad in inspecting the southeast, toward Freundorf and Michaelsbuch. It was now 0330. Dawn would be about 0615. Each detachment would take one of the new radiomen along, and leave two more to keep in control of Uttenkofen.

In Uttenkofen they had found two operable vehicles, a beaten-up old Unimog truck used for farm work, and a van from a local bakery. Varakin took the van. Isakov and 2d Squad got into the truck. The squad leader, Bohdan Donchuk, took the driver's seat, with Isakov next to him. The other six soldiers piled into the open rear flatbed. Much to their chagrin, its last duty appeared to have been manure hauling, and the flatbed stank. The Unimog slowly clattered its way down the road, without lights, passing a small cemetery. The road intersected Route 11, which ran east and west, about a kilometer from the village, before entering Michaelsbuch. Donchuk pulled the truck off the road before the intersection, and the squad dismounted. There didn't seem to be any traffic on Route 11 at the moment. Michaelsbuch was a good deal larger than Uttenkofen. It was very quiet, but there seemed to be more vehicles. There was no evidence of military vehicles. The squad cautiously advanced through the town, reaching the southern edge in a few minutes. A few hundred meters to the south was the A92 autobahn. Some military traffic was moving on it, mainly eastward toward Deggendorf. Michaelsbuch probably had some occupants still in it, but the town did not seem to pose any threat to the landing scheduled for later in the day.

Isakov decided to survey the other towns from the truck. It was a quiet night, and anyone seeing the truck would probably mistake it for one carrying NATO troops. The spetsnaz wore the new camouflage battle dress of the airmobile brigades, which was close to the American woodlands pattern camouflage. The squad mounted up again and set off down Route 11 toward Freundorf and the junction with Route 8. Freundorf was much the same picture—a small village either abandoned or with few occupants. On approaching Route 8, it was obvious that there was some military traffic. Route 8 connected Straubing, and the other towns to the northwest, with Deggendorf. After observing the traffic for a few minutes, Isakov had Gudkov turn the truck around to reconnoiter through Rettenbach and Mainkofen. They too were abandoned.

Isakov decided to leave two observers with a radio near the junction of Routes 11 and 8, overlooking the autobahn. This would keep most of the traffic at the southern end of the landing zone under watch. Another team was assigned to Michaelsbuch, stationed in the village's church belfry. This team could monitor any traffic coming off the autobahn toward the landing zone. Finally, one team was left in an industrial building near the Mainkofen railroad station to keep an eye on the autobahn and rail lines. This scattered the 1st Squad over a large area. But most of the teams could probably scrounge a car later in the day. It was important to cover all the likely avenues that enemy forces might use to attack Landing Zone Afrika.

With the teams in place, Isakov returned to Uttenkofen in the truck. Isakov was more familiar with German trucks than was the rest of the platoon. As a regular spetsnaz officer, he occasionally had been assigned to drive Soviet Avtotransport commercial trucks into West Germany while in civilian clothing. It gave him a clearer picture of the road nets and terrain than was ever possible from the sparse material provided in spetsnaz courses. Isakov reached Uttenkofen as dawn was breaking. Konchin and the 3d Squad had returned from the supply site. There were only two LuAZ jeeps, instead of the promised three, but they were heaped with supplies.

"Comrade Lieutenant, beg to report!" said Konchin. Isakov nodded. "Comrade Lieutenant, we met Captain Vavilov near the station about a half hour ago. He instructed me to tell you that our platoon would be receiving only two jeeps. They lost three jeeps, probably an overshoot of the drop zone. We have our full complement of Metis missile launchers and other supplies."

Isakov responded. "Konchin, your men will be our unit reserve and remain here for the time being. Prepare the missile launchers. We will deploy them later in the day. Unload the other supplies into that garage."

Isakov found one of the other radiomen he had left behind and instructed him to raise Grigorii Varakin with the 1st Squad.

"Bantu 1, this is Bantu 4, over."

The radioman was unable to raise the other squad. The channels seemed to be jammed. He tried several different frequencies, without luck. Isakov decided to drive down toward Stephans-posching to determine the situation, and the radioman accompanied him. The road led toward the hamlet of Steinkirchen, breaking off at the last minute toward Stephans-posching. At the intersection, Isakov spotted two of the 1st

Squad soldiers signaling him. He pulled the truck over. It was WO Ivan Gudkov, the squad leader.

"Comrade Lieutenant, Warrant Officer Varakin is over in Stephans-posching with three more men. There are some German troops in the town. It looks like some sort of engineer unit with bridging equipment on trucks. Varakin said he thinks they are only staying there for the evening."

Isakov told Gudkov to sent a runner to Varakin and tell him of the radio problems. If the problems continued, Varakin should send a runner with a report to Uttenkofen. Isakov got back into the truck and drove back down to Uttenkofen. He wished his men had not been so methodical in ripping down phone lines. It might have been possible to use them to communicate with his scattered scouts.

At about 0815, a tan German taxi began approaching Uttenkofen. Konchin's squad prepared to ambush it if necessary, but guessed it was a runner from the 1st Squad. It was Varakin himself.

"Good morning, Comrade Lieutenant!" Varakin seldom used the prescribed military greetings, but he and Misha Isakov were good friends. "The Germans have left Stephans-posching. But we will have to keep an eye out there. They seem to use that road pretty regularly. There are still some Germans in the town, mostly around a hotel and filling station. I've positioned one team in the church belfry, which looks out over the Danube River ferry. I've left another at the other end of the town, and one near the ferry. I've told them to stay under cover and keep their eyes open. I'm sorry I had to drive up here myself, but I was the only one who knew how to drive except for Gudkov."

Isakov nodded. "Nice car you picked out."

He turned to the map and pointed out the disposition of the squads. The unit was very scattered—too much so if there was any fighting to be done. The two men talked over plans to hold this sector while the airlift brought in troops later in the day. The drop area seemed suitable. There was very little evidence of German forces here. But things might change if the Soviet tank forces on the other side of the river began approaching. The fields would provide little defense against tanks. But it would probably be possible to hold a narrow bridgehead at the river itself from the small towns dotting the riverbank.

To get around the radio jamming, Isakov instructed one of the radio-men to use the R-350 burst-communication set to reach the HQ. A message came through about five minutes later indicating that someone from

HQ would be visiting Uttenkofen in a short time to determine the situation. They requested information on whether it was safe to pass through Stephans-posching. Isakov had the cipher operator reply that there were civilians present, but no military.

About thirty minutes later, a small postal truck appeared on the road from Steinkirchen, and the company zampolit, Captain Gelman, stepped out. He was brought into the small house where Isakov had set up shop. "Good morning, Misha!"

"Good morning, Comrade Captain." Isakov was more polite in his response. He was always careful with the "organs," as they called the "Organs of State Security." Zampolits were often a contact point between smaller army units and the KGB.

Isakov explained the situation of his unit. So far, so good. Very few signs of heavy enemy military presence. Considerable evidence of enemy activity all around the area. Heavy artillery firing, jet aircraft, and truck traffic on the autobahn. The area over the river seemed to be the scene of very heavy fighting, judging from the smoke and sound. Gelman indicated that the situation in the other sectors also seemed favorable. The only problem area was the main town of Strasskirchen, a large town that sat astride Route 8 at the northwest edge of the area. There was a lot of military traffic through the town, MPs to control traffic, and some permanent military presence. However, Irlbach, near the river, was quiet. Gelman indicated that Major Danilov was recommending that the air assault proceed on the basis of the scouting, but they would have to wait until later in the afternoon for the final verdict. The Germans might move more equipment into the area later in the day.

Aside from a few German military trucks passing through Stephans-posching, the day was mostly quiet. The scouts near the A92 autobahn reported continuing military traffic—mostly trucks, but an occasional tank column. Most were moving toward Deggendorf, where a major fight seemed to be brewing. In the early afternoon, a German Bo-105 scout helicopter appeared in the area, snooping around, but it continued on without incident. Isakov pulled back some of the scout teams from the southeast edge of the area, and deployed Konchin's missile teams to cover the A92 autobahn exit near Michaelsbuch and the approach from Deggendorf on Route 11.

Trouble showed up at about 1430, when a German artillery unit pulled off Route 8 and began setting up shop outside the Stephans-posching train station. The enemy unit consisted of a battery of M109 self-propelled howitzers, a command vehicle, and a few trucks. At 1500, the company headquarters radioed Isakov to get a final situation report before the decision was made to proceed with the assault. Isakov mentioned the artillery. Major Danilov recommended that he keep an eye on it. Once they fired, they would probably move, to avoid counterbattery fire. If the artillery remained in the area, Isakov's platoon would have to eliminate them before the helicopters arrived at 1600. They would have to act quickly, and probably would have surprise in their favor at least.

Isakov drove into Stephans-posching in the Unimog truck. He assumed the Germans would treat the truck as a "friendly." Isakov collected four more riflemen to add to the two in the back, along with Warrant Officer Varakin. Gudkov was instructed to capture any remaining German civilians in the area over the next few minutes, in anticipation of the helicopter assault at 1600. The artillery battery was located in a small clearing on either side of the road. The building hid the road the Soviets were traveling on from their view. The Germans had been very careless. Scanning the area with his binoculars, Isakov could see no evidence of a perimeter defense. His plan was to drive to the edge of the railroad station buildings and dismount the squad there, where a clearer view would be possible. His squad would be considerably outnumbered, but a lot of the artillerymen would probably not be carrying their small arms.

The Unimog bumped along down the road. It was a little more than a kilometer from Stephans-posching to the railroad station, but the drive seemed much longer. After crossing the railroad tracks, Varakin pulled the truck into a small parking lot, and the troops disembarked. Isakov entered a switching building that overlooked the enemy artillery unit, and went upstairs. The artillery battery was scattered in a field unloading ammunition and preparing to fire. They were about fifty meters from the road at the closest. If they tried to attack the artillery on foot, they would have to cover a fair amount of open field, and they'd probably be spotted by the Germans. Isakov and Varakin decided instead to drive the squad out to the side of the German position. Four of the men were told to get their RPG-22s ready by pulling out the tube and cocking them. As they got off the truck, they were to fire at the self-propelled howitzers. The rest of the squad would use their assault rifles and charge the German positions.

Varakin was driving the truck as they pulled out into the open. The Germans seemed to be paying no attention at all. They probably did not suspect that any Soviet troops were operating on this side of the river, and so had not taken even elementary defense precautions.

"Misha, what do you say we try to get closer?" asked Varakin.

Isakov nodded. Varakin drove the truck off the side of the road, and across the field toward the artillery battery. They headed toward the side of the German position. The M109 artillery vehicles were to the left and the German trucks to the right. When they were about thirty-five meters from the nearest vehicle, Varakin stopped. A German soldier, apparently an officer, began walking toward them. Varakin carefully got out of the cab, keeping the door open to hide his uniform. The troops jumped out of the rear, and the grenadiers deployed quickly. Isakov shouted to them to fire. The rockets hissed off in an ear-piercing roar, accompanied by the clatter of AK-74 assault rifles. The troops were bunched up at first, but when Varakin shouted "Urra!" and began running forward, they followed.

The Germans were in complete confusion. The rockets had hit three of the artillery vehicles. A great deal of ammunition and propellant were lying about, and it began to ignite. A second salvo of rockets hit the M577 command post and one of the trucks. Few of the artillerymen had their rifles at hand, and they were cut down by the charging Soviet troops. Two Bundeswehr soldiers near the truck did have their assault rifles and fired at the Soviets. Two spetsnaz were hit, but in turn they drew fire from a Soviet grenadier with a BG-15 grenade launcher. Varakin had spotted the two Germans and hit one with rifle fire. He then hurled a grenade, starting a fire in the trucks and wounding the other German soldier. Isakov tossed a grenade into the undamaged M109. There was a muffled blast, and the vehicle began to burn. He directed his squad away from the burning vehicles toward the trucks. By now some of the unarmed German soldiers were fleeing across the field, and a small group of German soldiers managed to escape in a jeep. There was a flurry of raised arms as the surviving artillerymen surrendered. Of the sixty German troops, about twenty-five were wounded or killed, ten or twelve escaped, and the rest surrendered. Surprise had worked in the Soviets' favor.

Isakov ordered the squad to remain near the station during the upcoming air assault. They managed to salvage one truck from the German vehicles. The prisoners were herded into one of the nearby station buildings and frisked down. Varakin remained with this group, while Isakov drove back to the main platoon positions at Michaelsbuch. The two wounded Soviet paratroopers stayed behind. One had been hit in the arm and was in considerable pain. The other soldier had been hit in the chest and was in shock. Varakin and one other soldier attempted to administer aid as best they could.

Isakov arrived in Michaelsbuch as the first signs of the air assault began. A flight of Mi-24 Gorbach attack helicopters flew overhead, attacking the traffic along Route 8 and the A92 autobahn. They were low to the ground and firing rockets. It was comforting to see the big attack helicopters. Their size and high speed made them seem omnipotent. Isakov went over to the church and climbed into the belfry to get a good view of the action. The Mi-17 transport helicopters were approaching the landing zone (LZ). He could see the first helicopters land, and several of his own men run out to give them directions.

The force setting down in LZ Afrika was the 1st Company of the 123d Air Assault Battalion. The air assault troops were well trained like his own men, and began to deploy rapidly. The Mi-17s seemed to be on the ground for only a few seconds before they were fully unloaded and off in the air again. Isakov climbed down from the belfry to greet the new arrivals. The officers from the 1/123d Air Assault Battalion were easy to pick out. A cluster of radiomen followed in their footsteps, with the whip antennas of their radios all too obvious. It was a good thing no enemy snipers were in the area.

The company commander, Capt. Vasily Bondarchuk, told Isakov that his company had been put, temporarily at least, under his command. Isakov led him to the Michaelsbuch church, where he had reestablished his command post. Using the maps, he explained his deployment. Bondarchuk told him to reassemble his platoon; it was too widely scattered to be useful in the upcoming fight. The 123d Air Assault would take over their positions in Stephans-posching. Bondarchuk indicated that the battalion commander expected the main attack to come in this sector from the southeast. Once his men reassembled, Bondarchuk wanted Isakov to position his platoon in the small hamlet of Hettenkofen, which was on the outskirts of Michaelsbuch. After asking about his antitank equipment, Bondarchuk reminded Isakov how important antitank defense would be in the forthcoming fight.

Isakov radioed to his squads, and by 1800, they had all reported to Hettenkofen, which was not so much a village as a collection of houses and other buildings along a secondary road. The houses would offer a certain measure of protection against enemy tanks, but not much. Basically, the idea was to hold the river perimeter until the main Soviet forces arrived on the northern bank. Then, a bridging operation would link up and seize the main A92 autobahn intersections. The main Soviet force was expected to arrive the next morning and begin bridging operations. Until then, Isakov's platoon would have to hold the easternmost edge of the bridgehead.

Isakov had the soldiers plant antitank mines along Route 11 to deny the road to enemy tanks. Some more were laid in front of their positions, but there were not enough to make effective barriers. The three Metis antitank guided missile teams were evenly spaced along the 500 meters of the perimeter. All troops were issued RPG-22s. There were about 30 RPG-22s left, enough for one man each, plus a half dozen extra. There was little point in trying to set up ambushes, since the terrain was too flat and exposed to permit it.

As night settled in, the fire over the river grew more intense. The night sky was illuminated by artillery flares and explosions, which was some comfort, since it was evidence of the approaching Soviet forces. Isakov was very pleased by the performance of his men against the German artillery position. But fighting tanks would be harder. The Germans obviously were preparing something. There was activity in the neighboring hamlet of Rettenbach and Mainkofen, and tanks were operating in the area, judging from the high-pitched metallic squeal of their tracks.

In the adjacent village the enemy was preparing a counterattack. The Germans were following an absolute rule learned at officer school. Soviet bridgeheads must be smashed as soon as they are formed. The one lesson learned five decades before during the war on the Eastern Front was that Soviet bridgeheads had to be rooted out, not just isolated. Reconnaissance had indicated that the Soviet airmobile force was located between Deggendorf and Strasskirchen. It would be light on armor, if it had any at all. And it would probably be light on antitank weapons. The Germans decided to hit it with a night tank attack supported by infantry. Artillery would be a dicey proposition due to the proximity of the German forces. Several scattered tank companies were rounded up, along with some mechanized infantry originally slated for the front against the main Soviet attack.

The German attack force began moving at about 2200. The night was nearly pitch black, owing to the clear skies and lack of moonlight. This was a serious problem for Isakov's ATGM teams. Their launchers had passive night sights, but a little moonlight or starlight was needed to make them work properly. There was damn little tonight. Flare pistols could provide some light, and Bondarchuk promised to get a little illumination from the battalion's mortars. There was considerable tank noise coming from the autobahn. About 2215, the attack began.

German tanks spilled off the autobahn in a wave aimed at cutting through Michaelsbuch and pushing to Stephans-posching. A similar attack was launched from the other side out of Strasskirchen toward Irlbach. The attack in this sector consisted of about two companies of tanks, numbering twenty-six in all, supported by thirty-four troop carriers and sundry other armored vehicles. There were three companies of infantry, although not enough vehicles to carry them all. The tanks were a mixed bag of twelve Leopard 2s, and various models of Leopard 1s culled from stragglers or units that had gotten separated from their original units. The plan was to envelop the area in smoke, with the Leopard 2s sitting back and using their thermal imaging sights to pick out targets. The smoke should blind the enemy gunners, giving the other tanks and infantry time to close rapidly on the Soviet positions. No one looked forward to street fighting at night, but neither town was very large.

Isakov's platoon could not see the German tanks, but could hear them. There was a slight flash of light as the smoke mortars were fired. Isakov gave Varakin the signal to fire several flares. All that was evident was a billowing white cloud from the German smoke grenades. One flare dropped slowly to the ground, casting an eerie glare on the scene. From out of the mist came the ugly snouts of several tanks. One of Konchin's Metis crews fired at it, but lost the tank due to the lack of light. Varakin tried firing more flares, but it was too late. The missile impacted harmlessly on the ground. Konchin's fire provoked the German tanks to begin firing. A Leopard 2 had spotted Konchin's missile team and obliterated it with a single 120mm high-explosive round. The German tanks alternated between cannon fire and machine guns as they charged forward. Another Metis team fired at a Leopard 1 tank that had outrun the smoke cover. It made a solid hit on the hull, stopping the tank. But again, the missile launch gave away the team's position and it was hammered mercilessly by tank fire.

The platoon had lost two of its three ATGMs in the first minute of fighting, and the German tanks were still 800 meters away. The RPG-22s were useless at more than 150 meters, especially at night. The German fire seemed to be directed mainly at Michaelsbuch, but three tanks had peeled off and were heading for Hettenkofen. All three were out of the smoke cloud and completely exposed, and the last surviving Metis team could see them clearly as long as the flares lasted. The missile spurted out of its tube and struck the Leopard squarely on the turret. It was a Leopard 2, however, and the puny missile warhead was ineffective against the thick-skinned beast. The Leopard 2 swung its turret toward its tormentor and snuffed out the last Metis team with a single fiery blast. As the German tanks continued to fire, the buildings where Isakov's troops were crouched were relentlessly pulverized. Casualties were mounting fast. The lightly armed infantry was unable to respond until the tanks reached point-blank range, if any of them survived that long!

The tanks reached the edge of the village in another minute, firing all the way with machine guns. Three RPG-22s were fired, one hitting. It did little damage, and the machine gun fire from the tanks intensified. The tanks seemed to be probing for a location to pass through the village. Eventually they headed for the opening between Hettenkofen and Michaelsbuch. Varakin was at the southern edge of the perimeter where the German tanks were passing through. He got a clear shot against the rear of a Leopard, setting its engine on fire. But the blast from the rocket gave away his position, and he was cut down by a Marder infantry transporter that had been following behind. The German infantry transporters then disgorged their foot soldiers, who charged into the village. Isakov was in the center of the perimeter. He fired his RPG-22 at one of the infantry carriers, without success. The Marder turned its 20mm cannon on the building he was in. One round clipped away a large chunk of masonry, which smacked Isakov in the head. He was knocked unconscious.

Lieutenant Misha Isakov regained consciousness about twenty minutes later. He could feel the sticky traces of blood congealed on his forehead. Standing in front of him was a German soldier with an assault rifle pointed squarely at his face. The German motioned him to move over to the wall. Sitting there were three members of his platoon, including Bohdan Donchuk of the 2d Squad. For Misha Isakov, the war was over.

## Analysis

The Soviets have a wide range of special forces, many of which would be used in any war with NATO. The fictional scenario takes a look at two of these forces, the spetsnaz and the heliborne air assault units. Of the two, the spetsnaz are the more controversial. Elite forces are an enduring source of fascination, even though their actual combat records are often dubious. In an age of computerized precision-guided munitions, it's satisfying to think that a well-trained band of brave men can change the course of wars.

*Spetsnaz* comes from the Russian words *spetsialnoye naznacheniye*, which roughly translated means "special purpose." Spetsnaz are the special operations forces of the Soviet GRU. The Soviet Union, like the U.S., has two intelligence agencies, the GRU, which corresponds to the U.S. Defense Intelligence Agency (DIA), and the KGB, which corresponds to the CIA and FBI all wrapped up in one. The GRU is a part of the military establishment, while the KGB is separate from both the Communist party and the Soviet Army, although deeply involved with both. The spetsnaz forces are intended to bridge the gap between conventional intelligence-gathering personnel such as spies, and tactical reconnaissance units attached to tank and motor rifle divisions.

The exploits of spetsnaz have been trumpeted by Viktor Suvorov, a former Soviet GRU officer who defected to the West in the late 1970s. Until Suvorov began writing his books on the subject, little attention was paid (publicly at least) to Soviet special forces aside from rather obvious elite units like the Soviet airborne divisions. Certainly, there has always been some appreciation for Soviet partisan warfare and unconventional tactics, but not for the extensive types of special operations portrayed by Suvorov. He luridly depicts spetsnaz as a bunch of highly trained professional, multilingual sportsmen-killers, with a bent for assassination and other mayhem. He has elevated spetsnaz to mythical proportions, suggesting that they will be used in missions to eliminate VIPs within NATO in the event of war, as well as to carry out more conventional commando-style operations against key NATO facilities. However, there is a lack of evidence as to their real importance, and many contradictions can be found in his claims about their activities.

Suvorov has suggested that the Soviet Army would have up to 30,000 spetsnaz troops available for operations in the event of war with NATO. These consist of spetsnaz brigades at front level, spetsnaz companies at army level, and various types of naval spetsnaz forces. In judging the quality of special forces, there is always a conflict between size and elite training. The larger the force, the more likely that its recruitment and training will be less demanding. While no one would deny the quality of the U.S. Marines as a fighting force, they do not compare in training and specialized skills to a unit like the Navy's SEALs. Likewise, British Paras are among the world's finest light infantry, but they are not equivalent to the SAS (Special Air Service), nor are they intended to be. The type of force described by Suvorov is an elite force, but its sheer size suggests that it is more like the U.S. Army's LRRPs (long-range recon patrols) or Rangers, rather than a Delta Force, and probably not even that well trained.

It must be remembered that spetsnaz, like most of the rest of the Soviet armed forces, is still largely a conscript force. In a spetsnaz company like the one depicted in the fictional scenario, fifteen of the twenty men are conscripts, three are conscript sergeants, and only two are professional soldiers. The scenario presumes that the Soviets will gradually upgrade spetsnaz training by including professional praporshchiks (warrant officers) rather than conscript sergeants. But it's worth noting that in the late 1980s 90 percent of spetsnaz tactical units were made up of eighteen- to twenty-year-old conscript soldiers with less than two years of military training. This does not imply the sort of James Bond characters that many people in the West now associate with the word *spetsnaz*.

To better understand how spetsnaz fits into Soviet special operations, it's necessary to briefly examine the many major components of Soviet special forces. It is a complicated matter, since special operations have been undergoing a major change due to the lessons of the Afghanistan war and to the introduction of special helicopter assault units.

## The Air Assault Force (VDV)

The largest Soviet special force is called the VDV, which is the Russian acronym for Air Assault Forces. The VDV is a semi-independent branch of the army, under central Moscow control for strategic operations. The core of the VDV is the seven air assault divisions stationed around the Soviet Union. The air assault divisions are paratrooper formations, like the U.S. 82d Airborne Division or the British Army's Parachute Regiment. The VDV is a select, elite force and receives a high priority in recruitment. Emphasis is placed on a clean record, and most Soviet paratroopers are recruited out of the Slavic majority: Russians, Ukrainians, and Byelorussians. Athletic ability is prized, especially evidence of leadership skills, such as team leaders in secondary school sports teams. The training is much more rigorous than that in ordinary Soviet units, and is similar to U.S. Marine or airborne training.

Soviet air assault divisions are smaller than tank or motorized rifle divisions but are more heavily mechanized than American or British airborne units. The Soviets use the airmobile BMD armored infantry vehicle as the basis for these formations. However, the Soviets have significant shortages of large transport aircraft to carry so much equipment in a single sortie. So the VDV troops are trained for operations with little mechanized equipment. They are a light infantry force first and foremost, capable of using mechanized equipment if available.

The role of the VDV divisions is to provide the Soviet General Staff with a deep operations force for special missions. A typical operation might involve seizing a bridgehead in advance of a mechanized column. The usefulness of an airborne division is constrained by two factors. Soviet airlift has decided limits, which probably means that airborne divisions will be used minus their BMDs. When used as light infantry, airborne divisions, in spite of all their fine training, suffer from serious military weaknesses compared to mechanized infantry divisions with less vigorous training. Light infantry divisions are only as mobile as human feet will carry them, and so are less mobile than mechanized infantry in most Western European terrain. More importantly, airborne divisions are very light on firepower. Airborne divisions have little capability to withstand tank attack. They cannot carry sufficient weapons for this contingency by the very nature of their organization. The best enemy of the tank is another tank, and airborne tanks have never really panned out. As was suggested in the fictional scenario where tanks overran Isakov's unit, this problem is endemic to light infantry, and not peculiar to airborne forces alone.

The Soviets concluded as much after World War II. Their study of World War II operations suggested that airborne units are valuable only when used against enemy forces that are already broken, or in peripheral operations. The battle for the Arnhem bridges was one of the clearest examples of the severe limitations of airborne forces during World War II, and the Soviets had several of their own examples with similar outcomes. So in view of these limitations, why do the Soviets still have seven airborne divisions?

The VDV still has its use as a Praetorian Guards. They are an elite force that is more reliable than the rest of the army rabble in the eyes of many Soviet leaders. Like most NATO leaders, the Soviets do not think that a war in Europe is particularly likely. More likely are wars outside of Europe. It is for these wars, not a confrontation with NATO, that the VDV is most useful. The VDV is used in ticklish situations where regular

Ground Forces units might be a bit too clumsy. In 1968 in Czechoslovakia, it was the VDV that took over the Prague airport and captured much of the Czech leadership. It is significant that no VDV division is stationed in Central Europe. They are stationed in the USSR itself, and while they may be used in Europe, their orientation is worldwide.

In Afghanistan in 1979, it was a VDV task force that spearheaded the invasion. The VDV units also formed the heart of Soviet counterinsurgency forces in Afghanistan. Many of the regular Ground Forces units were good for little more than guarding towns or conducting futile sweep operations. It was the VDV, with its combination of rugged training and high expectations, that carried out the more successful missions against the mujihadeen.

A recent study of the Afghanistan fighting by the Rand Corporation provided a good example of VDV skills. A mujihadeen unit in Nangrahar province had taken up positions in a mountain overlooking a Soviet base. They had laboriously moved rocket launchers and mortars up the mountain and in September 1986 were bombarding the Soviet base in the valley below. One morning, the mujihadeen was suddenly surprised by a group of about ninety VDV troops, who had scaled the mountain the previous night. One of the soldiers fighting them remarked: "Before that I had thought that the Soviet soldiers are not worth anything, but I must say that I have never seen anything like that. We had good food there and I was in good shape, but I would not have been able to climb that mountain. It was simply impossible for me. These were really tough guys."[5]

The Soviet leadership uses the VDV where the other tough guys fail. The Soviets have a special paramilitary Interior Army (VV), which acts like a state police force. If they need to bust heads during urban disturbances, they call in the Interior Army. But in situations where the Interior Army is unable to quell the rioting, the VDV is put into action. Soviet citizens know when they see the blue berets of the VDV that party time is over. In Azerbaijan and Armenia in 1987, ethnic disputes got out of the control of the local police. The Interior Army was called in. They couldn't handle it. The VDV was called in.

---

5. The Rand Corporation conducted interviews with Soviet deserters from Afghanistan to prepare an account for the U.S. Army of Soviet military experiences there. Authored by Alexander Alexiev, and entitled "Inside the Soviet Army in Afghanistan," it provides one of the most detailed looks at the capabilities as well as the problems of the Soviet Army today.

The VDV are classic examples of cold war soldiers. Their training is the best traditional sort—tough, demanding exercises with a focus on the basics of light infantry. This might not be so useful on a mechanized battlefield, but a mechanized battlefield in Europe is not very likely. Low-intensity wars are probable, and the VDV is the Soviet shock force for these contingencies.

## Airmobile: The New Generation

The problem with paratroop operations is the method of delivery. It is strictly one way. You drop them in, then they fight their way out. Or you have to fight your way in to get them out. The Soviets had several airborne operations in World War II in which they dropped a force in and then could not extract it. Helicopter technology is a better solution. Helicopters provide the ability to deposit forces deep behind enemy lines with considerable precision—even better than parachutes, since you don't have to worry about the wind. And better yet, you can extract them once they have completed their mission, or if the going gets too tough.

The Soviets began playing around with airmobile forces in the 1970s. These units are called Desantnaya Shturmvaya (assault landing forces). The concept is closest to U.S. air cavalry or airmobile forces. These forces are organized into brigade-sized formations rather than divisions, called DShB (Day-Shah-Bey) for assault landing brigades. The Soviets have tried a variety of different organizations. The DShB troops are recruited and trained like VDV troops, and appear to be under a similar organization. They are trained in parachuting, but their main means of delivery is the helicopter. There are at least two types of DShB brigades: units that have their own helicopters, and units that depend on regular air force helicopter units to provide the lift. The 123d Airmobile Battalion depicted in this fictional scenario is a DShB formation.

The DShB do not have the long lineage of the VDV paratroopers, but their combat role in Afghanistan was every bit as bold. Afghanistan became a helicopter war favoring Soviet airmobile forces just as Vietnam spurred American interest in helicopters. Helicopters give the infantry an incomparable degree of mobility in the worst terrain. Although physical training is still important, an airmobile unit in a helicopter will be better ready for battle than a crack special forces unit that has just trudged up and down the mountains.

It remains to be seen what the Soviets will do in the wake of Afghanistan with the VDV and DShB. The VDV has lost at least one division, disbanded after Afghanistan. The trend seems to be in favor of the heliborne forces. The question is not one of combat role or training, only the mode of delivery. The traditional silk, or the contemporary rotor?

## Recon Forward!

Although not a distinctly different branch of the Ground Forces, Soviet reconnaissance units have long been treated as an elite force. Called *razvedchiki* in the Soviet Ground Forces, they are the finest troops in their division or regiment. Razvedchiki are recruited from the conscripts on the basis of their athletic skills, intelligence, and composure under stress. They receive continual and more vigorous training than normal Ground Forces troops. Each regiment has a company of razvedchiki, and each division has a battalion. The razvedchiki are scouts. They are placed in the vanguard of the attack to determine the location of enemy positions, or to locate undefended avenues of advance. They are more lightly armed than other combat forces since their main role is to locate the enemy, not engage in battle.

Because of their superior training and leadership, the razvedchiki are also used for any especially demanding missions. For example, if a forward detachment is needed to seize an objective in advance of the main formation, it will usually be assigned to the razvedchiki. If a division plans a sneak raid against enemy positions, the razvedchiki will be the basis of the raiding force.

The practice of incorporating an elite formation within the ordinary divisions is due to several factors. On the one hand, the organization of large numbers of "elite" formations with an armed force has a detrimental effect on the quality of the army as a whole. Elite units tend to draw away the more adventurous and talented soldiers who seek the prestige of the specialist units. These units often boast that their privates are as good as the sergeants in regular units. This is precisely the problem. Elite formations concentrate the best soldiers and leave the main combat formations with mediocre soldiers. This is especially critical in the Soviet Ground Forces, where the NCO ranks are weak already due to the lack of a professional cadre. By establishing an "elite" formation like the razvedchiki within the ordinary divisions, the normal formations can continue to attract talented young soldiers who might otherwise be lured away into specialist units.

In addition, the Soviet Army has severe training shortcomings due to its sheer size and the turmoil of its draft system. The razvedchiki units allow the Soviets to isolate a portion of the combat units and lavish more attention on it. It gives the divisional or regimental commander an especially capable force for occasions when normal motor rifle troops might be too clumsy. Like the VDV and DShB, the razvedchiki were extensively deployed in Afghanistan. They are more difficult to distinguish than the VDV and the DShB, since they do not wear distinctive uniforms or an insignia, but they are often mentioned in the Soviet military press.

## The Legendary Spetsnaz

Much has been written about the spetsnaz, but much of it has been fanciful. The role of the spetsnaz appears to bridge the gap between elite special force combat units like the VDV and DShB, and the divisional razvedchiki. The fact that the spetsnaz are under GRU intelligence control suggests that their main role is operational reconnaissance. Spetsnaz units exist at two levels, companies at the army level and brigades at the front level. The unit described in this fictional scenario is an army-level spetsnaz company.

The composition of these units undermines many of the exaggerated tales that have been told about them over the past few years. As mentioned before, they are conscript units, much like any other Soviet unit, but with higher priority in recruitment and training. They are undoubtedly high-quality units. But it is difficult to believe that they are sophisticated enough to carry out disguised sabotage missions. It is highly unlikely that these troops have either the language skills or experience to convincingly blend into a Western European environment. This is not to say that the Soviets do not possess such forces. But such forces demand long-term, professional personnel and are inevitably much smaller in number than the 20,000 to 30,000 figure quoted for spetsnaz. It is more likely that such forces are under the jurisdiction of the KGB due to its control of intelligence and agent networks outside the USSR.

The role of spetsnaz is probably more akin to American LRRP units. That is to say, the units carry out deep reconnaissance missions, far behind enemy lines, but still in uniform. While they may be used in sabotage missions, their primary task is scouting. It is pointless to send a small, highly trained company with modest firepower to attack a large NATO installation when it could be more effectively neutralized by air or missile attack.

Spetsnaz finds the target and can conduct post-strike damage assessment. Spetsnaz may be used to attack smaller, high-value targets such as nuclear delivery systems (Lance missile units), nuclear storage facilities, or vulnerable ammunition dumps. They could also be used to carry out selected commando-style operations such as attacks on key communications links like bridges.

Nevertheless, front and army commanders will probably be reluctant to fritter away a valuable special force unit on a lot of pinprick commando attacks that may have little if any consequence on the conduct of the ground operations. For this reason, they may be consolidated for special high-risk missions directly connected with the offensive ground operations. As the scenario suggests, one such mission would be to act as the vanguard of army-level special forces operations, such as scouting and securing landing zones for critical air assaults.

It should be noted that there was hardly any evidence of spetsnaz operations in Afghanistan. Many of the operations associated with the spetsnaz were simply VDV or DShB operations, or the activity of the razvedchiki. Spetsnaz operations may have been few because of the small number of large-scale (army and front) operations. Assassination of mujihadeen leaders in Pakistan was mostly in the province of the KGB and their Afghan counterparts, the KHAD, not spetsnaz.

The scenario suggests that special forces, whether VDV, DShB, or spetsnaz, have distinct limitations on a mechanized battlefield. In spite of all their training, special forces units are invariably poorly equipped to deal with tanks, armored vehicles, and artillery. The histories of special forces units are filled with examples of elite formations being sent into missions where their reputations offered no protection against superior firepower and mobility. The attempt to seize the Arnhem bridges is one of the more obvious examples, but the Soviets have their own bloody reminder, the ill-fated Dnepr River operation of November 1943. The primary advantage of a special forces operation is surprise. And once that precious commodity has run out, special forces units had better hope for quick relief from regular, more heavily armed formations.

## Soviet Naval Special Forces

The Soviet Navy has its own special forces, the Naval Infantry and the naval spetsnaz. The Naval Infantry is the Soviet equivalent of the U.S. Marines or Royal Marines. Each of the Soviet fleets has a Naval Infantry brigade or, in some cases, a division. The Soviet Naval Infantry has much the same task as other marine forces: Their primary role is the conduct of amphibious landings. However, Soviet Naval Infantry forces are very small compared to their U.S. counterparts. While the U.S. Marines have about a third the number of divisions of the U.S. Army, the Soviet Naval Infantry is only about one-hundredth the size of the Soviet Ground Forces. This is largely due to the landlocked nature of the USSR, and the lack of a clear mission for the Naval Infantry in a European war.

In the event of a war with NATO, the Soviet Naval Infantry would probably be involved in peripheral operations. The 36th Naval Infantry Brigade of the Baltic Fleet most likely would be used in operations against Denmark in conjunction with similar Polish and East German naval assault units.[6] The 63d Guards Kirkenneskaya Naval Infantry Brigade of the Northern Fleet would probably be used in operations against northern Norway.

The Soviet Navy also deploys a spetsnaz diversionary brigade with most of the fleets. These units have a variety of roles, including special reconnaissance, like their land-based counterparts. The units are trained in underwater demolition and coastal raiding. The naval spetsnaz brigade of the Baltic Fleet probably has had the most active "peacetime" career of any spetsnaz unit; it has been used in a peculiar series of special reconnaissance operations along with Baltic Fleet submarines in Swedish coastal waters since the early 1980s. The actual mission for these deep-penetration operations is unclear. It is not certain whether the missions had a distinct military purpose, such as scouting Swedish ports and coastal waters, or whether the missions were of a more political nature, intended to intimidate the Swedish government.

## What About *Really* Special Operations?

The depiction of the spetsnaz here is a good deal less exotic than in many other published accounts. As mentioned earlier, this is not intended to discount the possibility that the Soviets have specialized deep-cover

---

6. The Polish Army fields the 7th Lusatian Naval Assault Brigade, and the East German Army usually assigns one of the regiments of the 8th Motorized Rifle Division in northern East Germany to the naval assault role. Recently, this has been the 29th "Ernst Moritz Arndt" Motorized Rifle Regiment at Proro in the Baltic.

assassination squads, but to suggest that a large force like the spetsnaz is unlikely to have such a high level of sophistication.

The Soviet KGB and its predecessor organizations, the NKVD and OGPU, have a long tradition of special units for "wet" operations such as assassination. It is worth noting that when the Soviets decided to kill the Afghan leader Hafizullah Amin before their invasion in 1979, it was the KGB that headed the operation. There is a certain competitive tension between the KGB and the military GRU, which might lead the GRU to encroach on this KGB territory; but it is the KGB that would organize most deep-cover sabotage and assassination operations in the support of combat operations in Europe.

Another question is whether the Soviets have organized special operations forces, disguised in NATO uniforms, to disrupt NATO rear areas. The German Wehrmacht in World War II was very active in such operations, with its Brandenburg units. However, the best-known example was Otto Skorzeny's improvised "Operation Griffon" during the Battle of the Bulge in the Ardennes in December 1944 with German troops dressed in American uniforms. The Brandenburg and Skorzeny operations highlight the difficulty of such missions, as well as their potential. It does not take a great many soldiers in disguise to seriously confuse and disrupt an opponent's operations, but it is difficult to organize large diversionary units of this type due to language barriers. Few soldiers have the language skills or the experience to convincingly pass themselves off as soldiers of another army.

The Soviets have another alternative in this respect, and that is to use East German troops to mimic West German troops. There have long been reports that the East German Army does indeed have a special diversionary battalion, equipped with M113 APCs and M48 tanks captured in Vietnam, and in German markings.

Soviet special forces are large and diverse. Some seem better suited to the demands of cold war contingencies, and not to confrontations with NATO. Others play an important part in Soviet operational planning, like the new DShB. The KGB special units, and to a lesser extent the spetsnaz, follow a long Russian tradition in rear area sabotage and diversion. And the razvedchiki, while not a special force by uniform and insignia, represents a Soviet counterpart to American Rangers. Nevertheless, their importance should not be exaggerated by romantic delusions of heroic derring-do. They have their place, but they have distinct limitations on the deadly modern battlefield.

# CHAPTER 5

## Attack Helicopters: The Air Assault at Irlbach

0600, 6 October, Chaloupky Airfield, Czechoslovakia

"Comrades, take your seats."

The aircrews of the 1st Squadron/69th Attack Helicopter Regiment (1/69 AHR) had been milling around in the ready room of the Chaloupky Airfield for fifteen minutes. The airstrip was too small to have a regular meeting hall, and this building had been taken over from an agricultural spraying operation. The squadron commander, Maj. Aleksander Frolov, tried to get his pilots to settle down. As the usual chatting ended, Frolov began the briefing.

"Pilots, as you know, our squadron has been held in reserve by the 1st Army for special missions. Our comrades from the other squadrons of the 69th Attack Regiment have already seen extensive combat in the fighting."

This was a bit of an understatement. The 69th Attack Regiment had been committed since the first day of the war. The Mi-8 transport helicopters[1] from the regiment's 3d Squadron had been flying repeatedly back to Chaloupky to get spare parts, ammunition, and crews. The 2d Attack Squadron, equipped with Mi-24M Gorbach helicopters[2] like the

---

1. The Mil Mi-8, code-named "Hip" by NATO, is roughly similar to the American CH-46. Although mainly used as a transport helicopter, there are armed gunship versions as well as electronic warfare and communication models. The Mi-8 formed the basis for the Mi-24 attack helicopter.

2. The Mil Mi-24 attack helicopter is known by its NATO code name "Hind"; the Mi-24M is the Hind-F. Soviet crews call the Mi-24 Gorbach (hunchback) due to the shape of the large engine compartment over the front cockpits.

1st Squadron, had seen the brunt of the fighting. The crews from the 3d Squadron reported that the attack boys were down to six helicopters from their original twenty-one Mi-24Ms. They had seen heavy fighting and had lost many helicopters to gunfire, missiles, and accidents. The pilots of the 1st Squadron were eager to learn everything these pilots could tell them about combat conditions. What were the main enemy threats? Were they encountering enemy helicopters? How strong were the enemy air defenses? Unfortunately, the transport pilots knew little of the real details of the past two days of fighting. Frolov could see that his men were anxious for action, but concerned over the heavy losses suffered by friends in the other squadron.

"We will have our first mission later today," he continued. "We will be supporting an air assault mission over the Danube River near the town of Irlbach. Our troops will be seizing a bridgehead on the south bank of the river. We will provide fire support and cover. Captain Dmitri Panchev from the front aviation command group will provide us with the details."

Although each army had an aviation staff, it was the front aviation group that had to approve the allotment of helicopter units for any large-scale heliborne operation. Panchev had been standing in the front of the room, fiddling with a large briefing board. He wore the camouflaged flight suit of assault helicopter pilots, but most pilots guessed he was just another weenie staff officer.

"Comrades," he began, "the operation will start at 1600 this afternoon. We plan to deploy the 123d Air Assault Battalion over the river just before sunset. This will give them the cover of the night to establish the bridgehead. We will be using the front's 14th Helicopter Transport Regiment[3] to ferry the battalion into action. You will be supporting them. The assault will be launched from a forward base at Dorfl. Your squadron will move forward to Dorfl at 1400, refuel, and prepare for the mission. Your helicopters will be armed here at Chaloupky before you leave. You will carry a full load of S-5 or S-8 rockets, and antitank missiles as well. You will not carry a flight technician on board, only the pilot and weapons officer. We do not expect heavy opposition. However, our intelligence has

---

3. A helicopter transport regiment would normally have two to three squadrons of Mi-8 medium transport helicopters (twenty-one per squadron), and a squadron of Mi-6 Hook or Mi-26 Halo heavy transport helicopters. The Mi-8s are used mainly to transport troops, whereas the larger helicopters could transport vehicles, artillery, and light armored vehicles such as the airmobile BMD infantry combat vehicle.

learned that the Germans have been moving more of their own PAH-1 attack helicopters[4] into the region. So don't focus only on the ground. Make sure your high flight keeps an eye out for enemy aviation. I'll turn you over to your Air Direction officer, Captain Kurasov."[5]

Captain Vasily Kurasov stood out among the assembled pilots if for no other reason than his age. Forty-five years old, a combat veteran of Afghanistan, he commanded the attention of the helicopter pilots who were a decade younger. Several of the pilots in the 1st Squadron knew Kurasov from lectures he had given to attack pilots during refresher courses for the helicopter units of the Central Group of Forces. He was an experienced and talented pilot, and was widely respected by pilots in the regiment.

"Comrades, I envy you. I'll be stuck on the ground later today with those *chuchmyek*[6] riflemen, while you boys will be flying overhead!"

The assembled pilots laughed at the racial slur. The aircrews were mostly Russians or Ukrainians. So were most of the elite air assault troops Kurasov would be accompanying into the drop zone. However, the pilots looked down their noses at *all* ground soldiers, even the elite DShB, as though they were ordinary motor rifle blockheads.

"Pilots, the first part of the mission is the most straightforward. Right out of tactical exercises. Even you nitwits from Leonov's flight should be able to manage this."

Senior Lieutenant Dmitri Leonov looked around sheepishly as the rest of the squadron pilots burst out laughing. He didn't think the remark was so funny. He was the flight leader of the 2d Flight, and he had already

---

4. The PAH-1 is the antitank version of the MBB Bo-105 light utility helicopter. It is armed with four HOT antitank missiles, but does not normally have a gun system. It roughly corresponds to the McDonnell (Hughes) 500MD. It is much smaller than the Mi-24.

5. The Air Direction officer (ADO) is a forward controller stationed on the ground to direct the attacks of helicopters and strike aircraft. The head of the Air Direction team is usually an experienced pilot. The Soviets use ADOs in a more rigid fashion than do most NATO forces, which usually allow the pilots a certain measure of freedom in picking out targets of opportunity.

6. *Chuchmyek* is a common racial slur directed mainly against Central Asians. Another popular expression in the Soviet Army for Central Asians is *chernozhop*. The worst is probably *zhopomordyi*. There are a variety of other common slurs, such as *khokhol* for Ukrainians, *yevreichik* or *zhid* for Jews, *katso* for Georgians, and *kosoglazyi* or *ploskomordyi* for Asians. The Russians have not entirely escaped this. The Poles, western Ukrainians, and Balts sometimes call the Russians *katsap*, suggesting they are provincial hicks.

lost one of his four helicopters. During the low-altitude training flight the day before, a Mi-24 had run into power lines. Fortunately, the crew survived. Earlier in the morning Kurasov had flown in on a reserve Mi-24 that would be turned over to Leonov's wingless crew. Kurasov was not the type to humiliate his junior pilots, but he knew how tense these greenhorns were. A joke at Leonov's expense seemed a small price to pay.

"All right, settle down," said Kurasov. "The objective is the area here, on the south bank of this turn on the Danube. The terrain is very open. The 14th Transport Regiment will be dropping the 123d in three areas, marked on these maps. Our reconnaissance from yesterday afternoon shows very few enemy concentrations in the area. That's why we selected it. We will be carrying out a ground reconnaissance this afternoon; it will be completed by 1400 and we will forward your commander the results. Unless something major turns up, we propose to conduct the attack as follows. The first three flights will each cover one of the three drop zones. Captain Nalepka, you and the 1st Flight will cover Landing Zone Kanada to the west. Lieutenant Leonov, your 2d Flight will cover the center Landing Zone Peru. Do a good job there, Dmitri, that's where I'm landing! Lieutenant Reiter and the 3d Flight will cover Landing Zone Afrika to the north. Lieutenant Dudarek's 4th Flight will be in reserve and cover any targets of opportunity we discover. We expect that the landing zones themselves will be clear. This is a secret so keep your mouths shut: We

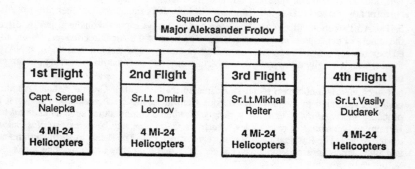

1st Squadron
# 69th Attack Helicopter Regiment

| Squadron Commander **Major Aleksander Frolov** | | | |
|---|---|---|---|
| **1st Flight** | **2nd Flight** | **3rd Flight** | **4th Flight** |
| Capt. Sergei Nalepka | Sr.Lt. Dmitri Leonov | Sr.Lt.Mikhail Reiter | Sr.Lt.Vasily Dudarek |
| **4 Mi-24 Helicopters** | **4 Mi-24 Helicopters** | **4 Mi-24 Helicopters** | **4 Mi-24 Helicopters** |

have a special spetsnaz team in there to look over the place. We expect that the main targets will be enemy convoys and other activity along autobahn A92, and along the roads that border the drop zone, like Route 8 and Route 11. You should aim to eliminate anything on these roads, or beyond them away from the landing zones.

"The attacks should be conducted in two passes. On each pass, empty one rocket pod per pylon. Save your cannon ammunition for later. The transport helicopters will follow you about ten minutes after your first attack. Pull back over to our side of the river. Once my team lands, we will give you directions from the ground. Captain Panchev will provide you with maps of the area. The enemy has few forces in the landing zones, but there are heavy concentrations here around Straubing to the west, and Deggendorf to the east. So be careful. Are there any questions?"

Most of the pilots wanted to ask about why the 2d Squadron was suffering such heavy losses. But they were afraid that asking such questions would display cowardice, or a lack of confidence in the equipment. Lieutenant Leonov, having been mocked earlier, was not so reluctant.

"Comrade Captain, as you know, our 2d Squadron has suffered heavy losses against the Germans. Can you tell us what has been causing these losses? Do the Germans have any new weapons?"

"We at the front aviation command group have been getting a lot of reports back from our forward attack squadrons," answered Kurasov. "Losses have been heavy, but we think that we are finally breaking through the thick crust of the German defenses. As far as specifics . . . I have to warn you pilots again to keep your eyes out for power lines. Your 2d Squadron lost two Mi-24 helicopters to power lines in one day. Flying low is a good tactic to limit your losses, but it requires real attention. You must instruct your gunners to keep watch for these. On the maps we're handing out now, the main power lines are clearly marked. But remember, there are apt to be smaller telephone and electrical lines elsewhere, like along road and railroad tracks.

"Now, regarding artillery. This is a sensitive subject. We have had real problems coordinating the helicopter attacks with the artillery boys. The forward artillery observers and the Air Direction officers have sometimes been working at cross-purposes. We've had several accidents where helicopters were called in for fire support when an artillery fire strike was occurring. This is especially a problem with the BM-21 Grad rocket knuckleheads. They have bad dispersion problems. We have lost a number of helicopters to friendly fire from this. You get the picture. Incoming artillery, incoming helicopters, and boom . . . no more helicopter. You do not need to worry about this on the assault today. The enemy defenses appear to be very modest, so there will be no artillery preparation before the landing. I don't want to worry you needlessly about this. Frankly, there's nothing you guys can do about it.

"Now, as far as weapons are concerned. If you encounter enemy tanks, there's a good chance there will be Gepards.[7] We've had a lot of complaints from the forward squadrons about the radar warning receivers — there is so much radar activity out there, they are always going off. A lot of flights are turning off their Syrena receivers.[8] Officially, I cannot recommend this procedure. But I can inform you of the problem. If you turn off the Syrena, you will have to keep a very sharp eye out for Gepards. They can hit you from 2,000 meters. Don't try to duel them with missiles. Those of you on Mi-24Ms, use your 30mm guns. The missiles take too long to get to the Gepard, and their guns will hit you before your missile gets there. The Gepards have proven very dangerous. Our electronic countermeasures have not been entirely successful.

"But don't ignore the ordinary guns. The Germans have a lot of 20mm AA guns with optical sights. You'll run into these when you attack bridges or other targets like these. Your Syrena warners won't do any good. Look for the tracers.

"Now, the missiles. The Germans are using an improved Stinger, what they call Advanced Stinger.[9] It didn't give us much of a problem the first day, since our multispectral flares seemed to work. But it seems as though they can adjust the seeker to filter out our new flares. Yesterday was a bad day. We've been taking a lot more hits to Stingers since the first day. I can't recommend much new on this beyond what you should already

---

7. Gepard is the German antiaircraft gun vehicle based on the Leopard 1 tank chassis. It is armed with twin 35mm autocannons, and uses radar fire direction. Although first fielded in the 1970s, it is still effective, especially against helicopters.

8. Syrena is the Soviet name for a type of radar warning receiver (RWR). They are a more sophisticated version of the radar detectors carried in cars to warn of radar speed traps. The receiver picks up radar emissions and warns the pilot that his aircraft has been illuminated by the radar. As in the case of automobile radar detectors, they can be set off by other microwave sources. The modern battlefield has so many radars and microwave sources operating that RWRs can be rendered useless by the sheer number of false alarms.

9. The latest model of Stinger, called the Stinger RMP, has a reprogrammable microprocessor in the seeker, which allows the missile crews to adjust the guidance to overcome new Soviet infrared countermeasures.

know. Don't waste your Hot Brick.[10] Turn it on when you're in the battle area, not too soon before. A lot of helicopters have been keeping them on, and they've been wearing out fast. Then when you need them, they're worn out. Use your flares only in the combat areas. Don't go wasting them on the approach. Don't shoot them off every time you see a flash on the ground. This is not peacetime. There's going to be a lot of activity under you, and a lot of weapons going off. Not every flash is a Stinger!

"Finally, keep your eyes open for enemy helicopters. Yesterday one of our squadrons lost almost an entire flight of helicopters to German PAH-1 helicopters. They are very small and hard to see. They popped up and fired antitank missiles at the flight, and hit three helicopters. I know all you hotshots have been waiting to gun down enemy helicopters with your cannon. But remember, what you don't see can kill you. Those lousy little PAH-1s don't have a gun, but their missiles can be deadly."

The crowd of pilots rustled a bit as the maps were passed out. But they listened intently to Kurasov. Their lives depended on his advice. Mikhail Reiter from the 3d Flight raised his hand.

"Comrade Captain, we've heard there are American Apaches in our sector."

"That's correct, Lieutenant. Last night, one of our tank units was hit by an Apache unit.[11] I don't know if you will encounter them today. The enemy seems to be committing them mainly at night. These things are much worse than the PAH-1s. They're a lot more like our new Mi-28s. They have a good cannon. But at night, they have radar and FLIR sights, and operate as easily as in the day. And their missiles are a lot worse. The Hellfire is faster than the TOWs and HOTs. If your laser warning receivers go off, take evasive action. The Americans have been using Hellfire air to air. They also have Stinger air to air. Don't mix it up with these people unless you have to. You are out there to support our riflemen.

---

10. "Hot Brick" is the slang expression for infrared (IR) jammers using modulated IR sources. The main tactical problem with many of these systems is that the IR lamp that provides the heat source has a short operating life. The Hot Brick cannot be used continuously or the lamp will wear out, so usually it is only used in high-risk areas or when a missile launch has been seen.

11. The AH-64 Apache is the U.S. Army's current attack helicopter. It is armed with laser-guided Hellfire antitank missiles, and newer versions will carry a millimeter wave-guided Hellfire. The Apache is superior to the Mi-24 in most respects, and comparable to the new Soviet Mi-28 Havoc.

You're not out there to become 'helicopter Kozhedubs.'[12] Look, I have to leave in five minutes for the staging area in Germany. Captain Panchev from the front's command group will stay here and answer any more questions. Good luck, chums!"

The pilots were sorry to see Kurasov go. He was a real helicopter pilot. Panchev was just a staff officer twit with no flying experience in attack helicopters. He was just a lousy truck driver, hauling riflemen around in Mi-17s (an improved version of the Mi-8). He parroted the official policy lines, which were boring and possibly dangerous in the circumstances. Kurasov had the balls to buck official policy and express his opinions about useful new tactics and maneuvers.

After twenty minutes of milling around, Dmitri Leonov collected the other three pilots from his flight and left for the field to prepare the helicopters. The 2d Flight had consisted of four Mi-24 helicopters, at least until they lost number 34 yesterday. Yevgeny Kunayev was the pilot of number 34 and was ferrying the aircraft forward to Chaloupky when he ran into the power line. The line caught on the rotor head assembly, and the helicopter slammed into the ground. Fortunately, they were flying slowly, and Kunayev and his weapons officer got out of the wreck. Kunayev was the least experienced pilot in the flight, a pilot third class. Leonov's wingman, Mikhail Popov, was a pilot first class, as was the other pair leader, Pavel Demichev. Leonov himself had won the distinction of "sniper" pilot due to his performance.

The flight operated in two pairs, and tactics stressed that the wingmen follow the maneuvers of the leaders. Leonov led the first pair in number 31, with his wingman, Popov, in number 32. The second pair leader, Demichev, in number 33 was saddled with the hapless Kunayev in number 34. However, with number 34 now a heap of tangled wreckage in a forest clearing east of Klatovy, Kunayev would be getting a new helicopter. As the four pilots walked out to the flight line, they could see Kunayev's machine already sitting there. It stood out from the other three Mi-24s because of its different paint scheme. The three helicopters were finished in a pale sand color with camouflage patches of dark green. The new helicopter, number 57, was painted in the alternative scheme of gray and

---

12. Ivan N. Kozhedub was the top-scoring Soviet fighter ace of World War II, with sixty-two aircraft claimed (including one jet fighter).

green. It was an older Mi-24V, fitted with a chin machine gun instead of a side-mounted twin 30mm cannon.

The pilots walked to their helicopters to look over the arming and fueling process. Each helicopter had six hardpoints on its stub winglets. The four inner pylons were for rocket pods, either the older S-5 57mm rockets, or the larger S-8 80mm rockets. For this mission, the larger rockets were fitted. On the outboard pylons were pairs of Drakon (Dragon) radio-guided antitank missiles. There were four per helicopter. The three original helicopters, all Mi-24Ms, had two 30mm cannons stacked one on top of the other on the right side of the fuselage. These were more powerful than the 12.7mm rotary cannon on number 57, but the whole helicopter had to be aimed to fire the guns. The older 12.7mm turret could be traversed by the front gunner, and so was a bit more precise and agile.

The seating arrangement in the Mi-24 was in tandem style. The weapons operator sat in the front cockpit, behind a panel of armored glass. Behind him, and slightly above, sat the pilot. The whole cockpit was enclosed in an armored titanium tub that would protect the crew from most small arms fire. There was a cargo compartment behind the cockpit. It

**2nd Flight**

**1st Squadron**

# 69th Attack Helicopter Regiment

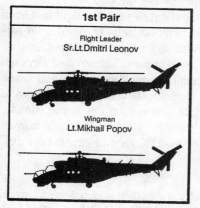

1st Pair

Flight Leader
Sr.Lt.Dmitri Leonov

Wingman
Lt.Mikhail Popov

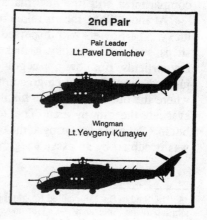

2nd Pair

Pair Leader
Lt.Pavel Demichev

Wingman
Lt.Yevgeny Kunayev

was large enough to accommodate eight riflemen, but usually was used to transport additional ammunition and a flight technician. For short-range missions, the helicopter could land behind friendly lines, rearm, and carry out an additional attack. For the current mission, this was impractical due to the ranges involved. The objectives were about twenty-five kilometers from the forward airstrip, so the added weight of another crewman and stores would reduce the range and loiter time of the helicopter. It would be better to have a bit of added fuel in case the helicopters had to stay in the area, providing gunfire support for the assault group.

Leonov was not keen on the idea of having to wait until early afternoon before moving forward to the staging area. There would be little to do, since inspection of the aircraft would take only an hour or so. He was anxious to get into action and get it over with. At times, the waiting seemed worse than going into battle. The long interlude between the briefing and the attack was due to the time required to prepare the transport helicopters and assault teams. The briefings for the assault group would be considerably more complicated. The most time-consuming missions involved regular motor rifle troops. Then the procedure had to include special training on debarking off the helicopter, proper loading and unloading procedures, and a few drills. At least today, the attack would involve regular air assault troops who were already familiar with helicopters.

He found his gunner at helicopter number 31. Warrant Officer Aleksander "Sasha" Bershko was sitting in the front cockpit, fiddling with the main gun sight. Leonov signaled to him, and they got into the rear cargo compartment with the new maps to review the mission.

At about 0800, the air raid siren blared out. So far, the field had been lucky. The Soviets had dispersed their aviation units to small civil airstrips, such as Chaloupky, to make it more difficult for NATO to eliminate key airfields. But now it was going to be their turn. Leonov and Bershko jumped out of the rear cargo compartment. Leonov looked around to see where the other crews from his flight were located. He signaled them to evacuate the runway area. The 2d Flight was not on the actual runway, but in a flat grassy clearing at the outskirts of the airstrip. The main runway was occupied by an assault regiment of Su-25K ground attack aircraft.[13]

---

13. The Sukhoi Su-25K, called Frogfoot in NATO, is a specialized ground-attack aircraft, similar to the American A-10 Warthog. Its Soviet nickname is "Grach," a type of bird.

The helicopters did not need the runway to operate and so were based away from the tarmac.

No one had bothered to dig air raid shelters or slit trenches at Chaloupky. Most of the time had been spent handling the overload of equipment and stores brought into this tiny provincial airport. Leonov and Bershko ran a few hundred feet into the field and hid in a depression. The area around the helicopters was littered with ammunition, rockets, and fuel. One good hit, and the whole mess would go up. The first flight of enemy aircraft appeared to the northwest. It looked like Tornados. They were moving very fast, and very near the deck. To his relief, Leonov saw them pass over the north end of the airfield by more than two kilometers. Probably hunting another target. But as he got up to head back, he saw another flight of aircraft coming directly over the airfield. He hit the dirt.

Four Tornados came screaming over the field at about 100 meters. There was little to stop them. Four ZU-23 23mm towed antiaircraft guns were positioned around the airfield, but they were too slow to track the aircraft at such close ranges. A battery of S-125 Pechora missiles had been brought in, but the aircraft were too near the ground for them to be effective. As they passed over the field, the large dispenser under the Tornado's fuselage sprayed out submunitions. It looked as though the aircraft were seeding a field. As the submunitions tumbled, small parachutes emerged from each one, and they gently floated to the ground. As the submunitions hit the tarmac, the runway erupted in a staccato of explosions.

The Tornados had dropped several STABO runway cratering munitions. Each bomblet is small, about thirty-seven pounds. But the charge can blast through reinforced concrete, and leaves a deep crater. One of the aircraft had delivered a load of fragmentation munitions and bunker-busting charges near the main hangars. These blanketed the parked Su-25K attack aircraft, bursting in a furious succession of small explosions. The Tornados left as abruptly as they came, the four 23mm guns futilely firing after them. In less than a minute, the airfield had been ruined. The enemy mission had been well planned.

Leonov got up off the ground and surveyed the airfield. It was hard to see the main building complex, since the whole field was enveloped in clouds of dust and smoke. To his utter amazement, the helicopters still stood in front of him, apparently undamaged. The NATO squadron must have based the attack on reconnaissance from a day or so before the helicopters arrived. The attack had concentrated on the aircraft regiment, and had left the other corner of the airport, where the helicopters were located, unscathed. The Tornado pilots had dumped their whole load in a single pass. But they must have noticed the helicopters. They'd probably be back to finish the job.

As the dust settled, it became evident how much damage the Tornados had done. The runway was a complete mess, with big, jagged slabs of concrete strewn about. The hangar area, the center of the attack, was burning furiously. Most of the Su-25K looked like they had been hit. Several were crumpled to the ground, their landing gear shattered by explosions. The large collection of fuel drums nearby was aflame, and there seemed little prospect of putting the fire out with the limited amount of equipment on hand. The base commander called the local fire department, but the fire chief acted as though he didn't speak Russian. It took several minutes to find one of the Czech Air Force personnel at the base to arrange for the fire trucks.

Leonov warned his men to stay away from the runway. These submunition systems usually mixed in delayed-action bombs or mines with the main runway cratering bombs. There was no telling what sort of munitions still remained on the field, waiting to explode. It seemed heartless not to run over to the hangars and help the Su-25 regiment, but Leonov didn't want any of his men needlessly wounded. The rest of the squadron, including its commander, Major Frolov, gathered around the helicopters. Frolov echoed Leonov's warnings. Stay away from the runway! Frolov attempted to contact the control tower to get instructions about the disposition of his helicopters, but telephone communications, including the field phones, were useless. He sent runners over to the control tower.

About a half hour later, the runners returned in a civilian jeep with some of the staff from the regimental HQ. They agreed that the Tornados might be back to finish off the helicopters. So it was decided to fly them into a small clearing about two kilometers from the airfield to await developments. Frolov asked whether the Tornados had been busy over the forward airfield at Dorfl. The staff said an attack had been made, but the air defenses and local fighter cover had forced back the attack, with few casualties to the helicopters. The helicopter regiments had been pretty lucky so far!

The crews had already cleared most of the ordnance-handling equipment and refueling trolleys away from the helicopters. They decided to take some of the technical staff along with them in the cargo compartment in case further work needed to be done on the helicopters. Fortunately, most had been completely armed before the air strike had hit. Leonov put on his flight helmet and adjusted the seat belts. A runner from the staff came over to each aircraft, warning them not to overfly the main runway for fear of detonating any MUSPA bombs on the field. Leonov nodded, and prepared for takeoff.

"Red Two, this is Red One, do you hear? Over."

Popov, in helicopter 32, responded affirmatively, as did the second pair.

"Red Flight, this is Red One. We will take off in pairs. I will lead. Wait for my instructions over the landing area. Over."

The big Isotov turbines behind the canopy whined loudly as Leonov prepared for takeoff. The Mi-24 is a massive helicopter, but its engine matches its bulk. In such cold October weather, the Mi-24 would have no problems lifting off, even with a full combat load. Leonov signaled to the ground crew and lifted his helicopter off smoothly. Popov got his helicopter off the ground seconds later, and fell in line behind him. From the air, the airfield was a bigger mess than he imagined. It looked as though the whole Su-25 squadron had been hit. Most of the aircraft seemed to be burned or broken. He switched his attention to the mission at hand and turned the big helicopter to the northwest.

It took no time to arrive at the new base, and he waited for the instruction of the 1st Flight commander, Capt. Sergei Nalepka.

"Kontsert One, this is Blue One. We will land in order. We'll go down into the northwest corner. Red One, put your chickens down in the northeast corner. Green One, you land near that farmhouse. Yellow One, you put your birds down in the southwest corner. Over."

The helicopters followed in order, about eighty meters from one another. Formation flying in such proximity was one of the more dangerous aspects of combat flying. But the crews were well trained, and the mission went without a hitch. Fortunately, the ground was damp. Otherwise, the helicopters would have kicked up a great deal of dust in the farm fields, making it increasingly more difficult for the later helicopters to land.

Before he had wound down the engine, Leonov had seen Captain Nalepka running toward his helicopter. He opened up the side cockpit door and removed his helmet. Nalepka, as experienced as he was with helicopters, still instinctively crouched as he ran under the big rotor blades.

"Dmitri, Major Frolov's in the back of my chopper. He's a bit concerned about us losing touch with the main attack group at the forward airstrip. He wants one of our boys to fly down there in advance to act as liaison. You're it. Misha Popov will take your flight down there this afternoon. Tell Kurasov and the command staff what happened, and give him these notes from Frolov about communicating with us. We will set up a temporary ground station here."

Leonov nodded. He turned back into the troop compartment, pushing aside the small curtain that divided the cockpit from the rear section. He signaled his flight technician in the back.

"Stefek, we're heading down to the forward strip ahead of the squadron. You get off here and help out the other crews."

Leonov's flight technician opened up the side cargo doors and jumped out. After securing the doors, he ran to the right side of the cockpit and gave Leonov the thumbs-up sign to let him know he was clear. At that signal, Leonov gave the rotors power and lifted off again. He heard the solid clunk of the main gear retracting and pushed the controls forward. The Mi-24 responded well and soon reached cruising speed. Leonov kept the helicopter at an altitude of about 100 meters. He was familiar with the terrain in this area, all the way to the border. It was very rugged countryside, covered with thick woods. He got on the intercom.

"Sasha, keep your eyes out for enemy aircraft. Let me know if you see anything. I'll keep us well over the treetops until we arrive in Germany."

It took the helicopter only four minutes to reach the Czech-German border. The flight was uneventful. The roads below were clogged with traffic. There was some air activity to the north, but little evidence of hostile aircraft. Dorfl was just across the Czech border, in a valley below a large reservoir. It proved easy to find, and Leonov radioed ahead for permission to land. This was quickly approved, although he did notice that his Khrom Nikel IFF set[14] was interrogated as he made the final approach to the staging area. From the looks of it, the landing site at Dorfl was not the main airstrip for the attack, probably only a forward base for the helicopters of the 69th Attack Regiment. He saw the long tadpole shapes of Mi-24s at the edge of the clearing, and landed well away from them.

---

14. Khrom Nikel is the Soviet name for the identification-friend-or-foe (IFF) system code-named Odd Rods by NATO. Ground defenses beam a signal at approaching aircraft, which triggers a coded response from friendly aircraft.

After doing a quick post-flight check, Leonov opened up the cockpit door and climbed down out of the helicopter. A small truck arrived to tow the helicopter to the shelter of the woods. The Air Direction group was located in a small mill building. When he arrived, he did not see Captain Kurasov. One of Kurasov's men, a young lieutenant, was the only member of the team there. Leonov dutifully conveyed the instructions from his squadron commander, then walked out to talk to the pilots from the other Mi-24 squadron of his regiment.

The pilots were out near their helicopters, most of which were covered with camouflage nets. There were only six left of the original twenty-one. The pilots seemed exhausted. The big Mi-24s showed evidence of their recent combat experiences. Many of them had patches from small arms fire, and several had evidence of more extensive damage that hadn't been fixed. Leonov found a friend, Sr. Lt. Roman Shurko, near number 54. Leonov was taken aback by Shurko's appearance. Normally very prim and neat, the small pilot looked like he hadn't slept or shaved for three days, which it turned out was close to the truth.

"Hey, Roman Ivanovich! The 1st Squadron's here to save your ass."

Shurko did not look amused. It was a bad joke in the circumstances. Leonov tried to make amends.

"Can I give you a hand?"

Shurko was up on the engine platform with a couple of ground crewmen looking at the rotor head assembly. He climbed down to talk to Leonov.

"Hello, Dmitri Mikhailovich. Sorry to be so abrupt with you. But we've been having problems keeping these helicopters in operation. We're supposed to be getting a few new machines later today out of the front reserves.[15] So what are you doing here?"

Leonov explained his squadron's mission and began questioning Shurko about the past few days' operations.

"I'm the last survivor from our flight. We were on a fire support mission the first day when Lavarev's bird was hit by ground fire. It plowed into the woods. Nobody got out. Yesterday, while we were carrying out a rocket pass, my wingman's bird just blew up in midair. No warning, no smoke, no nothing. The goddamn artillery had laid in a Grad rocket strike

---

15. Soviet helicopter regiments usually have a reserve of six to ten helicopters to replace battle casualties and helicopters suffering from extensive mechanical failure.

at the same time and in the same area we were operating. Then Vasily Abramovich's machine was hit on the way back by a Stinger. He was lucky. The missile really smashed up his engine, but he managed to crash-land it in a pasture. Some of our troops were nearby . . . they pulled him and his gunner out. He ought to be here later in the day.

"You know, Dmitri, we've been doing a good job. But we've really paid the price for it. It's about time you guys are finally being brought in. It's a tough situation out there. The ECM doesn't work as well as it should, and I really don't think the countermeasure flares are worth a shit. Stay low and move fast. That's all I can tell you. Once they get you in their sights, you don't have much chance."

Leonov was a bit taken back by his friend's pessimism. With a few hours to kill before the squadron arrived, he assisted Shurko in repairing and checking the aircraft. At about 1430, the 1/69 AHR arrived over the field and landed. Fuel trucks were quickly sent out to tank them up. Leonov rejoined his unit.

The attack was launched at 1530. The four flights of helicopters made an impressive sight in combat formation. Their light-colored camouflaged fuselages stood out sharply against the dark fir trees on the mountains below. The big Mi-24s stayed up high near the ridges. Not too high to be silhouetted against the sky, but high enough to avoid the inevitable humps and bumps of the mountainous terrain. Fortunately, during the final approach, the valley fed right into the landing area, and the helicopters were able to make a smooth transition to low altitude.

The helicopters made the final approach to the landing zone in two waves. Three flights were in line, up front, with Dudarek's flight in the second wave behind. The flights were several hundred meters apart to prevent the helicopters from running into each other. Nevertheless, it would be necessary to make tight turns exiting the target area to prevent collisions.

As they approached the landing zones, the pilots tensely awaited enemy fire. There was none. They had taken them by surprise! The landing zones had a small number of farmhouses and other buildings. The roads were quite visible beyond the landing zones, and had a fair amount of traffic. Leonov called over the intercom and told his gunner that he would trigger the rockets. On the approach, they had been flying at an altitude of about 300 meters, at a speed of 200 kilometers per hour. On the attack, Leonov popped the helicopter up to get a better view, then nosed it down into a dive for the firing run. He rotated the switch for rocket pods 1 and 4. The S-8 rockets hissed and whined in succession as they cleared the pods. It took several seconds for the rocket salvo to hit. Leonov could see his first salvo spatter the road, with one salvo hitting a large truck. He pulled his helicopter back around in a 180 degree turn, and the second pair began their firing pass.

This was a classic Soviet ground attack maneuver, sometimes called the "wheel of death." The idea was to continue to revolve around the target, giving it a continuous stream of bombs or rockets. As the second pair cleared the target, Leonov and his wingman, Mikhail Popov, made another firing pass. The 1st Flight leader, Captain Nalepka, radioed the squadron.

"Kontsert One, this is Blue One. Let's make a final firing pass with cannon. I want all flights to wheel around and go down the road west to east. After that, pull back to the north and let Bison land."

The final firing pass was more destructive than the first. By paralleling the road, it was possible to put more rounds on target. By this time the German truck convoys were a shambles. Trucks were scattered pell-mell on either side of the road, and many more were smashed and burning in the center of the highway.

At the end of the cannon pass, the three flights pulled back over the Danube. The first wave of the transport helicopters was right behind them. Several flights of armed Mi-17 transport helicopters went in first. As they orbited the river, Leonov could see why it had been chosen for the crossing. The river was not particularly wide at this point, and the banks on both sides were open, with little tree cover.

Kurasov's Air Direction team had been in the first wave. Kurasov was using the code name Indyuk One for the main Air Direction center. He reported that the helicopters had landed without encountering enemy troops. After all the apprehension about Stingers and Gepards, the attack had gone almost unmolested by the enemy.

By 1630, the flight was securely landed. It was an eerily attractive autumn evening. There was thick cloud cover at about 4,000 meters, and the setting sun had burned through near the horizon. It bathed the clouds in a pale salmon pink, a curious contrast to the dismal gray of the day preceding. It looked as though the weather would clear up that night. The

1st Squadron headed back to Dorfl for refueling and to await further missions.

Leonov and his gunner decided to sleep in the rear compartment of the helicopter. It was cold, and smelled of aviation kerosene. But it was better than a muddy tent. At about 0400, Leonov was woken up.

"OK, my fine princesses, time to get going. We're back in business."

It was his friend Shurko. Leonov was still in his flight suit. He put on his boots and numbly stumbled out into the cold night air. There were faint lights coming from a building several hundred yards away. He could barely see other members of the squadron making their way there, cursing as they stepped on cow turds or slipped into muddy puddles.

In fifteen minutes, the pilots from the 1st Squadron and the survivors from the 2d Squadron were gathered together, and Major Frolov began the briefing: "Comrades, we will be taking off at daylight for the bridge-head at Irlbach. The air assault battalion there has been subjected to a strong enemy counterattack. It doesn't look like our troops on the eastern side of the Danube have managed to reach the river. We have to try to give the bridgehead some fire support. If the situation gets bad enough, we may have to extract them.

"The enemy reacted very quickly last night. They must have been expecting an operation like this. They threw an armored unit against the bridgehead from Deggendorf in the east and Straubing to the west. They overran Landing Zone Afrika near Stephans-posching about two hours ago. We lost contact with Kurasov's team in Landing Zone Peru about thirty minutes ago. We don't know if they have been overrun, or if it's just because of the enemy radio jamming. The artillery boys have their hands full trying to cover the attack on the eastern bank of the river. This map here shows you the main artillery areas. We will have to avoid these on our approach. We will come in from the southeast and send in one flight from 2d Squadron about ten minutes in advance to do a quick recon-naissance. When we receive word back, we will provide each flight with instructions about their objectives. The air assault boys are very weak in antitank weapons. Our primary objective will be to eliminate enemy tanks. We have no word on enemy air defenses, but you will have to be careful. The enemy is fighting for the river on both sides. The east bank yesterday had few enemy troops. Today, there will be plenty. Supervise the arming of your aircraft. We will lift off about 0530. Questions?"

"Comrade Major, could you please explain the attack approaches? If we attack parallel to the river, won't that expose our left flank to enemy fire?"

"Lieutenant Dudarek, you are quite right. We will be attacking westward, not southward like yesterday. The main enemy attack seems to be from the east, from Deggendorf, against Landing Zone Kanada. Kanada's rear is protected by a wooded area. But the enemy may be attacking from the west as well. Our communications with Kurasov were interrupted by jamming, and we didn't get a complete situation report. However, the lead elements of the main attack assure us they will reach the opposite bank of the Danube this morning. So the air assault boys have been told to hold the bridgehead on the west bank at all costs. We're being sent in to help them do that. If that's all, let's get to our aircraft and get ready. It's going to be a busy day!"

Leonov stumbled out into the dark. He was a bit more awake than before the meeting. But the bright lights of the meeting hall had deprived him of night vision: The farm field now looked totally black. He thought about wandering back into the building for a flashlight, but then he noticed that the ground crews had begun to turn on the position lights on the helicopters. It looked like a feeble attempt at Christmas decorations. The little red and green lights on the stub winglets flickered in the distance, outshone by the main position lights on the top of the fuselage. Leonov trudged forward.

It took about thirty minutes to prepare the helicopters for action. The weather was finally changing for the better. It wasn't so overcast, and there were large clear patches with starlight shining through. The sky to the southeast was beginning to turn a dirty pink as the dawn arrived.

Shurko and the remnants of 2d Squadron took off at the first signs of dawn. They would perform the first scouting mission. As the landing zone had been narrowed, Major Frolov ordered the squadron to make a linear approach, with the four flights following in succession. Each flight would be separated by about three minutes. Once the firing passes had been made, the flights were to pass over the east bank of the Danube and circle around for another firing pass. Each helicopter had four Drakon antitank missiles, and they would probably fire one per pass.

"Kontsert One, this is Orkestra One, over." It was Roman Shurko over the battlefield. The 1st Squadron was already airborne and heading for the bridgehead. "We are in sight of the bridgehead. The enemy has overrun Landing Zone Peru. Our boys are around Landing Zone Kanada, mostly on the outskirts of Irlbach. The enemy has about a dozen tanks. We have already been fired on by at least one ZSU.[16] We will try to eliminate the ZSU before you arrive. Out."

Leonov could see Captain Nalepka's 1st Flight about a kilometer in front of him, silhouetted against the dawn sky. The squadron was approaching the objective at treetop level, very fast. The sun was still not fully up, and the forest below looked black. The crews were using low-light television due to the darkness. In the distance, Leonov could make out three Mi-24s pulling to the right and over the river as they exited from their firing runs. There should have been four. Who had been hit?

Nalepka's flight was staggered in two pairs, with the wingmen slightly behind the pair leaders. The squadron had slowed down a bit to permit more accurate sighting. Nalepka's flight began firing off countermeasure flares about four kilometers from the landing zone. The flares dropped away in patterns of four, brilliantly white against the dirty pink dawn sky. They didn't do any good. Before the helicopters reached firing range, two Stinger missiles came leaping up from the ground. The helicopter on the far left was hit near the rotor, suddenly lurching and falling to earth. The second Stinger missed, but kept coming toward Leonov's flight. Leonov felt helpless as the smoke trail of the Stinger came closer and closer. Before it reached the incoming flight, it exploded harmlessly several hundred meters in front of them. The three remaining helicopters from Nalepka's flight began firing their Drakon antitank missiles. A stream of heavy tracer fire began to spray into the formation. Two more helicopters were hit, and pulled off to the right, in flames. The damn Gepard was still there!

Leonov checked to make certain his electronic jammer was switched on. He would take care of countermeasures while his gunner steered the antitank missile. He got on the intercom and told Sasha to try to pick out the Gepard. He instructed his flight not to use flares. They didn't seem to work, and they only attracted attention. He could be reprimanded for this, but he would take the risk. About four kilometers from the landing zone, they zoomed over the last bit of woods and finally were over clear pastures. The scene ahead was confusing. There were a great many flashes and explosions from the fighting below. A slight mist from the river made it hard to pick out targets. The tanks revealed themselves by the occasional

---

16. ZSU is the Russian acronym for self-propelled antiaircraft guns like the German Gepard.

blast from their guns. The Gepard seemed to be down near a clump of trees. Sasha triggered the first Drakon missile and guided it toward the Gepard. He had indeed picked out the right target. A stream of 35mm tracer came up out of the trees toward the helicopters. Steaming red fireballs . . . they seemed like harmless fireworks. The tracer fire hit the left side of the flight, raking Yevgeny Kunayev's helicopter. The Mi-24 number 57 toppled over to the right and crashed into the ground in a large fireball. The Gepard turned its attention one aircraft inward, hitting Pavel Demichev's helicopter. That was its last victim. Both Leonov and Mikhail Popov's helicopters had targeted the Gepard with Drakon missiles, and they slammed into it nearly simultaneously. Leonov made a hard turn to the right, with Popov following shortly after. No Stingers so far. They swung around to the tail of the formation, behind Roman Shurko's flight.

The next two flights went in, losing two more helicopters to Stingers. There seemed to be two or three Stinger teams, but it was impossible to locate them. It took them time to reload, however, so it was possible to evade them if the flights went in fast enough. In the process of the attack, the squadron claimed eight tanks and the Gepard. It was very hard to tell. The battlefield was awash in smoke and dust. Leonov and Popov made a firing pass without incident, claiming two more tanks. The Stinger fire abated, probably because they were running out of missiles. Two more flights went in without resistance. On the final flight, Mikhail Reiter radioed that he had spotted reinforcements coming in from the west. Another armored column.

Leonov was over the east bank of the Danube when he noticed something moving in the tree line about three kilometers to the west of the landing zone. Then he saw the flashes. Enemy helicopters! The enemy was making a major counterattack from the west, with helicopter support. He radioed a warning to Dudarek's flight, but it was too late. The two surviving helicopters of 4th Flight were hit solidly on the side by antitank missiles. Leonov could now make out two enemy attack helicopters. Apaches! He and Popov broke out of the circle heading toward the enemy helicopters. He steered his helicopter toward the lead aircraft. As he was about to squeeze off the first round, he saw the helicopters fire at least two missiles. Much to his chagrin, the helicopters simply dropped into the forest in a fast vertical descent. His Mi-24 was approaching too fast to follow them, and he turned aside, trying to evade the oncoming missiles. The first missile struck the tail area of Mikhail Popov's helicopter. It spiraled into the forest in flames.

The second missile struck the stub winglet of Leonov's helicopter. It shook violently from the impact. At first, Leonov could not determine where he had been hit. But the helicopter was responding strangely to the controls. Looking back into the troop compartment, he could see jagged holes in the side of the fuselage. Fragmentation from the explosion had apparently damaged the left engine as well. He was getting warning signs of an oil leak. He decided to try to make it back to friendly lines. The enemy helicopters did not follow. They turned their attention to other Soviet aircraft.

Leonov crossed the Danube again, but there was little evidence of Soviet forces. The Germans began firing small arms at his helicopter. He could hear the pitter-patter of rifle fire cutting into the rear fuselage. The main line of fighting became evident about four kilometers east of the river. Judging from all the flashes and fires, an intense land battle was going on. Leonov passed over the main battle area, only to be hit by more small arms fire. This time the right engine simply gave out. A quick landing was called for. He spotted a large open pasture, littered with several destroyed armored vehicles. The landing gear refused to retract, so he tried to slow down his speed to about fifty before impacting.

The helicopter skidded for several hundred meters before hitting a low stone wall. The impact sheered off the remaining stub winglet, and the helicopter smashed over onto its left side. The rotor blades hit the ground, shattering off in large, frightening pieces. The helicopter finally came to rest.

Leonov and his gunner were strapped in, but were still smacked about by the abrupt landing. Leonov's door was above him, and proved hard to open, but he finally struggled free. Sasha was trapped in the front cockpit. His canopy opened to the left side, which was now jammed against the ground. He took a wrench from the tool kit and began punching a hole through the Plexiglas canopy. Leonov helped him pull away the Plexiglas, and Sasha Bershko wiggled out of the cockpit. They jumped down off the wrecked helicopter and began walking away. A small fire had broken out in the engine, but there seemed little danger of an explosion.

Just then a Soviet BTR-80 troop carrier pulled up and several riflemen came running forward. A short Kirghiz private ran up shouting *"Stoi."* Leonov put his hands up, but in an irritated voice shouted, *"Yestem sovyet-skim letchikem."* The soldier lowered his assault rifle and signaled him to follow.

Leonov wondered what had happened to the rest of the squadron.

# Analysis

Helicopters are a relatively new innovation in land warfare. Although they first saw action in World War II (in very small numbers), it was not until the advent of turbine-powered helicopters in the 1960s that they really caught on. American use of the helicopter in Vietnam cemented its place in the modern arsenal. Soviet experience with the helicopter in Afghanistan has shaped their own interest in this new technology.

Like most novel military technologies, there is considerable controversy over how the new machines should be used. In many respects, the turmoil over helicopter doctrine today resembles tank doctrine in the 1930s. There are many varying viewpoints, and little consensus on key issues. As was the case with tanks in the 1930s, recent combat experience with helicopters has been mainly in peripheral regions, not entirely resembling the nature of warfare between two well-equipped forces. For example, in the case of both Vietnam and Afghanistan, only one side had helicopters, and the opposing side was not well equipped to deal with them. The question remains how helicopters would fare in a war against a first-rate opponent.

## The Conservative Approach

The Soviet tendency has been more conservative than the American. The Soviets came into the helicopter business later than the United States, and there are many organizational differences. In the U.S., helicopters are the property of the U.S. Army. They are viewed as an integral part of the ground forces. In the Soviet armed forces, helicopters have remained in the Air Force. They are attached to the Ground Forces for operations, but are trained and equipped by the Air Force. As a result, there are striking differences in the configuration of combat helicopters and the way they are deployed.

In the U.S. Army, attack helicopters are deployed at divisional level. United States armored and mechanized divisions have large organic helicopter units. A typical U.S. division will have more than one hundred fifty helicopters, consisting of about forty-five attack helicopters, forty-five transport helicopters, and sixty-five scout and utility helicopters. In contrast, only a small percentage of Soviet divisions have any helicopters at all. And the few divisions that do have organic helicopter units have only about twenty helicopters, mixed between attack, transport, and light utility helicopters.

## Worth the Price?

The difference between the U.S. and Soviet approach can be traced to two main sources—the Soviet tendency to hoard scarce, high-technology systems at higher echelons; and the cost and maintenance burden posed by helicopters. Since helicopters are air force assets, the Soviets tend to place them under the control of army or front aviation command groups. The Soviets have argued that this allows the army and front commanders to better concentrate these valuable weapons, in much the same way that fixed-wing tactical air support is concentrated. In some respects they see an analogy to the debate over tanks in the 1930s. Then, tanks were usually deployed in small quantities, so-called "penny packets," where their firepower and shock value were diluted. They tended to be subordinated to the infantry for local actions and were not available to higher echelons for grand mobile operations.

While this argument certainly has some merit, it is not particularly illuminating. The U.S. Army not only has divisional helicopter units to provide support in small-scale tactical operations, but it also has larger, independent formations, attached at corps level, for use in large-scale operations by higher echelons of command. The Soviet tendency to argue in favor of concentration above divisional level to some extent masks certain Soviet problems in the combat use of helicopters.

To begin with, helicopters are exceedingly expensive weapons. An attack helicopter will typically cost four or five times as much as a main battle tank. So a battalion of attack helicopters attached to a division costs nearly as much as all of the tanks in a division. For the Soviets to contemplate equipping each division with such precious equipment mandates a major escalation in the cost of each division. It is doubtful that the Soviet Ground Forces will be able to afford this luxury for some time. Instead, an attack regiment (roughly the same size as an American attack helicopter battalion) is attached at army level, to be shared by its three divisions as the situation warrants.

Exclusion of helicopters from the divisions is probably also based on the difficulty and cost of maintaining an aviation branch distinct from the

Soviet Air Force. Although helicopters can operate from grass strips, in peacetime they usually operate from paved runways, with prepared hangars and extensive support equipment. For the Soviets to allot helicopters to army divisions would necessitate a major expenditure to build up airfields adjacent to army bases to better integrate the forces. For reasons of economy, it is cheaper to keep the helicopters under air force control, operating out of air force bases and facilities. Expansion of existing air bases is a cheaper alternative to the dispersion of helicopters to a large number of new air bases.

## The Maintenance Burden

The Soviets also suffer from serious problems in maintaining modern military aircraft. This is in no small measure due to the use of a short-term conscript force. The bulk of ground crews are enlisted personnel who enter the Soviet services with no experience in aviation repair. In the U.S. and much of NATO, teenage boys have access to motorbikes, automobiles, personal computers, CB radios, and other equipment that familiarizes them with the basic concepts of machinery and electronics. Soviet society is far poorer in these consumer products, and Soviet teenagers are more apt to be technologically illiterate when they are drafted into the service. Furthermore, the skills learned in the service are quickly lost as the Soviet NCOs return to civilian life after two years of duty.

The backbone of U.S. Army aviation is a large pool of experienced NCOs and warrant officers. The U.S. can deploy helicopters in the division because it can organize the critical manpower needed to keep the infrastructure running. The Soviet Ground Forces, with low priority in the Soviet manpower pool, has a harder time recruiting suitable personnel for a sizable aviation branch than does the more elite Air Force. The Soviets have tried to alleviate the problem by an emphasis on maintenance simplicity in their helicopter designs. Western operators of civil versions of Soviet military helicopters have found them to be very suitable for use in remote areas due to the ease of maintenance.

On the other hand, Soviet helicopters, like most Soviet aviation products, tend to have much shorter operating lives than comparable NATO designs. For example, the rotor blades of the Mi-2 Hoplite utility helicopter have a retirement life of 1,000 hours. In contrast, the German Bo-105 has a blade life ten times as high, some 10,000 operating hours. The overhaul schedule for the rotor head is 1,000 hours for the Mi-2, and 10,000 hours for the Bo-105. The difference in engine overhaul schedules is less dramatic, but still significant—1,000 hours versus 3,500 hours. The problems are not entirely technological. When queried about the reason for the short blade life, a Soviet engineer indicated that blades were manufactured at factories separate from the helicopter plants where the main incentives are to increase the quantity, not the quality, of blades. Although the designers felt that the blade life could be extended, to do so would lead to a large surplus of rotor blades, endangering the bonuses of the management of the rotor plant. Therefore, the helicopter plant was discouraged from designing more durable rotors. This problem is endemic in the centrally planned economy, which tends to favor quantity of output over quality.

The relative lack of durability of Soviet helicopters also affects the training of pilots. American helicopter pilots who have met their Soviet counterparts in international helicopter sporting events have been favorably impressed by their training and their capabilities. What has shocked the Soviet pilots has been the age of their American counterparts. American helicopter pilots are a good deal younger. The reasons for the difference are easy to trace. American pilots get a great deal more flying time, and therefore build up flying experience much quicker than the Soviets. The Soviets, although as capable as the American pilots, take a longer time to gain experience, due to the restrictions on the number of hours they are allowed to fly. This is directly related to the low durability of Soviet helicopters, and to the high cost of training.

In a wartime situation, these tendencies are likely to have an effect in several areas. To begin with, the Soviet helicopter forces are likely to be the most capable during the initial phases of the war. The relative quality of their forces is likely to drain away faster than that of NATO helicopter units due to the lower durability of the equipment, and to maintenance shortcomings in the ground crews. Furthermore, the Soviet tendency to hoard helicopters at upper echelons of command, and under air force control, implies that Soviet use of helicopters in supporting ground forces will be less flexible than in NATO forces, where there are stronger organic links between the ground and aviation elements. The U.S. Army troops expect helicopter support, since they train regularly with it. Divisions expect scout helicopters to provide divisional reconnaissance, for example. But in the Soviet case, the helicopters are farther up the chain of command, and are less likely to be available for support missions at divisional level. For example, the Soviets still tend to rely on ground units, not on helicopters, for reconnaissance.

## Soviet Helicopter Design

Soviet helicopter design is also affected by the orientation of the helicopter forces. Attack helicopters are a good example. A comparison between the AH-1S Cobra gunship and its Soviet counterpart, the Mi-24V Hind D, makes this very clear. The Mi-24 is much more massive than the AH-1S Cobra. The Hind weighs about 10 tons, fully loaded. The Cobra weighs about 7.5 tons fully armed and loaded. The armament load of both helicopters is similar. The difference in weight stems from design factors. The Hind is designed as a fast fire support aircraft, with greater horsepower. It usually fires its weapons during a fast pass, much like a fixed-wing aircraft. The Cobra design places less emphasis on speed and more emphasis on maneuverability in the ground-hugging environment. On antitank missions, the Cobra will usually fire its TOW antitank missiles from a hover. The Hind is not well designed for this role and has difficulty hovering due to the configuration of its stub wings. The mission for the Hind places emphasis on the artillery fire support role in which hovering performance is less important. Typical attack profiles for the Hind call for a fast approach at low altitudes, a pop-up maneuver close to the target, followed by a diving pass and weapons release. Indeed, Soviet helicopters have been used to drop bombs, a practice virtually unheard of in U.S. helicopter units.

The design differences between the American and Soviet helicopters have an odd history. The Mi-24 Hind and its mission closely resemble the notions held by the U.S. Army in the 1960s before the Vietnam experience. Had the American AH-56 Cheyenne helicopter program succeeded, the aircraft would have been very similar to the Soviet Hind. According to Soviet sources, the Mil design bureau was heavily influenced by the Sikorsky entry in the Cheyenne program. Like the Sikorsky S-67 Black Hawk, the Hind has a troop compartment in the center of the aircraft. This allows the Hind to transport eight troops or additional supplies. However, it also makes the helicopter a good deal bulkier than its American counterpart, the AH-1S Cobra.

The next generation of attack helicopter, the American AH-64 Apache and Soviet Mi-28 Havoc, exhibits a greater convergence in design philosophy. The Mi-28, like the AH-64 Apache, places greater emphasis on tank fighting, and so would be better suited to the standoff and hover role. This has real advantages in an area full of antiaircraft defenses like the scenario depicted here. A helicopter that can stand off two or three kilometers from the target and hide in the trees is far less vulnerable to air defenses than one that continues toward the target during the firing pass.

## Can Helicopters Survive?

The fictional scenario also illustrates two of the major questions about the nature of helicopter fighting in a future war: the vulnerability of helicopters to air defenses and the probability of helicopter versus helicopter fighting. Although the U.S. lost many helicopters to ground fire in Vietnam, the losses per sortie were so low that they never seriously compromised the use of helicopters in the fighting. In contrast, in 1986–87, the Soviets began losing so many helicopters to the mujihadeen once the Stinger missile appeared, their support missions were seriously curtailed. The presence of man-portable antihelicopter missiles like the Stinger will force attack helicopters to use standoff tactics like those described. A helicopter with a long-range antitank missile can remain masked behind trees, nearly invisible to enemy missile gunners. Furthermore, an infrared seeking missile like the Stinger, or the Soviet SA-16, has a harder time tracking a helicopter flying near the ground, due to the presence of extraneous heat sources such as burning vehicles, building smokestacks, and the like.

The other approach to lessening the threat of the missiles is infrared countermeasures. There are two approaches to this. The simplest is to drop infrared flares, designed to emit heat at the same frequency as the sensitivity of the antihelicopter missile's seeker. These lure the missile away from the helicopter. The other approach is the so-called "Hot Brick" systems, which emit a heat signal that confuses the missile seeker. The problem with these approaches is that newer missiles have multispectral seekers, which look for emissions in several frequencies. The countermeasures may jam one but not the other. The Soviets adopted both approaches in Afghanistan. They proved very effective against old antihelicopter missiles like the SA-7 Grail but not very effective against the Stinger. The best defense against these missiles may prove to be tactics rather than technology, tactics such as low-altitude flying and standoff weapons attacks.

The proliferation of helicopters on the battlefield also will lead to encounters between helicopters. This already happened in 1982 in the fighting between Israel and Syria in Lebanon, and in the Iran-Iraq war. Helicopters do not have to worry much about fixed-wing aircraft, since they tend to operate so close to the ground and can easily outmaneuver a fixed-wing aircraft. But there are very good chances of running into other helicopters. There has been some talk of special antihelicopter weapons. The first type to be adopted by NATO and the Warsaw Pact is a simple adaptation to carry antihelicopter missiles like the Stinger. Although they were normally designed to be launched from the ground, it has proven fairly easy to design a system to launch them from helicopters.

Many helicopter forces have been slow to adopt specialized weapons for helicopter dogfighting, however. The reason is that existing helicopter weapons may prove adequate for these chance encounters. During encounters with Syrian Gazelle helicopters, the Israelis used TOW wire-guided antitank missiles to shoot down at least one Syrian helicopter. Many attack helicopters also have turret gun systems, which can be used in dogfighting. Reportedly, an Iraqi Mi-24 Hind shot down an Iranian F-4 Phantom jet fighter that was chasing it, using its turreted gun!

One of the most interesting aspects of the helicopter dogfighting controversy is the role of the new Soviet Kamov Hokum helicopter. Many Western analysts see the Hokum as a helicopter fighter, designed primarily to attack NATO helicopters. The Hokum has yet to enter service, and its intended role is not at all clear. It remains to be seen whether the Soviets really think it is worthwhile to invest so much money in a specialized antihelicopter aircraft when existing attack helicopters can perform this function. It is also not clear how survivable such a helicopter would be, since the helicopter role implies that it would be operating over NATO lines where it would be vulnerable to missiles and other air defenses.

## Soviet Helicopter Tactics

In spite of these new threats to the helicopter, the Soviets remain deeply committed to heliborne warfare. The main attraction of the helicopter is the mobility it offers to ground forces. In the transport role, the helicopter offers an alternative to paratroop forces, and paratroop operations are always very risky. The wind can scatter the attacking force, or they can be dropped into the wrong landing zone. Heliborne landings have the classic advantages of paratroop operations—surprise and deep penetration—but the helicopter can reduce the risks of the landing itself. In the fictional scenario, the Soviets used a helicopter force in an operation that probably would have involved paratroops in World War II.

Soviet interest in this type of operation has increased dramatically since the Afghanistan fighting. Afghanistan favored the use of helicopters, as did Vietnam, due to the rough terrain. The Soviets found that they could move combat units rapidly to counter the elusive Muslim guerrilla forces only by helicopter. In mountainous terrain, road traffic is forced to use narrow mountain roads, which can be easily ambushed. Helicopters have far fewer problems operating in such conditions.

During the Afghanistan war, the Soviets began using their airmobile units for the first time in combat. Prior to this fighting, the Soviet Ground Forces had planned to use normal motor rifle troops to carry out airmobile operations. However, Afghanistan convinced them that specially trained units, more familiar with airmobile tactics, were more effective. Airmobile units also have to have a different organization than regular motor rifle troops. Airmobile units do not have armored vehicles or motor vehicles to provide fire support and logistical support during most missions. So the units have to be more self-contained, with additional antitank weapons, mortars, and other fire support to make up for the lack of other weapons. The Soviets also found that airmobile tactics require a higher caliber of troops than the run-of-the-mill motor rifle troops. So far, Soviet airmobile troops are part of the DShB branch of the elite VDV Air Assault Force. These units have far stricter training demands than normal motor rifle troops and also have higher priority in recruitment. In the Soviet Army, the airmobile units are elite formations, intended for specialized, high-risk operations. It would not be surprising to see the number of Soviet air assault (paratroop) divisions decrease over the next few years, while the air assault (heliborne) and other airmobile units increase.

At the moment, Soviet helicopter units are in a period of transition. There are a number of different types of helicopter units in service, some on an experimental basis, as the Soviets try to determine which style is the most effective. Divisional helicopter units, when they exist, tend to have eighteen to twenty helicopters. Usually there are three flights of four helicopters each, equally divided among Mi-24 attack helicopters, Mi-8 transport helicopters, and Mi-2 utility helicopters. In some units, there are eight Mi-8 transport helicopters instead of the usual six. The more common formations are the helicopter regiments under army or front jurisdiction. Transport helicopter regiments, like the fictional 14th

Helicopter Transport Regiment in the scenario, are used to transport air-mobile forces. They will typically have two or three squadrons of medium transport helicopters (Mi-8 or Mi-17) and one squadron of heavy (Mi-6 or Mi-26) transport helicopters. These will number about fifty-two helicopters, with as many as a dozen spares.

The picture regarding attack helicopters is somewhat more complicated. There appear to be several different types of attack helicopter regiments, varying in the number of squadrons. The typical attack helicopter regiment, like the fictional 69th Attack Helicopter Regiment in the scenario, has two attack helicopter squadrons and one transport helicopter squadron. Some attack helicopter regiments at front level will have four attack helicopter squadrons, or three attack and one transport squadron. There is also a variety of other specialized helicopter formations.

## Air Assault Forces

The Soviets have also been experimenting with a variety of airmobile forces tailored to helicopter operations. The airmobile brigades, first organized in the 1970s, are the first Soviet attempt to directly integrate helicopters and ground forces in one unit. The brigade has an air force helicopter regiment attached to it for airlift operations, and its fighting strength centers around three light infantry battalions. The helicopter regiment is not sufficient to lift the whole brigade at once. It would need either the assistance of another helicopter regiment or two sorties of its own helicopters. These brigades permit the Soviets to train ground forces troops in airmobile operations in peacetime, and are probably used as experimental formations to investigate the future of airmobile operations. In many respects, the airmobile brigades are pioneer formations, like the early mechanized units of the Red Army of the 1930s. They are the experimental basis for future, and probably larger, Soviet heliborne formations.

Another type of unit tailored to heliborne assault is the air assault brigade. Because it has no helicopters of its own, for heliborne operations the air assault brigade would depend on helicopters obtained from front-level aviation units. The air assault brigades are trained for either paratroop or heliborne assault. Depending on the circumstances, they can be airlifted into the landing area using either technique.

The Soviets added these two types of brigades in order to give front and army commanders highly mobile forces for specialized operations. The airborne (paratroop) divisions require so much airlift support that they remain under high command control from Moscow. In contrast, the new brigades are at the disposal of front and army commanders as "keys to unlock the stability of the enemy defense." They would be husbanded for critical missions, like seizing key bridgeheads as described in the scenario. These heliborne brigades give the Soviet front and army commanders the ability to project forces twenty kilometers into the NATO rear to disrupt key defenses.

It remains to be seen whether helicopters will live up to their potential. They remain very vulnerable to ground fire and missiles. They have never been used in a conflict where both sides had substantial helicopter units and equally substantial antihelicopter missiles and guns. As suggested in the fictional scenario, helicopters do have an important role to play on the battlefield, but their accomplishments may come at a considerable cost in men and machines.

# CHAPTER 6

## Red Artillery: The God of War

2100, 8 October, Deggendorf Bridgehead, near Huterhof

"All right, comrades, try to make some room."

The officers of the 155th Artillery Battalion tried to crowd, as best they could, into the back of a Ural-375 maintenance truck. It was cold and raining, and there were no houses in the dispersal area in which to conduct the staff briefing. The battalion commander, Maj. Pyotr Yefimov, and his deputy, Capt. Pavel Gonchar, sat on a workbench at the front of the van. The officers were drenched from the incessant rain; their boots were soggy and their moods were foul.

The major continued his briefing. "We're going across the Danube tomorrow." Fine, most thought. Only five days late. What a relief to get out of the forests. Finally onto flat ground! "We'll be crossing here near the town of Ainbrach. The engineers are erecting another pontoon bridge tonight. So much for the pleasant news. The new bridge is going to have to handle a lot of traffic tomorrow morning. You all saw how much equipment is in this area. That means the 2S1s and the 1V12s are going to have to make the crossing in the water."

The officers were not keen on this idea. Their 2S1 armored howitzer vehicles[1] and the 1V12 armored command vehicles[2] were designed to be

---

1. The 2S1 is an armored self-propelled howitzer vehicle, armed with a 122mm gun. It uses a tracked suspension and is amphibious. It is also known as the SO-122, or by its project name, Gvozdika (Carnation).

2. The 1V12 is a family of armored artillery command vehicles, based on the same chassis as the 2S1 artillery vehicle, but armed only with a single machine gun. There are several different versions, designated 1V13 through 1V16. They are better known in NATO as the ACRV M-1974 armored command and reconnaissance vehicle.

amphibious. But it would take an hour or so to get them ready for swimming, and any swimming operation with armored vehicles was risky, especially if the river was fast.

"I don't want to hear any complaints about this. There's plenty of engineer equipment around, so if anybody gets stuck in the riverbank, we will tow you out. All of the battalion's trucks will go over the pontoon bridge. We have priority. The boys on the western edge of the bridgehead need our support."

Although the 155th Artillery Battalion was normally attached to the 55th Guards Motor Rifle Regiment, their parent regiment had been pretty badly shot up during the forest fighting. The divisional artillery group assigned them wherever they might be needed. The battalion was in much better shape than the 18th Guards Motor Rifle Division's tank and motor rifle troops. Out of the twenty-four 2S1 howitzer vehicles the 155th had started the war with, they had lost only four to mechanical breakdowns or mines. Normally, the battalion had four batteries, but these had been consolidated to three due to the loss of equipment.

"We will be crossing around daybreak, at 0615 tomorrow morning. That means we start moving out of here at about 0530. You'll get all your trucks onto this road leading to Huterhof, and all the tracked vehicles will form up on the southeast edge of the village. The trucks will have a code painted on the front bumpers to help the MPs sort out the traffic.

"Now, on another matter. All tracked vehicles will have a large white triangle painted on the roof. We're going to be up close to the edge of the battle line. The fly-boys have been having problems sorting our tanks and vehicles from those of the enemy. So for your own good, paint the triangle in a prominent position and keep it clear of tarps and the usual junk.

"When we get to the other side of the river, we'll take this road down to Schambach, and then over to Amselfing. We're going to be deployed on the eastern side of Aiterhofen. Our first fire missions should come in at about 0900 if all goes well at the crossing. The batteries will be deployed in straight lines. Nothing fancy. Our fire control computers have been acting up. We'll have to move around a bit. The enemy has been doing a lot of counterbattery firing against our artillery in this area. Now, get some sleep!"

That was an easier thing to say than to do these days. Senior Lieutenant Viktor Belov and his 2d Battery were weary to the bone. The previous day had been a long and tiring series of fire missions in support of the bridgehead. They were firing at maximum range, and their howitzers were beginning to show the strain. They would take a lot of maintenance, but there was neither the time nor the equipment to permit it.

Belov walked back to his battery along with his deputy, Lt. Aleksander Durnov. "Are the men bedded down yet, Sasha?"

The young lieutenant indicated that they were, but promised to make a final check. The battery was huddled in a big clump off the road. It would make an ideal target for enemy aircraft or artillery. Nobody cared. There just wasn't enough space here for dispersal, and NATO had better things to shoot at nearer the bridgehead—like the bridges themselves.

No rail or road bridges were still standing in this section of the Danube, so all the crossings had to be made with pontoon bridges or ferries. The river here was too deep and the bottom too soft to allow the tanks to make a crossing on their own using snorkels. So they had to be laboriously ferried over using special GSP tracked ferries, an amphibious vehicle fitted with folding pontoons. Holding the bridgehead was difficult since the flow of tanks into the area was very slow. Most of the light armor, like infantry carriers and artillery vehicles, as in Belov's battery, was amphibious. They could swim over. Artillery was needed more than ever to make up for the lack of tanks.

Belov was awakened the next morning at 0500 after about four hours of sleep. It was the most he had gotten in one night since the beginning of the war. He had slept curled up inside his 1V14 armored command vehicle.[3] It was cold inside, but at least it was protected from the rain. There were five other soldiers assigned to the vehicle, but at night usually only Belov, the driver, and the two radio operators remained inside. There just wasn't enough space for the scout or the artillery surveyor.

It was still dark outside, but at least it wasn't raining. Belov's battery had six 2S1 artillery vehicles, all parked near the two armored command vehicles. There were also six big Ural 375 five-ton trucks, which the battery used for supplying ammunition. A single GAZ-66 truck was used to provide meals for the battery, and it was in that direction that Belov now headed. Sergeant Badarian had lit up the small stove and was preparing water for tea. There were nearly seventy men in the battery, most of them

---

3. The 1V14 is a version of the 1V12 family of artillery command vehicles. It is designed for battery commanders. This version carries a laser range finder in the turret as well as other specialized equipment. It is called the ACRV M-1974-2a by NATO.

## 2nd Battery
# 155th Self-Propelled Howitzer Battalion

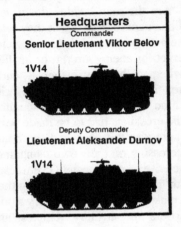

### Headquarters

Commander
**Senior Lieutenant Viktor Belov**

1V14

Deputy Commander
**Lieutenant Aleksander Durnov**

1V14

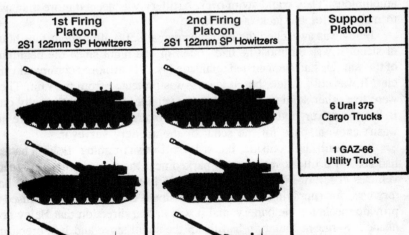

**1st Firing Platoon**
2S1 122mm SP Howitzers

**2nd Firing Platoon**
2S1 122mm SP Howitzers

**Support Platoon**

6 Ural 375
Cargo Trucks

1 GAZ-66
Utility Truck

trying to get some tea and bread. There was one line for the enlisted men, and another for the senior sergeants and warrant officers. The battery officers simply walked to the front of the lines.

The artillery battery was a microcosm of Soviet Army life. Artillery units require highly trained personnel in many of the posts. Computing firing missions and other technical responsibilities are the tasks of the officers, but many other chores require technical expertise. Artillery pieces are difficult to keep in service when a lot of heavy firing is done. The technical positions were usually filled by Russians or Ukrainians, but there were also a large number of bright teenagers from the Baltic republics, mostly from the cities. The draft boards kept their eyes out for youth with a good mathematics background. Most Russians would be scooped up by more prestigious services, whereas the youth from the Baltic republics, Armenia, and other regions would be left out. The Ground Forces were only too happy to have them for tasks like these. On the other hand, artillery units have a lot of heavy, mindless work as well. Somebody has to load and unload the ammunition. This was work for the battery's second-class citizens, mostly Uzbeks or other Central Asians.

By 0530, the engines of the 2S1 artillery vehicles were warmed up. Belov had had the troops prepare the vehicles the previous evening for the river crossing. The 2S1 and the command vehicles have special "gill skirts" that have to be attached to the front fenders. This helps direct the water flow from the tracks to propel the vehicle when it is swimming. He also had them check the various ports where water could seep in. He didn't want to lose any of his vehicles by sinking.

Second Battery was not the only unit on the move. Other divisional formations were moving forward in anticipation of the river crossing. Belov took the lead of his column in his 1V14 command vehicle, riding up in the turret to get a better view. In front of him was a PKT 7.62mm machine gun, the vehicle's only defense—hardly enough to ward off an infantry attack!

As they approached the crossing point at Huterhof, the road became jammed with vehicles. A sergeant in a black leather uniform approached Belov's command vehicle. He wore the usual traffic-control uniform with a white helmet and red band. "Comrade Lieutenant, could you give me your control papers?" Belov handed him down the papers, which assigned priority for the bridge crossing. Using a small flashlight, the sergeant inspected them and handed them back up to Belov. "Comrade Lieutenant, your tracked vehicles should proceed across the field over there to the right to prepare for the crossing. Your trucks can remain here, and we will get them across as soon as possible."

Belov looked around. The column ahead didn't seem to be moving. "Sergeant, have they completed the bridge yet?"

"Yes, Comrade Lieutenant. But we had an air strike here about an hour ago and we're just finishing clearing the wreckage."

Damn, the NATO people were already attacking the bridge. And at night! Belov was very anxious to get his vehicle across. When the dawn came up in an hour or so, the bridge would attract NATO artillery and air strikes like bees to honey. Belov used the intercom to instruct the driver. He was followed by the six 2S1 artillery vehicles; at the tail of the column was Lieutenant Durnov in the other battery command vehicle. As they passed around Huterhof, Belov could dimly see the shapes of a battery of 2S6 air defense vehicles.[4] These big vehicles each had a pair of long radar-directed 30mm cannons. On top of the turrets the surveillance radar rotated at a slow rate, hunting for targets. Nestled on the sides of the turrets were tubes for antiaircraft missiles. A formidable vehicle. At least Belov hoped so. They would have to protect his unit during the crossing operation.

Belov's battalion arrived near the river's edge. The Danube glistened in the early dawn hours. The moon occasionally peeked through the clouds, its light reflecting off the water. The opposite shore was totally black except for the signs of small fires and the occasional flicker of electric lights. Belov got out of the command vehicle and made his way over to the 1V13 command vehicle of Captain Gonchar, the deputy battalion commander. "Good morning, Comrade Captain."

"Hello, Viktor. So are you ready to get your feet wet?"

Belov did not laugh. He was very concerned that some of his vehicles might have problems crossing. "How soon do we go over, Pavel? I'd just as soon get this over with." Before Gonchar could answer, the sky lit up.

The 2S6 antiaircraft vehicles had found a target and were hammering away at some unseen enemy over the river. Belov, like all artillerymen, was used to noise. But the gun flashes were prolonged and spectacular.

---

4. The 2S6 is a new Soviet air defense vehicle, replacing the earlier ZSU-23-4 Shilka. The associated radar system is code-named Hot Shot by NATO. It also carries four missiles, designated SA-19 by NATO. The system was called SPAAG M-1986 by NATO until its Soviet designation 2S6 became known.

It seemed like a duel of fire-breathing dragons. There were six of these vehicles around the perimeter. They were firing in two- or three-second bursts. Each burst contained a lot of tracer ammunition, and you could see the tracer hurtle over the river in the dark dawn sky. Belov could not make out any sort of target. He walked away from his vehicle to get a better view of the scene. It was fascinating. Then the unseen enemy responded. Two or three huge glares appeared in the sky, about a kilometer over the river. Tracers began coming back in the other direction! Whatever was out there had a big gun.

A tracer from the enemy aircraft impacted against one of the 2S6s near the river's edge. It looked like a fireworks display as the depleted uranium slugs from the 30mm cannon of the attacking American A-10 aircraft slammed into the steel armor of the 2S6.[5] The contact of steel and uranium at such speeds throws off pebble-sized chunks of metal that glow like sparklers. The single burst smashed the turret, setting off the stored ammunition. The 2S6 began burning, with ammunition cooking off in little staccato bursts.

Two of the enemy aircraft screamed over Huterhof, dropping cluster bombs over the massed column. The bombs blossomed open, spraying the column with hundreds of tiny submunitions, each with the explosive force of a large grenade. The flurry of submunitions began exploding in a wave. It was a frightening sight. The whole area was engulfed in a fury of small explosions. Belov was thankful that his 2S1 vehicles were out of harm's way. And he hoped that his trucks were far enough back in the column to have escaped the air strike.

The Americans did not escape unharmed. As one A-10 began to bank away over the river, it was hit solidly along the belly and wings by one of the 2S6 antiaircraft vehicles. With flames licking out of its belly, the plane plunged into the Danube. The two A-10s that had dropped the cluster bombs came back over the town in the opposite direction, firing their big cannons the whole time. They raked the remains of the truck column, then turned their attention to the pontoon bridge. In the early morning light,

---

5. The Fairchild A-10 is a specialized ground-attack aircraft. It carries a large internal 30mm Gatling cannon, which is capable of penetrating the thin armor of light armored vehicles, or the side and rear armor of tanks. It can carry a variety of weapons, including bombs and Maverick guided missiles. The 30mm cannon fires special depleted-uranium projectiles. Uranium is used due to its density and weight.

Belov could see huge splashes of water around the pontoon bridge, but it was hard to tell whether or not it had been hit. The 2S6 antiaircraft vehicles fired three missiles at the departing planes, but the A-10s had been dropping a steady stream of infrared flares, which seemed to distract the missiles. The two A-10s escaped over the river, unharmed. Undoubtedly, they would be back.

A major from the bridging unit came up to Captain Gonchar's 1V16 command vehicle and advised him that the unit could begin crossing. He suggested that they wait until it was a little lighter. But after the recent display of NATO air power, Major Yefimov and Captain Gonchar decided to begin moving their equipment right away. The engineers had placed some type of matting on the riverbank. They had blown a hole in a wall along the river and bulldozed a ramp down into the water. The first vehicle to attempt the crossing was the battalion's PRP-3 scout vehicle.[6] It had

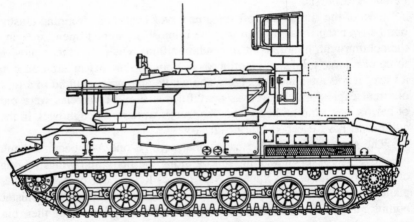

# 2S6 Air Defense Gun/Missile Vehicle

---

6. The PRP-3 is an artillery scout version of the BMP infantry vehicle. It has a large two-man turret, similar to that of the BMP-2. Its equipment includes a ground surveillance radar, code-named Small Fred by NATO, as well as a laser range finder and night vision sight.

a night vision device in the turret and so could see more clearly across the river. The driver let the tank slip slowly into the water. You could see only the roof and turret when it finally settled into the river. The driver had the engine going at full speed, and its diesel was howling.

The PRP-3 had small position lights on the rear, pointing back to the shore. The command vehicles and 2S1s of the 1st Battery went into the water next. Bobbing up and down, they looked like an awkward flotilla of drunken ducks, only a good deal noisier. The vehicles did not have propellers, but relied on the motion of their tracks to push them through the water. The drivers had to really crank up the engines to get enough track speed to keep the vehicles moving forward against the current. The river was about 170 meters across at this point, and it would take three or four minutes to cross.

Belov led his battery into the cold Danube next. The big 1V14 command vehicle rode higher in the water than the 2S1 artillery vehicles. It was not only boxier (and therefore more buoyant), it also was lighter due to the absence of the heavy howitzer the other vehicles carried. The spacing between vehicles was about twenty meters, and the first ones were already climbing ashore on the opposite bank. By the time Belov's vehicle entered the water, the dawn sun had already appeared.

About halfway across the river, Belov noticed to his shock that the 2S1 in front of him seemed to be settling lower in the water. The crew must have realized it as well, because soon Belov noticed three crewmen on the turret roof. The 2S1 was also losing speed. Belov shouted to them to pull the vehicle out of line, but it did little good with all the noise. He called down to his own driver to try to steer around it. Although it is nearly impossible to steer vehicles like these in the water with any precision, the driver managed to move it out of the line of traffic. Belov shouted down to his driver to proceed forward. By now, the water was well over the bow of the sinking vehicle and threatened to swamp it. The driver shut off the engine, and the four crewmen jumped off and began swimming toward the approaching vehicles—a dangerous business since a swimmer could get caught in the tracks. Two of the swimmers managed to grab onto Belov's vehicle, and the other two continued to dog-paddle in the hopes of catching onto the next 2S1.

The crewmen clung for dear life to the grab handles on the side of the vehicle. One of them managed to pull himself up and climb the side of the vehicle, using the grab handles. It was the commander, Sgt. Ivan Dombrovskiy. He crawled on all fours toward the turret where Belov was standing. Dombrovskiy pulled off his dripping wet padded canvas helmet so he could talk to Belov. (Armored vehicle crewmen's helmets are designed to be soundproof due to all the noise in armored vehicles; the crew communicates via headphones connected to the vehicle's intercom.) Belov had to remove his own padded helmet so he could talk to his water-logged guest. Dombrovskiy related the story: The vehicle apparently had begun to fill with water almost immediately upon entering the river. At first, he didn't notice it, but soon, water began lapping up into the turret. His guess was that all the firing they had done over the past few days had cracked open a weld in the lower hull, causing a leak. He felt lucky to be alive. Dombrovskiy looked back to see what had happened to his other two men. To his relief, they had been picked up by the 2S1 following behind Belov's vehicle.

The scene near the exit ramp was chaotic. The bank was very muddy from all the rain and traffic. When one 2S1 bogged down in the mud right at the shoreline, the other vehicles began backing up behind it. Amphibious armored vehicles are not agile like boats and cannot easily remain stationary in a river current. So several 2S1s were pushed a bit downstream by the current while waiting their turn to exit. They could not easily get onshore at points below because of the stone and concrete walls. Finally, the engineers towed out the bogged-down vehicle with an armored recovery vehicle. They stayed nearby to help in case other armor bogged down. They did. The whole process of clearing the exit took forty-five minutes—far more than expected.

The battalion lost a second 2S1 from the 3d Battery during the crossing. It flooded out also, probably from hull cracks. Belov was lucky that his battery had crossed intact. He also had an added gun crew from the drowned vehicle. The battalion was on dry land by 0740. The crossing point was about a half kilometer from the main pontoon bridge. Traffic began crossing the bridge in spurts around 0700, but the air strikes were seriously disrupting the operation. Belov could see at least one other pontoon bridge farther down the river near Pfelling. There were at least four more, all providing a steady trickle of equipment over the river.

The A-10s returned in strength at 0750. Their main target this time was the pontoon bridge itself. After having been stung by the 2S6 antiaircraft vehicles, they stood off at a distance, firing Maverick missiles against the bridge. Two missiles seemed to strike the bridge, and it began to lazily break apart. Portions of it began to move downriver with the current as

*A flight of four Hind D training helicopters. The Mi-24 is partially armored with some protection around the pilot and gunner's stations in the nose. However, it is an older design, not as hardened against antiaircraft fire as the more recent US Army AH-64 Apache.* Sovfoto.

*The Mi-24 Hind F has two 30mm cannons on the fuselage side instead of the turreted 12.7mm machine gun found on earlier models. It also uses the improved AT-6 Spiral antitank missile, similar to the US Army's TOW.*

*The pilot's station in the Mi-24, located behind the gunner's station, is partially armored to protect the pilot from small arms fire. The Mi-24 is crewed by Soviet Air Force personnel, a different practice than in the US armed forces where the Army controls attack helicopters.*

*An Mi-24 being armed in the field. Soviet military helicopters are sturdy and simple in an effort to make them easier to repair in the field. They are less durable than most NATO helicopters, however, and key components like rotors and engine transmissions wear out faster.*

*Soviet air assault tactics have been shifting away from the use of paratroop forces in favor of heliborne assault. The workhorse of the Soviet helicopter force is the Mi-8, and its improved derivative, the Mi-17, called the Hip by NATO. The Hip is larger than the US Army's UH-1 or UH-60, but smaller than the CH-46 helicopter.* Sovfoto.

*The Afghanistan experience has led to many changes in Soviet helicopter design and tactics. This Mi-17 is fitted with special infrared jamming equipment in an attempt to defeat the deadly man-portable Stinger antiaircraft missile. Soviet helicopters proved to be especially vulnerable to small missiles during the Afghanistan fighting, leading to the development of special countermeasure devices.* Sovfoto.

*The Mi-24 will eventually be succeeded by the Mi-28 Havoc. The Havoc entered production in 1989–90 and will not be available in large numbers until the mid-1990s. It is a much more sophisticated attack helicopter than the Hind, and more comparable to the American AH-64 Apache. Although well armed and well armored, it is not as well equipped as the Apache for night flying and night fighting.* Steven Zaloga.

*A deadly enemy of helicopters is the radar-directed air defense gun vehicle, like this German-designed Gepard of the Netherlands army. The Gepard, armed with twin 35mm cannon, is one of the most effective antiaircraft gun systems in NATO use.* Pierre Touzin.

*The Soviet airborne forces, or VDV, are the elite of the Soviet armed forces. Spetsnaz troops are similarly equipped, and trained to an even higher standard. The characteristic feature of the air assault troops is the pale blue beret, seen on this paratrooper/radioman during summer wargames in the mid-1980s. Sovfoto.*

*The Soviet VDV air assault force is a heavily armed intervention force. Their closest counterpart in the US armed forces is the Marine Corps, although the VDV are not trained for amphibious assault. VDV units are fully mechanized, using the BMD-1 armored transporter seen here, a smaller cousin of the BMP-1. This airborne trooper is armed with the stubby AKS-74U carbine, first seen in Afghanistan in the early 1980s. Sovfoto.*

*Soviet airborne units are expected to protect themselves from air attack. They are equipped with man-portable missiles like the SA-14 Gremlin, Soviet equivalent of the Stinger, and portable antiaircraft guns like this ZU-23 "Sergei" twin 23mm autocannon.*

*The staple of Soviet mechanized artillery units is the 2S1 Gvozdika 122mm self-propelled howitzer. Armored artillery has become increasingly necessary on the modern battlefield to protect artillery crews from the possibility of chemical weapons as well as the threat posed by enemy counterbattery fire.*

*Like many Soviet light armored vehicles, the 2S1 was designed to be amphibious. This permits the Soviet engineers to save their precious assault bridges and ferries for heavy, high-priority equipment such as tanks, which cannot swim.*

*The 2S1 is accompanied into action by the 1V12 series of armored command vehicles. These vehicles, better known by their NATO acronym "ACRV," house the artillery battalion's command personnel, computers, communication equipment, and specialized electronics.*

the Soviet engineers set out in small boats in an attempt to repair the rupture and prevent the bridge from disintegrating.

At this point Belov received a message from the battalion to move his vehicles away from the bridgehead toward the deployment area near Aiterhofen. The column passed through the ruined streets of Ainbrach. There was nothing but rubble. The road headed south through a small woods. Passing through it, they entered the remains of Schambach, a small town that had been caught up in the original fighting two days before. It was largely in ruins. There had been little time to clean up, and the road in the village was littered with rubble and debris. This created a bit of a problem: The road heading westward was supposed to be in the center of town, but because the area had been so obliterated by artillery shelling, there was no evidence of the road. The PRP-3 scout vehicle had pressed ahead and found an opening in the rubble.

The battalion spilled off the road into a large pasture to the east of Aiterhofen. They had been informed that targets were likely to be in the Geiselhoring area, and the three batteries deployed accordingly. The battalion commander, Major Yefimov, and the battalion reconnaissance vehicle set off to find the "assault group" they were supposed to support. Assault group was a fancy name for a collection of tank and motor rifle troops that had been cobbled up from the remains of other units. The

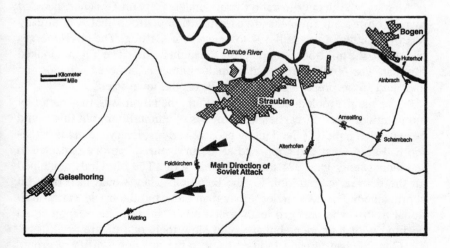

assault group was about the size of a motor rifle regiment, but did not have as much equipment. It was using the radio call sign Perina (featherbed) and so was being called the Group Perina.

Group Perina was holding the western edge of the Straubing-Deggendorf bridgehead. The main direction of the Soviet attack was out of Deggendorf, south along the A92 autobahn. Group Perina was attempting to hold a large chunk of farm pasture running south of the city of Straubing. The NATO forces had no interest in fighting in the streets of Straubing itself, which were held by another improvised Soviet battle group. Attacking across open fields wasn't too appealing either. However, on the southern edge of Group Perina was a small cluster of low hills, no more than 400 meters high; this area had been the scene of most of the fighting. Group Perina had a battalion of motor rifle troops and some tanks holding the small village of Metting in the hills. They were requesting artillery support urgently.

The battalion was ready to begin firing about thirty-five minutes after having reached the fields. Captain Gonchar placed the battalion in a triangular formation, with each battery deployed in a simple line. This was bad if the enemy should decide on counterbattery fire, but the urgency of the moment demanded a simple fire plan. Normally the battalion would deploy its reconnaissance team forward to locate the objective precisely and to observe the impact of the battalion's fire. Since it would take the PRP-3 and its scout team more than forty-five minutes to reach the vicinity of Metting, the deputy battalion commander, Captain Gonchar, decided to rely on a team from the divisional artillery group that was already nearby. The target was Hill 394 to the west of Metting. The NATO forces had seized the hill from Group Perina the night before. The hill overlooked Metting. The NATO forces had a small number of armored vehicles and appeared to be preparing for an attack on the town itself.

The main problem facing the artillery battalion was the matter of ammunition. The 2S1 carries forty rounds of ammunition, but this would be expended rapidly if the fighting became serious. Everyone in the battalion had seen what had happened at the bridgehead; no one expected to see their twenty Ural 375 trucks anytime soon. The big Urals contained all the reserve ammunition for the battalion. They would also be a bit shorthanded. The 2S1 carries a four-man crew, but the trucks carry additional troops who perform loading and other chores. The weapon could be fired with four men, but it would slow their rate of fire.

Gonchar had already radioed back to the divisional artillery group, explaining their predicament. An officer there had promised to send up some ammunition from Deggendorf, but the roads were crowded, and the main attack elements were clamoring for more ammunition as well. Gonchar told the battery commanders to have their drivers assist in firing the howitzers. It was a risk, since enemy counterbattery fire might catch them just sitting there. But the vehicles were armored, and Gonchar decided against moving the batteries around unless there was evidence of enemy artillery.

Major Yefimov was in transit to the headquarters of Group Perina, and had left it to Gonchar's judgment how the initial artillery strike should be configured. In view of the situation, Gonchar decided to register the target with a round from each battery. There was no sense wasting precious ammunition. A single howitzer from each battery fired a registration round. Gonchar waited in his command vehicle for word from the forward observers. There was nothing but the squawking of radio jamming on the line, which continued for several minutes.

Finally, the radiomen managed to reestablish communication. "Lev, this is Belka . . . you are short 100 meters . . . repeat, you are short 100 meters . . . confirm, over."

"Belka, this is Lev, adjusting plus 100, repeat, plus 100, over."[7]

Gonchar had the computer operator calculate the necessary changes, which were passed on to the three firing batteries. One of the radio operators was assigned to stand on the roof of the command vehicle and use flag signals to tell the batteries to open fire. The target was an area of two hectares, and the firing norms called for 300 rounds of 122mm ammunition for adequate suppression. This meant 100 rounds from each battery, about 15 percent of the ammunition on hand. At his signal, the batteries began firing. The fire strike would take about five minutes.

The forward observers reported that the artillery strike appeared to be successful. The enemy attack had been halted, although there was still sporadic tank fire. Gonchar was pondering whether to move the battalion; enemy counterbattery radar could have located them.

He was interrupted by one of the radiomen in his vehicle. "Comrade Captain, it's Major Yefimov, he wishes to speak to you urgently!"

"Pavel, the attack at Metting is just a feint. The enemy is launching

---

7. Belka=squirrel; Lev=Lion.

a major attack against the center of our positions at Feldkirchen. Tanks, infantry vehicles . . . the works. We will need everything you have to break up the attack. Stand by for coordinates."

Viktor Belov was listening in on the radio net and signaled to his six artillery vehicles to prepare for a rapid fire engagement. They could expect frequent adjustments to keep pace with the momentum of the enemy attack. In moments, the fire control computer in Captain Gonchar's vehicle had prepared the firing solutions and the data was passed to the batteries.

The first salvo was fired in less than two minutes from the original receipt of target data. The battalion had been firing for about a minute when the first adjustment came in. The NATO attackers were obviously moving very fast. Belov was observing the firing from the outside of the command vehicle when he saw what looked like small airbursts explode over the battalion. He lunged for the rear door to try to get inside the protective armor of the command vehicle. Enemy counterbattery fire!

The American forces launching the attack against the Straubing bridgehead were well prepared to deal with the Soviet artillery. They had moved a Firefinder radar into position the night before. It was directing a battalion of M109A2 155mm howitzer vehicles to the west of Geiselhoring. The Americans expected the Soviets to use armored artillery vehicles. Normal artillery would not be very effective against these, so they used M836 SADARM ammunition instead. The SADARM projectiles contain two submunitions about the size of a soup can. Each submunition separates from the projectile and is slowed by a special parachute configured to allow the submunition to rotate in a spiral pattern. At the front of the submunition is a millimeter wave and infrared sensor, which looks for a large, metallic, and actively infrared target (like an artillery vehicle). When it finds the target, it fires an explosively formed slug capable of punching through the thin roof armor of most armored vehicles.

The enemy counterbattery attack was sudden and lethal. Within a half minute, most of 1st Battery and nearly all of 3d Battery had been hit. Belov's 2d Battery, at the southern edge of the deployment, had about half its vehicles hit. Sitting so close together, the battalion vehicles had made a very vulnerable target to the enemy. In all, of eighteen howitzer vehicles, eleven had been hit and put out of action, as had four of the six command vehicles.

Belov had leapt into his vehicle at precisely the wrong moment. A SADARM submunition had homed in on the hot engine exhaust of the vehicle and had fired a penetrator at it. The slug ripped into the rear compartment, immediately above the radio operators. It smashed through one of the operators, leaving a gruesome trail, and careened into two of the torsion bar suspension arms, effectively jamming the center road wheels. Belov was hit in the shoulder by a small fragment of metal, which penetrated the muscle. It was painful but not serious. The back door of the vehicle remained open, swaying with the impact of the SADARM. Belov emerged from the rear of the vehicle in a daze and splashed with the blood of his hapless radio operator, who had also been hit. Captain Gonchar's vehicle had also been hit and was burning. Smoke curled out of the back door, and several survivors stumbled out. One of the nearby artillery vehicles was on fire.

The enemy artillery, not content with the havoc already wrought, fired in several salvos of DPICMs.[8] These sowed hundreds of little grenades over the area. Although not particularly lethal to crews in armored vehicles, they could break tracks and cause other damage. It would be some time before this artillery battery was ready for action again.

## Analysis

The fictional scenario presented here highlights two branches of the Soviet Ground Forces that are in many respects superior to their NATO counterparts—the artillery and the combat engineers. The artillery has always been the favored branch in Russian armies, whether Tsarist or Soviet. The Russians have traditionally regarded the artillery as the "god of war." Artillery in this century has been the primary cause of casualties, ranging from 60 to 80 percent in the Soviet experience. The combat engineers are the branch that "lubricates" the mobility of the army. They

---

8. DPICM stands for dual-purpose improved conventional munition. These artillery projectiles contain several dozen small submunitions, about the size of a roll of 35mm film. The submunitions act like small grenades. However, they also have a small shaped-charge warhead, so that if they strike armor, the blast can be channeled forward to pierce steel.

are responsible for ensuring quick passage through natural and man-made terrain obstacles such as minefields, fortifications, and rivers. The Soviet combat engineers received special attention as a result of the experiences of World War II, particularly the costly river-crossing operations of 1944–45.

## Soviet Artillery

The Soviet artillery branch is formally called the Rocket and Artillery Force. It is responsible for conventional tubed artillery, multiple rocket launchers, and tactical ballistic missiles. In spite of its favored position in the Ground Forces, Soviet artillery lagged behind NATO artillery for the two decades after World War II. The Soviets fielded enormous quantities of conventional towed artillery, but largely ignored the trend toward artillery mechanization. The NATO armies were converting their artillery forces away from towed guns to armored artillery vehicles, which provided the guns with more mobility and a measure of armored protection.

The lag in Soviet developments in this field was due to several factors. The artillery is one of the more conservative branches of the Ground Forces, and there was probably resistance to the adoption of mechanized artillery when towed artillery is so much cheaper. But even the most die-hard conservative had to admit that traditional towed artillery was far less suitable on a battlefield where chemical or nuclear munitions might be used. Furthermore, with advances in artillery detection radars, towed artillery is more vulnerable to counterbattery fire.

Ironically, one of the main impediments to Soviet artillery modernization was the prestige of this branch and its research and development organization, the Main Artillery Directorate (GAU). When the Kremlin decided to develop atomic weapons, it was the artillery branch that managed the program. And in the late 1940s when Stalin decided to push the development of intercontinental ballistic missiles, it was the artillery branch, not the Air Force, which headed the effort. These two high-priority projects drained away much of the artillery's finest talent. In 1960, the strategic missile force was finally broken off from the artillery and formed as an independent branch of the armed forces. This led to a renaissance in the Soviet artillery, which first became evident in the early 1970s.

After decades of neglect, the Soviet artillery branch began to modernize with a vengeance. The first armored artillery vehicles, the 2S1 Gvozdika (Carnation)[9] 122mm self-propelled howitzer and the 2S3 Akatsiya (Acacia) 152mm self-propelled howitzer, began appearing in large numbers. These vehicles look like tanks, but they are much more thinly armored—only enough to protect against small arms fire and light shrapnel. And their guns are designed for indirect artillery fire, not direct fire like tanks. Neither of the new Soviet vehicles was particularly innovative, but they were comparable in quality to NATO designs of the period. What was so surprising was the numbers of vehicles being produced. The U.S. Defense Intelligence Agency estimated that the Soviets produced in excess of 10,000 self-propelled guns from 1972 through the mid-1980s, which was far in excess of the total number of self-propelled guns in every army on earth. The U.S. Army has only about 2,400 self-propelled guns.

The modernization program was also surprising in terms of its depth. It included highly specialized long-range artillery vehicles, such as the 2S5 Giatsint (Hyacinth) 152mm gun, the 2S7 203mm artillery vehicle, and the 2S4 Tyulpan (Tulip tree) 240mm heavy mortar vehicle. The airborne forces received their own airmobile artillery vehicle, the 2S9 Anona (Anemone). New multiple-rocket launchers were also developed, such as the BM-22 Uragan (Hurricane), an equivalent of the U.S. Army's M270 MLRS (multiple launch rocket system). Besides the weapons themselves, the Soviets fielded a wide range of sophisticated support vehicles. They developed a specialized command vehicle, the 1V12 armored command and reconnaissance vehicle (ACRV), based on the same chassis as the 2S1 artillery vehicle. There are different versions of this vehicle for battery and battalion commanders, as mentioned in the scenario. Other armies use armored artillery vehicles, but no army has developed a vehicle specifically for this purpose the way the Soviets have done. In addition, the Soviets developed a specialized artillery radar scouting vehicle, the PRP-3 (Small Fred), and a mobile artillery location radar system, the SNAR-10 (Big Fred).

The Soviet Ground Forces differ in their artillery deployment from NATO practices. At a divisional level, Soviet artillery firepower tends to be lighter than that of U.S. Army divisions. The Soviets make up for it by heavier concentrations of artillery at army and front level, and by the sheer number of divisional artillery units. A typical forward deployed

---

9. Although it may seem odd, the Soviets traditionally use the names of flowering plants as code names for their artillery vehicles and some towed artillery pieces.

Soviet division these days, like the units portrayed in the fictional scenario, has about 192 artillery vehicles. Each tank and motor rifle regiment has a battalion of 2S1 122mm self-propelled howitzers, like the unit depicted in the scenario. In addition, there is a divisional artillery regiment with 72 2S3 152mm self-propelled howitzers and 24 BM-21 Grad (Hail) 122mm forty-barrel multiple rocket launchers. The U.S. divisional artillery has fewer vehicles, but of larger caliber and greater firepower. The U.S. Army relies on the M109 155mm self-propelled howitzer, rather than a 122mm howitzer, as its standard divisional artillery piece. There are 96 M109s in four battalions in each U.S. heavy division. For heavy firepower, the U.S. Army has battalions of 24 M110A3 203mm howitzers in the corps. The Soviets have 203mm artillery vehicles like the 2S7, and they are found at army and front levels, and not in the division. Finally, the U.S. Army deploys 36 M270 MLRS 227mm multiple rocket launchers in the division, compared to 24 of the smaller Soviet BM-21 multiple rocket launchers. To give some comparison, a single salvo by the howitzers of a U.S. heavy division delivers 6.2 tons of projectiles, while the Soviet howitzers in a division, though more numerous, deliver 4.9 tons. The multiple rocket launchers add considerably to divisional firepower—a 68-ton salvo in the case of the U.S. division and 12 tons in the case of the Soviet division.

Although the Soviet division's firepower is less than that of a U.S. Army division, in any confrontation in Europe, NATO divisions are likely to be faced by two or three Soviet divisions, often with additional artillery support from army or front level. Modest advantages at divisional level are meaningless if the NATO divisions are confronted by the artillery of several Soviet divisions. The NATO divisions attempt to counteract their quantitative inferiority with technical superiority and proficiency. The effect of artillery is not purely a matter of mass. The first salvo to strike a target is far more effective than any successive salvo. The reasons are simple. If the first salvo can catch the opponent unaware, the projectiles explode before the opponent can seek cover, whether in a trench or in an armored vehicle. Successive waves may continue to be destructive, but the opponent usually has taken defensive measures after the first impact, reducing the effect.

Therefore, the ability to strike a target accurately on the first fire mission is an important advantage in maximizing the impact and lethality of the artillery. The U.S. Army has some notable advantages in this area due to improvements in fire control data handling. The U.S. Army uses the

Tacfire system, which not only provides rapid computer-based firing solutions, but allows the transmission of critical firing data to the batteries more quickly and accurately than traditional methods.

## Precision-Guided Munitions

Although artillery remains the branch responsible for causing the greatest number of casualties on the battlefield, it remains largely ineffective against tanks when used in the normal, indirect fire mode. Tanks were largely developed as an antidote to artillery after World War I. Artillery has not been as decisive a weapon since the advent of the armored vehicle. Numerous attempts are being made, however, to increase the lethality of artillery against tanks. As a result, it is likely that in the future artillery will play a greater role in the antiarmor battle. The new artillery antitank projectiles include high-tech approaches, like precision-guided munitions (PGMs), and novel low-tech solutions, like artillery-scattered mines.

Precision-guided munitions have been the buzzword of advanced artillery since the late 1970s. There were glowing reports of technical advances that would permit artillery to fire guided projectiles capable of destroying a tank with a single round. The first generation of these weapons appeared in the U.S. Army in the early 1980s in the form of the Copperhead laser-guided projectile. A forward observer, equipped with a laser designator, aims the laser at an enemy tank. He radios to the artillery vehicle, which fires a Copperhead roughly into the area where the tank is located. The Copperhead picks up the coded laser light reflecting off the tank and guides itself against the tank.

First-generation PGMs like the Copperhead are an advance in the ability of artillery to oppose tanks, but such systems have many shortcomings. The Copperhead requires secure communication links between the forward observer and the artillery. If the radio link is jammed, the weapon is useless. The Copperhead can also be defeated by bad weather. Laser light can be absorbed or deflected by heavy rain, fog, and certain kinds of smoke. But the real problem is that the Copperhead does not provide any really unique capability on the battlefield. At the moment, it is useful only in attacking tanks along the forward edge of the battlefield, since it can be used only against targets that can be seen by the forward observer. Other weapons like antitank guided missiles can perform the same function. And an antitank missile like the U.S. Army TOW is about half the price of a Copperhead. For a PGM to have a revolutionary impact on the battlefield, it must be capable of striking targets beyond the front line, in the depths of the enemy positions. The Copperhead can be used in this fashion if there is a laser-equipped, remotely piloted vehicle (RPV) drone to designate the targets. At the moment, the U.S. Army does not have such a drone. So to be effective, a new generation of PGMs should be autonomous, that is, able to guide itself against the target without the need for a designator. This has proven to be very tricky.

The first weapon of this sort is likely to be the U.S. Army SADARM, an artillery projectile that contains two or more guided submunitions. The 155mm howitzer or MLRS rocket launcher fires the SADARM roughly into the area behind the lines where the enemy tanks have been spotted by reconnaissance aircraft or drones. The projectile opens up, dispersing the SADARM over the target. The submunitions, which are about the size of a soup can, have special plastic parachutes to slow them down. As the submunition falls to earth, the parachute device gives it a slight spiral motion. The first spiral is about 150 yards across, and then gradually grows smaller so that an area 150 yards in all directions is covered. The submunition has what is called a "hybrid" sensor, which uses a tiny millimeter wave radar and infrared sensor to pick up the target. When it finds a target, the submunition is detonated, firing an explosively formed metal slug at the top of the enemy vehicle.

It was originally hoped that the SADARM would be the long-range tank killer that artillery has long sought. It has not lived up to expectations, however. The "footprint" that its sensor sees is small, so it has little chance of engaging a moving tank formation. The SADARM is likely to be effective against stationary tanks and other targets. One of its main roles, as described in the scenario, will be counterbattery fire, for which the SADARM is ideally suited, since self-propelled guns are stationary when firing, and their gun barrels give off a very evident infrared signature that the submunition can easily see.

A third generation of PGMs is under development even before the second generation, like SADARM, has entered service. The third-generation systems are larger, more complex, and more expensive. They are large enough to incorporate guidance surfaces, so they can steer themselves into moving tank targets. They also are large enough to include highly sophisticated computer-processing systems to discriminate between low-priority targets (like trucks) and high-priority targets (like tanks). The first of these is likely to be the TGW (terminally guided warhead), being developed as a joint NATO program. It will be carried on the MLRS multiple rocket launcher. Similar systems are also being developed for conventional artillery howitzers, but they appear to be much farther down the road.

Systems like SADARM may enter service by the early 1990s, and systems like the TGW by the mid-1990s. Do the Soviets have such systems? Probably not yet. The Soviets do not appear to be as advanced as the United States in the critical microprocessor technologies that are needed for PGMs. From Soviet writing, it is evident that they are interested in such systems. Until their industrial base proves capable of developing them, however, Soviet artillery will have limited capability against armored targets.

High tech is not the only way to skin a cat. Low tech can work, though perhaps not as elegantly. There are two approaches to defeating armor using low-tech artillery: attacking the thin tops of armored vehicles and attacking the thin bottoms. Since it is nearly impossible to hit small targets like tanks with ordinary artillery projectiles, artillery designers have developed ICMs (improved conventional munitions). These are also called cargo rounds. Unlike normal artillery shells, these rounds contain dozens of small, unguided submunition grenades. They work like a shotgun. Before they hit the ground, a special fuse breaks open the round a few hundred feet in the air. Instead of one big explosion in one spot, they cover a much larger area with a lot of little explosions. There can be forty to one hundred of these in a projectile, each capable of punching through the thin roof armor of a tank. The warheads are not large enough to do a lot of damage unless they get a lucky hit; for example, they might detonate near ammunition stowage or fuel. The ICMs have not been used extensively in any recent war due to their novelty. But computer simulations have suggested that they could be very deadly against light armored vehicles like infantry transports or self-propelled artillery. But they must be used in heavy concentrations to ensure a good probability of hitting their targets.

Artillery-scattered mines attack the other Achilles' heel of tanks — their soft underbelly and tracks. Conventional antitank mines had to be laboriously emplaced by hand before a battle began. The new artillery-scattered mines can be delivered as the battle develops, covering only those areas where an enemy is attacking. A lot of mines are required to lay down a minefield thick enough to have a good probability of stopping most of the tanks. But tanks are very poorly protected underneath, and their tracks can be broken easily. Artillery mines can assist in stopping a tank attack, as was suggested in Chapter 3.

Little is known about Soviet low-tech antiarmor munitions like these. It seems likely that the Soviets do have such systems. They do not require sophisticated sensors, although they do require very careful quality control at the factory and precise light machining. Such munitions mesh with Soviet tendencies toward the employment of massed artillery. To be really effective, these munitions have to be expended in large numbers. The greater the density of the minefield, the more likely enemy tanks will run over it. The more submunitions scattered over a target, the greater the likelihood of lethal damage to enemy vehicles.

The Soviets see reconnaissance-strike complexes (RSC) as the wave of the future in artillery. An RSC is not a single weapon, but rather a group of weapons and sensors. The main emphasis is on new ways for the artillery to identify and target enemy vehicles and defenses. An RSC would consist of a conventional artillery unit, an airborne reconnaissance system (either aircraft or unmanned scout drone), and a communications and data handling post, which would coordinate the information collected by the reconnaissance system with the artillery unit. The NATO armies are already developing these systems, although progress has been slow. The U.S. Army's Aquila unmanned scout drone program proved to be overly complex, but the army has managed to put together an impressive artillery fire control system with Tacfire, and future systems like AFATDS (artillery fire and target designation system).

## Rocket Artillery

One area where the Soviets have shown more activity than the U.S. Army is rocket and missile artillery. The Soviets were among the pioneers in the use of rocket artillery in World War II. The legendary Katyusha multiple rocket launchers have remained a staple of the Soviet artillery since their initial use in 1941. Rocket artillery is an area saturation weapon and has less precision than conventional tubed artillery. A multiple rocket launcher like the BM-21 Grad can hurl nearly two tons of high explosive and metal against a target in a single salvo. Such an enormous amount of firepower hitting a target in a few brief seconds has tremendous shock value.

The disadvantage of multiple rocket launchers, aside from their lack of precision, is the time it takes to load them; it takes about ten minutes to reload a BM-21. Rockets are also inherently more expensive than artillery projectiles with the same payload. Rockets require more propellant than conventional artillery, so they weigh more and take up more precious cargo space than tubed artillery. Rocket artillery will never replace tubed artillery, but it acts as an important firepower supplement.

The U.S. Army used multiple rocket launchers in World War II, but on a smaller scale than the Soviets. They largely ignored this form of artillery until the late 1970s, when the M270 MLRS was developed. The MLRS is much larger than most Soviet systems, firing a more potent rocket. The Soviets are currently fielding a vehicle of somewhat similar size, the BM-22 Uragan, and have an even larger 280mm rocket launcher in development.

The Soviets also have had a more active interest in ballistic missiles for tactical artillery use. They have deployed the R-65 Luna-M (FROG-7) in divisions since the 1960s, and at army and front level have the R-300 (SS-1b Scud) and OTR-22 (SS-12 Scaleboard). The U.S. Army has the Lance, a FROG-7 equivalent. The Intermediate Nuclear Forces treaty of 1987 has altered the use of missiles in the artillery role. The SS-12 Scaleboard is being destroyed under the terms of the treaty, as is the new OTR-23 (SS-23 Spider). As a result, the missile weapons have been pushed up a notch in the organization hierarchy. The FROGs and their new replacement, the SS-21 Scarab, are now found at army level rather than in the divisions.

Missile weapons of this type are primarily intended for the delivery of tactical nuclear warheads. Older missiles, such as the Scud, are not accurate enough to be used with conventional high-explosive warheads. The Scud received some prominence in the late 1980s owing to its use by both sides in the Iran-Iraq war. The Iranian and Iraqi Scuds were fitted with conventional high-explosive warheads, but because of their lack of accuracy, they were used to bombard cities rather than smaller military targets. As missile accuracies improve, their use with nonnuclear warheads becomes more feasible. Because of their cost, they are usually reserved for high-priority targets. Typical targets in a conventional war would be communication and command posts, airfields, and major transport centers like rail yards.

The capabilities of Soviet artillery are often neglected in public discussion of the NATO/Warsaw Pact balance. Artillery has not played a decisive role in modern wars since World War I and has been overshadowed by the tank and other armored vehicles. Nevertheless, artillery is likely to remain the primary cause of casualties in future wars, and new munitions and fire control technologies are likely to increase its importance on the modern battlefield.

## The Combat Engineers

Soviet interest in combat engineers stems largely from their experience in World War II. Mobile warfare inevitably means that rivers will be frequently encountered. Rivers are the most formidable natural obstacle to mobile operations.

The Soviets have tried to diminish the impact of rivers on mechanized operations by making the lead combat elements, such as tanks and light armored vehicles, capable of crossing on their own. It is nearly impossible to make tanks amphibious due to their weight. The Soviets solved this problem by equipping tanks with "deep wading" equipment. Soviet tanks are designed so that all their major openings—engine grills, hatches, ventilation covers, and air intakes—can be hermetically sealed. Snorkels are fitted to the vehicle to provide air for the crew and the engine. The tanks can then be driven across the bottom of riverbeds.

This ingenious system is not without its faults. The Soviets have demonstrated tank river crossing operations during their annual war games, but have fudged the matter by laying concrete roadways on the river bottoms to prevent problems. In reality, riverbeds may be too soft or irregular to permit easy transit by tanks, and the water may be too deep for the snorkels. Even when the riverbed is suitable, the operation is hazardous. In spite of their weight on dry land, tanks retain a certain measure of buoyancy underwater. This makes them very difficult to handle and especially difficult to steer. As a result, a river crossing operation by tanks is unlikely to be a spontaneous affair, with the tanks leaping into the water at first opportunity. Combat engineer troops are provided with special amphibious vehicles, like the IRM, which have sensors capable of testing the river bottom. Armored recovery vehicles are also likely to be present to help tow tanks that become bogged down.

In the event that the river is unsuitable for deep fording with tanks, as in the fictional scenario, the Soviet engineers have special tank ferries. These are tracked vehicles with folding pontoons stowed on their roofs. It takes two of these vehicles, called GSPs, to make a ferry buoyant enough to support a tank. The vehicles drive into the water and are clipped together. They have their own ramps, and the tanks can drive aboard and be transported to the opposite shore. A tank division has only six of these pairs, so it would take some time to move a regiment of tanks across a river.

Light armored vehicles are less of a problem. They are light enough that they will float with the right hull design. Virtually all Soviet light armored vehicles are amphibious. Wheeled light armored vehicles like the BTR-80 infantry transporter have a water jet propulsion system. Water is drawn into a tunnel and pushed out the back end by a propeller. Tracked vehicles like the BMP infantry transporter or 2S1 artillery vehicle can use their track to propel themselves through the water, as mentioned in the fictional scenario.

The U.S. Army has paid less attention to these amphibious features, since it presumes it will be operating defensively with bridges intact behind its positions. American tanks are not designed for deep wading. Many light armored vehicles, like the M113 infantry transporter or the M2 Bradley, are amphibious like their Soviet counterparts. However, many other vehicles are not. The M109 armored artillery vehicle is not amphibious, unlike the Soviet 2S1 as seen in this scenario.

Tanks and light armored vehicles constitute about a fifth of the vehicles in a Soviet tank or motor rifle division. The rest are trucks, trailers, and other support vehicles. Very few of these are amphibious. To get these vehicles across a river, conventional combat engineer techniques are used. Pontoon bridge systems like the PMP are the usual method. The PMP is carried on a truck; the truck backs up to the edge of the river, and the pontoon sections are slid off into the water for the engineers to assemble. A typical Soviet division has enough PMP sections to make 120 meters of sixty-ton bridge, or 280 meters of twenty-ton bridge. The bridge takes from fifteen to forty minutes to assemble, depending on the type. In the event of a major river crossing operation, additional pontoon bridge units would be provided to allow several bridges to be assembled.

## Mine Warfare

Rivers are the main natural obstacle to mobile tank warfare. Mines are the most common man-made obstacle. The Soviets have paid more attention to rapid minefield breaching than any other army. Every tank regiment has its own minefield breaching equipment, and the division has specialized equipment. The standard method for minefield breaching is the mine roller, which consists of heavy cast metal wheels on special arms attached to the front of the tank. The tank is driven into the minefield and the rollers detonate the mines in front of the tank. The rollers can withstand more than a dozen mine explosions before they are worn out and have to be replaced. Soviet tanks can also be fitted with mine rakes – small plows that push aside tilt mines or other types of mines that the rollers do not detonate. As the mine-roller tank drives through the minefield, it leaves a trail of incandescent markers for the remaining tanks to follow. Minefield breaching of this type is slow and tedious. The mine-roller assembly is too heavy to permit tanks to always carry it. It takes time to bring it forward from rear supply areas and fit it to the tank. And the tank moves through the minefield slowly. If the minefield is properly protected with tanks or antitank missiles, the mine-rolling tank makes an easy target. The way around this problem is to use a rapid minefield breaching method. The Soviets use a specialized vehicle called the MTK, which has a special rocket launcher. Attached to the rocket is a length of explosive tubing. When fired, the rocket drags the explosive over the minefield and drops it. When it hits, the explosive line charge is detonated, destroying mines near it and blowing a path through the minefield. Such a system is very quick to operate, but it is complex and costly. A division will have only a handful of these vehicles.

Although the Western press is full of stories about "technology transfer" and the Soviet acquisition or theft of Western military technology, the reverse situation is not often discussed. One of the few areas where the U.S. Army has copied Soviet technology has been combat engineer equipment. The U.S. Army's ribbon bridge system is based on the Soviet PMP system. The U.S. Army and Israeli Army mine rollers and mine rakes are based on Soviet mine-clearing systems. None of these are high-tech systems, but they do demonstrate the Soviet attention to detail in this often neglected area.

Indeed, the amount of Soviet attention to combat engineering belies Soviet claims of the defensive orientation of the Warsaw Pact. An army does not need a lot of fast bridging equipment or minefield breaching systems if it is primarily interested in defense. An army that has an offensive posture, however, requires rapidly deployable bridging equipment, since it has to presume that its opponent will destroy his own bridges as he retreats, to hinder the passage of the enemy. This has even been recognized by Mikhail Gorbachev, who stated in his UN speech in December 1988 that he would reduce the amount of engineer equipment held by forward-deployed Soviet formations in Central Europe as part of the Soviet gesture to reduce cold war tensions in the area.

# CHAPTER 7

## Fighter Combat:
## The Battle for the Airfields

0600, 8 October, Milovice Air Base, Czechoslovakia

Senior Lieutenant Ivan Dushak adjusted the harness that strapped him into his MiG-29A fighter aircraft. He had flown this particular machine, number 21, several times before. It was pretty much trouble free in the hands of a good ground crew and had the red operating proficiency badge on the nose as a result. The high walls of the ready revetments blocked what little sunlight was available in the early morning hours. Dushak took a small flashlight from his flight suit to check the notepad he had strapped to his right leg. It was securely in place. He turned his attention to the cockpit instruments and began going through the engine warm-up procedures. He checked to make certain the inertial navigation system had been turned on. It would take several minutes of warm-up time to operate properly. The airfield support battalion brought a truck to tow the aircraft out of the revetments before the engines were started. As his aircraft was towed into the open, he felt exposed. The NATO air forces had been attacking Soviet airfields relentlessly, and the last thing he wanted to happen was to lose his aircraft on the ground. He hoped that his wait until takeoff would be brief.

Dushak's MiG-29 was one of eight from the 1st Squadron of the 176th Proskurovskiy Guards Fighter Aviation Regiment being prepared for this particular mission. Two flights, each with four fighters, would be escorting a strike group against an improvised NATO airfield near Ingolstadt. The Germans and Americans had converted a length of Route 16 to the west of Ingolstadt into an airfield from which they were flying A-10 attack aircraft. The A-10s had been hitting at Soviet ground columns during the fighting for the Danube bridgeheads for the past day or so. The army was demanding that they be stamped out. The proximity of the Ingolstadt field allowed the A-10s to make many sorties each day, and they had been wrecking the pontoon bridges and engineer equipment as fast as they were erected. The bitter complaints from the front commander had led the Air Force to allot two squadrons of the prized Su-24 attack bombers to the mission. The Su-24 was a two-seat strike aircraft with very sophisticated navigation and electronics. It resembled the American F-111 strike bomber. The Su-24 was not usually assigned to simple tactical strike missions, unless they had high priority. The strike force would be rounded out by a flight of Su-22s configured for the ECM jamming role. The Su-22s were sometimes called "Zubr" (Bison) by their crews due to their rotund shape and arched fuselage. Laden with jamming pods, they would be sluggish and vulnerable.

Dushak's fighter regiment had been brought into Milovice two days before from its normal operating base outside of Lvov in the Ukraine. Fighter losses in the past few days of air fighting had been heavy. It wasn't only the NATO fighter planes, it was also the damn SAM missiles like the Hawk and Patriot. The missiles were forcing the Soviet aircraft to operate at low altitudes, where NATO radars couldn't find them in all the ground clutter. But it was dangerous to fly below 1,000 meters. The terrain along the border was mountainous, and it was easy to run into a hill if you weren't careful. And at low altitude you attracted the attention of everybody with a gun. Modern jet aircraft are rugged, but at high speeds, even small damage can be lethal. A single bullet, in the wrong place at the wrong time, can bring down a multimillion-dollar jet. A bullet down the air intake, impacting the turbine blades, can lead to a catastrophic engine failure. A ruptured hydraulic line can lead to a loss of control. Such losses to small arms fire are not very common. Jet aircraft have been known to absorb more than a hundred small-caliber bullets and fly safely back to base. But when flying at low altitude, the "golden bullet" that can wreck your plane is always a worry.

Modern air defense missiles are another matter. Missiles like the Hawk or Patriot are so large that if they lock onto your fighter with their radar, your chances are not good. Electronic jamming is possible, but difficult. And the warheads on these missiles are so large that they nearly ensure an aircraft loss if they explode close enough. They are a major worry on a strike mission like this, since so many aircraft provide a juicy target. By staying at low altitudes, the strike group can stay under their radar cover. Without radar acquisition, the missiles are useless. It's a trade-off. If you go in high, you can avoid small-caliber gunfire and Stingers, but then you are out in the open against the Patriot and Hawk batteries. In view of the losses of Soviet aircraft to Hawks and Patriots in the past few days, this attack mission would be going in low.

Either way, the flight could be attacked by enemy fighters. The main problem in this area was F-16s, which were present in abundance and were a real menace. The F-16 was smaller than the MiG-29, but its performance was similar. Some were armed with the deadly AMRAAM radar-guided missile, but many still had only Sidewinders. The Sidewinder used infrared homing, and fighters were usually within visual range before the infrared seeker could lock onto the target. This limited their attack envelope. The AMRAAM was a different matter entirely. It was radar guided and didn't require illumination from the enemy fighter's radar like the older Sparrow. These were undoubtedly the most lethal weapon in the recent fighting, and more than one Soviet squadron had been massacred by AMRAAMs. Some F-16s had been modernized to fire these, but the F-15 was the primary AMRAAM platform. The F-15 was bigger than the F-16 or MiG-29. The F-15 pilots preferred to kill their adversaries at long range with the AMRAAM rather than mix it up in a messy dogfight at close range with the smaller MiG-29.

Dushak checked his own panel to make certain his missiles had been properly mounted. He carried the usual weapons load. There were two R-72 radar-guided missiles on the inboard pylons. These were like the NATO Sparrow missiles. You illuminated the enemy aircraft with your RP-29 radar, and the missile homed in on the radar reflections from your

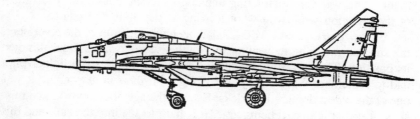

## MiG-29 Fulcrum A Fighter

target. They were good missiles, with good range. But you had to keep your radar locked onto your target the whole time—from missile launch to missile impact. If you had to break off the engagement due to the presence of enemy fighters, the missile would not hit. It also meant you could engage only one target at a time. With the AMRAAM, the missile had its own little radar and didn't need the aircraft to radar illuminate the target. And you could engage several aircraft at once, which was not possible with either the NATO Sparrow or the Soviet R-72. The other four missile pylons on the MiG-29 had R-60 infrared missiles slung from them. The R-60 operated like a Sidewinder, homing in on infrared energy from the target aircraft. It could even be launched from head on, picking up the leading edge of the fuselage and wings that had been heated by air friction. The main problem in dogfighting with the R-60 was that it had less range than the Sidewinder. The Soviet Air Force had the old K-13 with good range, but its seeker was not very sensitive. There was the new R-73 infrared missile with performance similar to that of the R-60, but it wasn't common yet, and Dushak's squadron had to make do with the older R-60s.

For real dogfighting, the MiG-29 had a 30mm autocannon in the left wing root. This was a very destructive weapon: A few solid hits could destroy most modern fighter planes. The gun was linked to a laser range finder, which told the pilot if the enemy plane was in range. Through the computer and heads-up display (HUD), it told the pilot how much elevation or deflection was needed. The HUD in the MiG-29 was a real advance as far as Dushak was concerned, especially over the old sights in the MiG-23. The HUD is an optical data system that is located in front of the pilot. The main element is a tilted glass panel that has data from the aircraft computer projected onto it. The main attraction of the HUD is that it allows the pilot to keep his eyes looking forward, through the canopy, and still be able to get vital information. In older fighters, you had to look down into the cockpit to get information from the various flight instruments. This was very distracting in a dogfight: You could lose your grasp of the situation while you were looking at the dials and gauges.

By the time Dushak's MiG-29 had been wheeled out of the revetment, the sun was creeping its way up the southeastern horizon. Dushak noted its position. The sun could be an ally in any dogfight, and a fighter pilot had to remember where it lay. Attacking with the sun at your back was one of the oldest dogfighting tricks. Even in the age of computers and missiles, it was still an excellent tactic. It is hard to see into the sun, and this blind spot can be exploited by a skilled pilot. Dushak had used this tactic often during peacetime training. He was about to find out whether peacetime training was anything like the real thing.

The warrant officer who headed the flight crew signaled to Dushak that everything was ready. He started the engine and closed the cockpit canopy. It made a solid clunk, and he locked it shut. He had already adjusted the aircraft radio to the mission frequency and was awaiting further instructions. Dushak's flight would be using the radio call sign Shashka (Sabre); the other MiG-29 flight would use Molot (Hammer). The Su-24 squadron was using the call sign Kirka (Axe), and the countermeasures flight was using Pika (Pike). Dushak's aircraft was Shashka 3; the flight leader, Sniper Pilot Nikolai Vlasov, was Shashka 1; his wingman, Pilot 3d Class German Burlakov, was Shashka 2. Dushak was the second pair leader, and his wingman, Pilot 2d Class Sergei Kostenko, was Shashka 4. Sergei "Seryozha" Kostenko was a younger pilot than Dushak,

**"Shashka Flight"**
**1st Squadron**

# 176th Proskurovskiy Guards
# Fighter Aviation Regiment

| 1st Pair | 2nd Pair |
|---|---|
| Flight Leader<br>Sniper Pilot<br>**Nikolai Vlasov**<br>*"Shashka 1"* | Pair Leader<br>Pilot 1st Class<br>**Ivan Dushak**<br>*"Shashka 3"* |
|  |  |
| Wingman<br>Pilot 3rd Class<br>**German Burlakov**<br>*"Shashka 2"* | Wingman<br>Pilot 3rd Class<br>**Sergei Kostenko**<br>*"Shashka 4"* |

twenty-eight years old. Dushak had flown on MiG-23 fighters in the 1980s, before transitioning to the new MiG-29 in 1991. Kostenko had flown the MiG-29 ever since he had been a combat pilot.

Dushak had a lot of problems with Kostenko as his wingman. The younger pilot was much more aggressive than Dushak. The Air Force had been trying to encourage pilots to show more initiative and daring, but Dushak felt that Kostenko carried this a bit too far. Dushak had been trained in the old-fashioned way, which placed more stress on central control from the GCI (ground-controlled intercept) handlers. Kostenko made it no secret that he wanted to be assigned to "free-lance" squadrons, which were used for offensive fighter sweeps. He was very unhappy with the escort missions and air defense patrols that the squadron had been assigned since the outset of the war. Kostenko seemed to imply that Dushak was cowardly for not engaging in more aggressive maneuvers during the missions. Dushak had spoken to the regiment commander about Kostenko, but was left feeling that the commander had more sympathy for Kostenko than himself. "New equipment requires new approaches, Comrade Lieutenant Dushak," the commander had said. Times and tactics were changing with the arrival of the MiG-29.

The day before, they had been flying an air defense mission over Czechoslovakia when a NATO air strike was occurring to the north at the Mimon airfield. The GCI told them to remain patrolling their sector, that other regiments were covering Mimon. Kostenko had badgered Dushak to move the patrol circuit a bit farther north so that they might engage any stragglers coming into their sector. Realizing that this would complicate the patrol patterns of other flights, Dushak had told Kostenko to shut up and stay in formation with him. They had an uneventful flight. But wars are not won by uneventful flights.

Dushak could see that they had prepared the rest of the flight. Captain Vlasov's plane, with a blue "04" on the air intake, was at the head of the flight. Looking in his rearview mirrors, Dushak could see Kostenko's plane behind him. The flight was all set up in a nice little row. He was hoping they would get off the airfield fast before the damn NATO people figured out an operation was planned and bombed the hell out of the base again.

Milovice airfield had already been bombed at least seven times since the beginning of the war. The runway had been cratered badly, and ground crews had spent the whole night repairing the damage. The German Tornados that had struck the airfield early the previous morning had dropped several delayed-action bombs with the usual cratering load. They had to be meticulously removed before the runway was declared safe for operations. Fortunately, runway 2 had not been hit as badly, and would be used for this morning's operation. The NATO attacks had not put the runways permanently out of action, but they had raised havoc with the ground support. So much fueling and support equipment had been destroyed, and so many men killed, that they were lucky to get two sorties a day out of the field.

Dushak listened for instructions from the control tower. He could see the sixteen aircraft of the Su-24 squadron already taking off. The MiG-29s were faster and would catch up. The Su-22 countermeasures aircraft were already airborne and waiting to join the Su-24 formation. They were intended mainly to protect the bombers, and flew in pattern with the sleeker Su-24s. The control tower finally told Shashka flight and Molot flight to begin taxiing to the runway approach. The runway was wide enough to accommodate two fighters at once, so they would take off in pairs in quick succession. Dushak had made certain that the engine intakes were set to the protective position. The MiG-29 has large doors that cover the main intake while the plane is on the ground and during takeoff, because the aircraft is so low slung that it risks sucking small debris off the runway. A pebble or other bit of junk, slamming into a jet engine turbine blade at high speed, would ruin a very expensive engine, and could lead to the loss of the plane. The air is drawn in through special intakes on top of the fuselage. Dushak admired the practicality of this design. In his old squadron, he had seen a MiG-23 eat some junk on takeoff and auger in shortly afterward due to engine failure. It was a hell of a way for a well-trained pilot to die.

The runway approach widened, and Kostenko pulled his plane over to the right side of Dushak's MiG. Molot flight took off first, banking to the right to join the attack group. The first pair of Shashka flight took off, and Dushak almost lost sight of them in all the heat shimmer from their engine exhaust. Dushak and Kostenko trailed behind shortly after, the aircraft bouncing about badly due to all the air turbulence caused by the previous flights.

Takeoff was exhilarating, even in this crummy weather. The cloud cover was low, about 500 meters. The plan was to proceed to the Czech border over the clouds, at 2,000 meters, then drop back down on the deck to 500 meters when they reached Germany. The Shashka flight would stay a bit high and to the right, while Molot would be on the southern side and slightly to the rear. As his MiG entered the clouds, the sides of the cockpit became smeared by rain rushing over its surface. This lasted only moments, and the flight burst out of the clouds into a clear blue sky above. They had left the dreary world of Milovice airfield behind and were now in their own environment, skimming so close to the clouds that their aircraft cast shadows on them.

The Su-22 countermeasures planes stood out like a sore thumb. They were painted in the usual three-color camouflage scheme of tan, brown, and green. The Su-24s looked elegant as usual in a blue-gray finish with bright white underbellies. The MiGs were in dogfighter colors with a blend of two grays. But it occurred to Dushak that when they went back down on the deck, the Su-22s would blend in, and the MiGs would look out of place. Kostenko was trailing behind Dushak's aircraft about a hundred meters back, and off his right tail. He looked at the rearview mirrors and spotted him bouncing up and down a bit. The air seemed wonderfully clear, but there was a lot of turbulence at this altitude.

Dushak began looking down at the Syrena radar-warning panels. The MiG-29 has several panels and antennas at the front and rear of the aircraft to pick up hostile radar emissions. They are designed to warn if the aircraft is being illuminated by an enemy fighter's radar, or, worse yet, by the radar seeker in an AMRAAM missile, by little flashing lights that go off, and a loud buzz in the pilot's earphone. The problem with the radar warner is that it often goes off from stray reflected microwave energy. Over the battlefield, there are so many radar emitters that the Syrena is screaming every few minutes. It's like the story about the little boy who cried "wolf!" too often: After a while, the pilot begins to ignore it; some simply switch it off. The problem in all modern fighter planes is that there is just too much information for the pilot to sort out and absorb. One wag describes it as like trying to take a drink from a fire hydrant. At some point, it becomes vital to ignore all the spurious junk coming in over the electronic sensors and just concentrate on what is happening outside the airplane. It's stressful trying to decide when to ignore the black boxes and when to give them special attention.

Dushak noticed the lead flight beginning to dip into the clouds ahead of him. It was business time! At high combat speeds, it takes no time at all to cross two or three European borders. He nosed his plane back down into the clouds, and in a few moments he reentered the dingy world of ground-pounding missions. So far there had been little sign of enemy fighter aircraft. Allegedly, there was an An-74 airborne warning aircraft in this sector acting as an airborne command post. But he had not heard any transmissions from it to the flight. NATO had been jamming it and sending in aircraft to shoot it down whenever they had a chance. More likely it was sitting on the ground in need of electronics repair.

They dropped down to 500 meters. It was impossible to keep a steady altitude, since the terrain below was so mountainous. The leading flight of Sukhoi bombers was trying to follow terrain contours and keep the strike force down below the higher mountain ridges. Dushak didn't like this kind of flying. It was fine for the bomber boys, but it was a bit claustrophobic for fighter jocks. Enemy fighters could jump them from above, and they'd have a hell of a time maneuvering out of these chasms.

The flight passed to the south of Regensburg, not far from the scene of the current ground fighting. They gave the bridgehead area a wide berth, since there would be enough artillery shells in the air to make mincemeat out of their flight. The terrain shifted abruptly as they reached the Danube. It went from mountainous forest to flat pasture land in hardly ten kilometers. Now they were in the open, with no mountains to hide them from the prying eyes of radars.

At that moment the Syrena radar warning started going nuts. It was blinking from three quadrants at once, indicating several different illumination bands. Dushak bent his head down to look into the RP-29 radar display. There was no evidence of enemy fighters ahead. His radio crackled: "Shashka and Molot Flight, this is Kirka Leader. Do you have crows? Over." ("Crows" was the nickname for enemy fighters; the Soviet fighters called friendlies "falcons.") It was the strike leader in one of the Sukhoi bombers! He must be getting the warnings too. He didn't have an air intercept radar, however, so he didn't have as good a chance to pick up enemy fighters beyond visual range.

"This is Shashka Leader. No crows. Over."

Captain Vlasov hadn't spotted any enemy fighters yet either: "Molot Leader, no crows here. We've got strong signals south. I'm swinging my cone. Over." The Molot MiG flight was going to bank off to the south. The RP-29 radar has a limited cone of view forward. It was possible the enemy fighters were outside of this visual range.

"Crows to the south! Crows at 9 o'clock. Break!" Before he could determine what to do, Dushak saw a missile impact against one of the Sukhoi bombers on the left side of the flight. It hit near the cockpit and blew off the whole nose—a frightening sight. The plane began an uncontrollable tumble, spewing burning fuel behind it. There was no way the crew could have survived. A second missile impacted another Sukhoi near the tail. The plane shuddered, and a big chunk of tail went sailing; it smashed into a trailing Sukhoi, which dropped off to the left. The crew of the first Sukhoi punched out with their ejector seats.

"This is Kirka Leader. Molot Leader, engage the crows. Shashka, you stay with us." The flight of four MiG-29s on the left banked southward to engage the enemy fighters. They peeled off in a fast climb, afterburners glaring. In a moment, they were in the clouds. The Sukhois dropped even closer to the ground. They had terrain avoidance radars and so could follow the ground contours a lot closer than the MiGs.

Dushak hated this kind of flying. Being tied to a bunch of turkey bombers made the fighters vulnerable to ambush. Over the earphones, he could hear transmission from Molot flight. "Break into pairs. Molot Four, stay with your wingman. Watch it, Molot Three." The transmissions were confusing. It was not at all clear who was winning or losing, or even if Molot had found the enemy. Fortunately, they were only about sixty seconds from target. No SAMs so far.

The target was difficult to spot; the road was covered with trees on either side. They were running parallel to the highway. The German air defense crews began firing 20mm cannons at the flight, but they were not very accurate. The red fireballs spit into the air over the flight. The aircraft were traveling at well over 500 kilometers an hour, so the fireballs whizzed right by. Several miles ahead, there was an obvious change on the road. The Germans had built a detour around the new airfield. The airfield seemed to have few aircraft, but there was equipment nearby.

"Shashka Flight, this is Shashka Leader. Break to the right and clear the target area." They banked to the right and gained altitude, not wanting to run into any stray bombs. The Sukhois began dropping their bombs with parachute retarders.[1] Dushak caught a glimpse of the bombers as the munitions separated and snapped behind when their retarders blossomed. Shashka flight was almost into the cloud layer by the time the bombs hit.

The Syrena began going nuts again. The flight was in a three-g turn,

---

1. Bomb retarders are either small parachutes or air bags called "ballutes," which open up behind the bomb to slow it down. These are used when aircraft bomb from a low altitude. If bombs without retarders are used, the bomb continues to fly forward at almost the same speed as the aircraft. This leads to the possibility that the bomb will go off on the ground below, not far from the aircraft that dropped it, possibly damaging the aircraft.

and Dushak found it difficult to move his head to look into the radar. As they pulled out of the turn, they saw two aircraft go by at high speed, followed by at least three others. "Shashka Flight, tallyho. We have crows! Break and fight in pairs."

Where the hell are they? Dushak pulled his MiG up over the clouds. To hell with the SAMs. It was time to get a little altitude and figure out what was going on. Kostenko followed, narrowing the gap between himself and Dushak's MiG. As they broke through the cloud cover, they could see a dogfight already in progress. The problem was, who was who? They all looked like MiG-29s! There seemed to be about six aircraft—a pair chasing a lone aircraft to the south and another pair chasing a lone aircraft some distance away. They all had the distinctive twin tails of the MiG-29. To his horror, Dushak saw one of the aircraft from the southern pair fire a missile from its wing tip. MiG-29s don't have wing-tip missiles! The missile went up the tail pipe of the lone aircraft, ripping off the right engine and the right stabilizer. The pilot punched out safely.

"Shashka Three, you take that pair that just hit Molot. Me and German will take the other pair." Dushak nosed his aircraft down to bring it closer to the cloud base. It was possible the crows ahead hadn't yet spotted him and Kostenko. The range was less than five kilometers. The radar was tracking the target, as was the little Sh-1 infrared tracker. Dushak told Kostenko to switch his radar into dummy load position so it wouldn't emit and be picked up by the enemy's radar warning receivers. The Sh-1 IR tracker would continue to follow the enemy aircraft. It was purely passive, unlike radar. The Sh-1 picked up the infrared energy of the hot engine exhaust of the enemy planes, but gave off no signal, so it wouldn't warn the enemy. It worked reasonably well, except in clouds. Then the radar would automatically turn back on.

As they approached the enemy fighters, Dushak suddenly realized that they were F-18 Hornets. Or to be more precise, CF-18 Hornets of the Canadian Air Force. They flew out of a field near Bad Sollingen or somewhere farther west. He was surprised to see them this far east. He uncaged the seeker on the number 4 R-60 infrared missile. He got a tone on his headset, and launched. The strong infrared signature from the tail pipes made it an easy lock-on. It was hard to see the flight of the missile because its white trail was lost against the bright white of the cloud base below. Moments before the missile impacted, the Canadians suddenly pulled up and to the left. They had been spotted! The missile adjusted its flight path, but the turn happened so fast that it did not impact, but exploded a short distance to the right of the trailing aircraft. The enemy fighter shuddered slightly, and some debris came spewing back. But the missile caused no lethal damage. The R-60s were just too damn small.

The Canadians pulled up in a fast banking climb with the MiGs in fast pursuit. The turn was pushing six g's, much too much to permit a missile launch. The range had closed to two kilometers. The Canadians pulled a snap roll, aiming for the cloud bank. They seemed to be trying to break off the engagement by running away in the clouds. Dushak and Kostenko followed, but somewhat higher up. As they entered the cloud bank, the RP-29 radar switched from dummy load back to active, emitting to take over from the blinded IR tracker.[2] The radar picked up the Hornets below in the cloud bank, heading west, about two and a half kilometers ahead. Dushak and Kostenko both prepared a missile. Before they could fire, the Canadians made a sudden hard bank, in an attempt to turn on their attackers. Dushak decided to make a firing pass on the Canadians before they could turn squarely around to face them. But with the action taking place so near the cloud cover, he couldn't get the missile to signal lock-on. The high sun reflection off the clouds was confusing the missile seeker. He prepared to use the gun. The pipper in the HUD display tracked the target. Dushak slammed the controls around trying to get the pipper to line up in the center of the target dial. It started to do so and Dushak squeezed off a burst. Missed! The Canadians were still pulling around, Dushak trying to swing his aircraft into them. He failed to get a suitable position, and the Canadians swept under them at very high speed. Dushak instinctively pushed the throttle forward and pulled the stick back, trying to get altitude. Where would he find the Canadians?

Shashka 1 and Shashka 2 were not having as much luck. They approached the other three aircraft, assuming they were two CF-18 Hornets chasing a MiG-29. Unfortunately, it was three CF-18s. The Canadians got on the tail of the MiGs, and Shashka 1 made a fatal error. He tried to make a level turn at high speed to push enough g to prevent the Cana-

---

2. The RP-29 is a pulse-Doppler air intercept radar, called "Slot Back" by NATO. It is the first Soviet fighter radar to have the ability to see small targets located below the fighter. On earlier fighters, the radar return from the ground created so much clutter, it was impossible to see aircraft below. There have been allegations that the RP-29 is based on espionage successes in gaining data on the F-18 Hornet's APG-65 radar. An employee of Hughes, which manufactures the radar, sold a considerable amount of technical data to a Polish intelligence agent. This presumably was done on the behest of the Soviets.

dians from getting missile lock with their Sidewinders. He succeeded, but the MiG-29 lost energy in the turn faster than the CF-18. One of the Canadian pilots pulled in close enough to Vlasov's MiG to get off a lucky shot. It clipped the wing root. At such high g, the damage from the 20mm cannon burst was lethal. The main wing member was damaged, and the pressure shattered it. The plane spun out of control with a crumpled wing. Vlasov did not manage to escape. His wingman, German Burlakov, was only a pilot third class. Pitted against three enemy fighters, he stood little chance. He managed to evade the Canadian who had downed his flight leader by making a sudden upward climb. But the other two Canadians were following close on his heels and launched two Sidewinders. One impacted in the tail pipe. The plane held together for several seconds, allowing Burlakov to eject.

Shashka 3 and Shashka 4 now found themselves at about 1,500 meters in a clear blue sky. They headed in the direction of the Canadian aircraft, but their radars picked up no sign of them. There was no warning sign from the Syrena and they could see nothing overhead. The first sign they saw of the enemy fighters was the glare of their tracers as they came sizzling by from down and to the left. The Canadians had managed to maneuver into their blind spot below and behind them. The CF-18s roared overhead. Kostenko's MiG had taken a hit in the outer wing panel, and Dushak's had taken at least one hit in the left air intake. The damage was not serious. Dushak and Kostenko tried to follow the Canadians into the climb, but then noticed the other three Canadian CF-18s coming up towards them. It was time for a fast getaway.

The MiGs had an altitude advantage and Dushak planned to use it. He nosed his aircraft down and aimed directly at the approaching Canadian formation. He radioed to Kostenko to release IR flares from the tail dispenser to distract any heat-seeking missiles. The rate of closure between the two groups was tremendous, more than 1,100 kilometers an hour. Dushak aimed at the left-most Canadian fighter with his cannon, and as they reached the 1.5 kilometer range, he fired. Although his burst failed to impact, Kostenko got a solid hit on the right tail surface of one of the Canadian planes. Although Dushak and Kostenko were pulling away too fast to see it, the tail eventually ripped off, and the Canadian pilot punched out.

The two MiG-29s headed to the ground at breakneck speed trying to evade their more numerous tormentors. Luckily for them, the Canadians were at the outer limits of their fuel endurance and had begun to head home. Dushak and Kostenko were under the cloud bank, approaching Mach 1. Dushak could feel his heart pounding, and he was soaking wet from his own sweat. His mouth had that metallic tang you get from too much adrenaline. His first concern was that they had escaped safely. But as he calmed down, he began to worry about the Sukhoi squadron they were supposed to escort. What had happened to them? Well, at least his formation had pulled the Canadians off the bombers. But at some cost: They had lost six fighters. The Canadians also must have lost some aircraft, judging from the odd five-plane formation they had encountered.

Dushak checked the fuel status. The high-speed fighting and the heavy use of afterburner had really eaten up fuel. They were already over the Czech frontier, only ten minutes from base. Dushak was glad to be alive; Kostenko was itching for a little revenge. "Shashka Three, this is Shashka Four, we have pigeons at 3 o'clock low." "Pigeons" was slang for slow flying, vulnerable enemy aircraft. It was remarkable that Kostenko had seen them—a flight of four fighter-bombers, hugging the ground to their right. "Shashka Four, we have to be careful. Let's confirm they're pigeons and not falcons before hammering them. Leave off the radar. Let's hit them with missiles."

The MiG-29s gracefully banked down. The enemy aircraft hadn't seen them yet. As they got closer, it was obvious they were hostiles. The peculiar bent wing and chevron tail of the F-4 Phantom are unmistakable. Dushak radioed Kostenko and told him not to use the Khrom Nikel identification system. They were apparently West German aircraft, and they had spotted the MiGs coming down on them. The four aircraft broke up into two groups of two. They jettisoned their payloads and began to pull up, trying to get some altitude for maneuver. Dushak took the right pair. The range was 1,500 meters, almost close enough for the gun. After the experience earlier, Dushak decided to salvo two R-60 missiles to have a better certainty. He heard a good clear signal of missile lock-on and fired two missiles. Kostenko had reacted slightly faster, and three missiles were tracking the two Phantoms.

Dushak's two missiles struck the rear of one of the Phantoms, in two nearly simultaneous explosions. The blast severed the left stabilizer. The airplane began a peculiar bucking motion, obviously brought about by the loss of the tail surface. The plane began to go out of control and the crew ejected. Kostenko's single missile impacted in the rear of the aircraft's tail pipe. There was a sharp blast, followed by a spurt of debris. The second Phantom continued flying, although obviously damaged. Kostenko had closed on his target and began firing with the 30mm cannon. The Phantom was probably flying on a single engine, as its speed had dropped considerably. It was unable to maneuver, and Kostenko hammered its left wing with cannon fire. Large pieces of wing panel flew back, and Kostenko shifted the gun toward the fuselage with a quick jerk of the stick. Hydraulic fluid or fuel began to burn, and the crippled plane nosed over. The crew ejected safely before the plane splashed all over the pasture below in a fiery smear of light and smoke.

The other two Phantoms had headed back to Germany and neither Kostenko nor Dushak could see any evidence of them. With fuel beginning to run low, Dushak ordered the pair home, and they were soon over Milovice air base. As they approached the base, it was obvious that it had been subjected to another attack. There were plumes of smoke from the repair hangars, and a pall of dust over the runways. The tower was not responding to radio calls. The usual secondary airfield for the regiment was Kbely, outside Prague, but that strip had been smashed up badly the day before and was probably not operating yet. Dushak radioed Kostenko to follow him to the Klecany-Vodochody strip north of Prague. There was a chance it had escaped today's fighting.

As they approached the airstrip, they received word from the tower that the runway was indeed open, but was still pitted from earlier attacks. They were told to be careful and use their parachutes to slow the taxiing. Dushak headed down first. They weren't kidding when they said the runway was pitted! The strip of concrete was decorated with a complicated pattern of little earth mounds where the craters had been filled. As Dushak set down his MiG, he heard a loud bang. The right tire had burst on landing, largely as a result of unobserved battle damage. The plane began skidding uncontrollably. He could do nothing to stop the skid, and the plane headed for the side of the runway. It crashed into a small stand used for landing light array, then plowed into the soft field beyond. The nose gear collapsed, bringing the aircraft to a sudden, jarring halt.

Dushak's heart was pounding wildly. As a trained pilot, he knew he'd escaped this mishap, but his other senses had been preparing for the worst. Some ground crewmen in their usual black coveralls and black berets were running to the aircraft. It suddenly occurred to him that he had better exit the plane before a fire broke out. He sprang the release on the canopy and unfastened his harness. The ground crew was shouting to him, but with his helmet on, he couldn't hear. He removed it as he got out of the cockpit. "Comrade Pilot, get out quickly! Enemy bombers!"

Before he could crawl down from his awkwardly tilted perch, Dushak heard the deafening roar of fighter-bombers immediately overhead. A group of about six F-16s screamed over, dropping cluster bombs and Durandal airfield-cratering bombs. The concussion from a nearby Durandal heaved Dushak out of the cockpit, hurling him against the ground below. He had broken a collarbone, but was otherwise all right. He staggered to his feet and began running away from his wrecked aircraft toward a nearby clump of sandbags.

The airfield hangars took a heavy pounding. Kostenko's aircraft had been taxiing near the hangars, but Dushak could see no signs of his wingman or his aircraft. He hoped he had made it safely before the attack began. No more planes would be flying from this field today!

## Analysis

There is a cartoon, popular on many American army bases, showing a couple of Russian tankers in a cafe in Paris, their tank parked outside. Their feet are up on the table, and they are sitting back, having a mug of beer. One tanker says to the other: "Tell me, Ivan. Who did win the air war?"

The Soviet armed forces are not as preoccupied with tactical air forces as the U.S. Although the Soviets have a large tactical air arm, the so-called Frontal Aviation of the Air Forces, it receives a smaller chunk of the Soviet budget than is the case with the U.S. Air Force and U.S. Army. Some of this has to do with historical experiences, and some of it is due to budget and technology constraints.

The Soviet Air Force in World War II was heavily oriented toward supporting the ground troops. The aircraft produced in the greatest numbers during the war was the Il-2 Shturmovik ground attack aircraft. The Soviet Ground Forces did not put as much dependence on tactical air support as did U.S. forces, since air superiority over the battlefield was usually in question. Although the Soviet Air Force could attain local air superiority in 1943, the Germans still managed to contest control of the air right into 1944. In contrast, the U.S. ground forces enjoyed air superiority almost from the outset in the European theater. The Soviet Ground

Forces came to depend more heavily on artillery for fire support than on air forces. The Soviet Air Force accounted for less than 5 percent of the German tanks destroyed during the fighting on the Eastern Front. In contrast, Allied fighter-bombers accounted for nearly 20 percent of the tanks knocked out in the Normandy fighting, and almost 50 percent in Korea in 1950. More importantly, Allied tactical air forces had played a vital role in smashing German logistics and supply efforts.

From 1945 until the late 1960s, Soviet tactical air forces received little priority. In the late 1940s and early 1950s, the accent was on strategic air defense. Fighters like the MiG-15, MiG-17, MiG-19, and MiG-21 were configured primarily for the antibomber role. The Il-10, successor to the Il-2 Shturmovik, ended production in the late 1940s and was not succeeded by a dedicated ground attack plane for more than a decade. In the post-Stalin period, the Soviets began shifting to the view that the battlefield in Europe would go nuclear, and so dedicated conventional attack aircraft would be of questionable value.

When the Soviets finally began to pay more attention to ground attack, they introduced a thinly rehashed fighter design, the Sukhoi Su-7, for this role. The Sukhoi Su-7B was viewed as a "frontal fighter" capable of being used as either a fighter or a light bomber. It was mediocre in either role. But the Soviets noted the critical role of air power in the 1967 Mideast war, in Vietnam, and in the 1973 Yom Kippur war. In the late 1960s, a major program to rejuvenate Soviet Frontal Aviation began. A new generation of MiG fighters, the MiG-23/27, was developed clearly for the tactical air role. The Su-7 was modernized into the more successful Su-17/20/22 family. And the Soviets began deploying attack helicopters in their Air Force for close air support.

Soviet tactical aircraft design has been heavily influenced by trends in the West. The Su-7 and the Su-17/22 Fitters were inspired by American strike fighters like the F-105, even though technically they have little in common. The MiG-23/27 Flogger emulated the highly successful F-4 Phantom. Like the Phantom, the Flogger was an attempt to develop a single aircraft capable of being employed in the fighter and fighter-bomber role. The Su-24 Fencer was a clear counterpart to the F-111/FB-111. This highly capable strike aircraft represents the high-technology end of tactical air support. It is a deep penetration aircraft, with an elaborate and sophisticated navigation system. On the lower end of the technology spectrum, the new Su-25 Frogfoot is a counterpart of the U.S. A-10 ground attack aircraft.

## The MiG-29 Fulcrum

The MiG-29 Fulcrum, which is the centerpiece of this fictional scenario, is a Soviet attempt to come to grips with the new generation of American fighter aircraft. The MiG-29 was developed in the early 1970s as a counterpart to the F-16 and F-18. In terms of size, it is closer to the F-18, and shares a very similar configuration. The Soviets also developed a counterpart to the larger American F-15 Eagle in the form of the Su-27 Flanker.

A bit more is known about the MiG-29 Fulcrum than many other new Soviet combat aircraft as a result of glasnost. In 1987, the Soviets displayed the MiG-29 at a Finnish air base, and in 1988, they took the unprecedented step of displaying it at the biannual Farnborough Air Show in England. This gave Western aircraft designers and pilots a chance to see it firsthand. While Western pilots were not allowed to fly it (at least as yet), they were able to get some sense of its capabilities.

The aerobatic performance of the MiG at the show was spectacular. Although some of the attraction was due to its novelty, its performance did put it in the same class as the F-16 or F-18. Instantaneous and sustained turn rates appeared to be comparable to Western fighters, but not necessarily any better. What made the performance especially remarkable was the nature of its design. Although it seems to offer performance approaching the best of Western fighters, the technology in many respects is of an earlier generation. The Soviet aircraft designers have shown an intriguing ability to push older technologies to the limit in order to extract performances and capabilities that Western designers obtain through the use of new technology.

One of the big surprises was that the MiG-29 does not use fly-by-wire flight controls. Fly by wire was pioneered on the F-16, and represents an important advance in this area. In the past, flight controls were directly linked to the pilot's controls. The pilot moved the stick or rudder pedals, and the control surface moved. In a fly-by-wire aircraft, the controls are linked to a flight computer and flight sensors. The computer takes the movement of the stick or pedals and then subtly manipulates one or more control surfaces to get the desired result by consulting, almost instantaneously, with the flight sensors. Such a system permits more precise control and makes the aircraft simpler to fly in a combat environment, where extensive maneuvering is necessary. In addition, it permits the designer to select aircraft configurations that are more maneuverable. Aircraft that are inherently stable are not particularly maneuverable, even though they are easy to control. Aircraft that border on aerodynamic instability can be very maneuverable. Such designs have not been used in the past, since they would be too taxing on the pilot. But with fly by wire, the computer keeps the control surfaces moving to ensure stability and, when hard maneuvering is required, it takes advantage of the aerodynamic instability of the design and provides complex changes in the flight control surfaces that a human could not manage.

The Soviet designers, recognizing the limited possibilities in their industry for mass producing the high-tech items needed for fly by wire, developed a more conventional flight control package and aircraft design, which permits maneuverability approaching that of Western fighters. The designer in charge of the MiG-29 project, Mikhail Valdenberg, stated that computers were used only where absolutely indispensable. Understood in the context of traditional Soviet defensive rationalizations, this means that the Soviet aviation industry could not produce sufficient flight computers to equip the MiG-29 with more sophisticated controls. The MiG-29 does employ a stability augmentation system, rate dampers, and automatic leading edge devices and flaps, which are only several steps away from true fly-by-wire controls.

How close the MiG-29 comes to Western fighter performance is not clear, and probably won't be until pilots who have flown the F-16 or F-18 get a chance to fly the MiG-29. What is clear is that the MiG-29 is more demanding of its pilots than comparable Western fighters. Fly-by-wire controls free the pilot's attention from many aspects of flight control; the plane cannot be maneuvered in a way that would lose stability. This means the F-16 or F-18 pilot can push the plane to its very limits without fear of losing control. The Soviet pilot, on the other hand, must be extremely careful to avoid maneuvers that stray from controlled flight regimes or the angle-of-attack limits. To do so would risk losing control of the aircraft. During cruising this is no problem. It becomes tricky when the fighter is engaged in maneuvering combat, where he can least afford to divert his attention. This is why the angle-of-attack indicator is red-lined at a modest 25 degrees, which places some limits on maneuvering. The matter of flight controls is so serious that in the MiG-29 cockpit the alpha/load indicator has a more prominent position than even the Syrena radar-warning receiver.

### The Man-Machine Interface

In view of its sizzling performance, other aspects of the MiG-29 design proved to be a bit surprising. The cockpit of the Fulcrum is a 1960s configuration with hints of 1970s technology. The instrumentation resembles that of the F-4 Phantom generation. The dials and instruments are straightforward analog systems. There are none of the digital displays or multifunction displays found on later Western fighters. The radar display is small and is covered by a viewing hood, which suggests that the Soviets have not yet managed to field sunlight-readable displays. This is awkward for the pilot, since he must bend forward to read the radar display. This may seem like a frill, but the interface between the man and the machine is proving to be increasingly important. Pilots today face a data overload. They not only have to fly the plane, they have to keep track of whether enemy radars are searching for them, whether someone is interrogating them with an IFF system, and whether all the complicated electronics systems are functioning properly. In peacetime flying, this can be managed. But in the confusion and stress of modern air war, this data overload can have fatal consequences. Ignore the radar warning system at the critical moment, and seconds later a missile will impact against your aircraft. Advanced displays are not gold-plating. They are an attempt to simplify the pilot's tasks by making the flow of data more coherent and easier to understand. Western fighters have an advantage in this regard.

The MiG-29 is typical of contemporary Soviet weapons design that accents machine performance but often takes shortcuts in the interface between man and machine. Another example: the pilot's seat is nearly vertical, while Western designs use an angled seat, which allows the pilot to better cope with high-g (gravitational) forces during combat maneuvering. The MiG-29 is stressed for nine g's, but its pilots are not. Although pilots can be trained in straining maneuvers to help them cope with high-g forces, their endurance can be enhanced by design features such as inclined seats. A pilot in an inclined seat will be more willing to push his aircraft into hard (and personally painful) eight-g and nine-g turns, knowing that he will not black out.

Other aspects of the design show that the Soviets have paid less attention to detail than the Western designers. The MiG-29 canopy configuration does not permit the pilot to "check his six," meaning he cannot swing his head around to check the six o'clock position directly behind him. On the early MiG-29s, there was a radio strip antenna in the upper canopy that obstructed upward vision. Designs like the F-15, F-16, and F-18 were purposely built to allow the pilot to see behind him and in all other directions with a minimum of hindrance. The Soviets originally fitted the MiG-29 with crude automobile-style rearview mirrors to give the pilot some rear vision. On the newer production MiG-29s like the one at Farnborough, they have adopted Western-style curved mirrors, which reduce obstruction. But mirrors are not as beneficial as good cockpit design to give the pilot a clear picture of the environment behind him. Also, the helmet for the MiG-29 pilot is outdated compared to Western designs and is about twice as heavy. The trend has been toward lighter and more comfortable helmets, to encourage pilots to keep their heads moving, surveying the sky around them. The Soviet helmet is heavy due to the padding needed to protect the pilot against the high levels of cockpit noise—it seems no attention has been paid to reducing the helmet's size and weight. Combined with the restricted space under the canopy, the helmet inhibits the pilot from moving his head rapidly, and often, to check for hostile aircraft.

## Situational Awareness

The buzzword in fighter combat these days is "situational awareness." It is fighter jock talk for the special skill needed to prevail in the modern dogfight. Situational awareness means knowing where you and your plane are, where the enemy planes are, and the status of your fuels and weapons. More than that, it implies an intellectual or instinctive ability to understand the dynamics of fighter combat. It is somewhat comparable to the instincts of a great chess player, who can see several moves ahead and who knows the likely responses an opponent will make to his own moves. Likewise, situational awareness implies a sharp foresight into how an enemy will respond to a pilot's actions. At the heart of this concept is a clear picture of the existing environment—where the enemy is, what he is doing. Good aircraft design cannot give the pilot situational awareness, but it can make it easier for a pilot to better hone his abilities. Soviet flight instrumentation and cockpit design inhibit situational awareness compared to Western designs.

Another feature of the MiG-29 design that proves rather surprising is the nature of the surface finish on the aircraft. The fuselage design is elegant and smooth, especially in the forward areas where it is most critical. Many control surfaces are made of advanced honeycombed or composite materials. But toward the rear surfaces, the finish is often very rough. There are exposed rivet heads where Western aircraft would use flush fasteners. On close inspection, it can be observed that the front screws that hold inspection panels in place have unusual blue lines painted across them. The explanation for this is indicative of continuing Soviet problems in keeping high-tech equipment in service: the blue lines are used to ensure that ground crews properly reattach the panels to the aircraft. If the blue line on the screw head does not match the edges of the blue line on the panel, they are not tight enough. Western fighters avoid the problem by using specialized fasteners. The Soviets use an older fastener technology and, combined with doubts about the skills and experience of their ground crews, it can lead to some concern about aircraft maintenance.

Overall, the impression created by the MiG-29 induces respect for what the designers were able to accomplish using such mediocre technology. The MiG-29 is testimony to Soviet design ingenuity, which has long been a trademark of Soviet aircraft design. The MiG bureau has turned out a remarkable aircraft considering the raw material they have used. In World War II, Soviet fighter designers pushed plywood fuselage construction to the outer limits, approaching the design qualities of German fighters using aluminum. But the MiG-29 design also highlights the fact that the Soviets are still behind in many aspects of aerospace technology. There appear to be continuing bottlenecks in the mass production of advanced electronics, and the fighter designers have adopted less desirable configurations knowing that better components would not be available.

## Soviet Dogfighting Missiles

Details of the MiG-29's weapons are less well known. The MiG-29 is usually armed with four R-60 missiles, better known by their NATO code names as AA-8 Aphids, and two R-72 (AA-10 Alamo) missiles. The R-60s are a new infrared guided missile, replacing the old R-3S (AA-2 Atoll). The R-60s are not as capable as current models of the Sidewinder missile, such as the AIM-9L or AIM-9M. Their seekers are not as sensitive, they do not have as much range, and their warheads are a bit suspect. As suggested in the fictional scenario, the Soviets may have to launch two at a time to ensure a kill. A recent incident in southern Africa confirms the problems with these missiles. A small British Aerospace-125 business jet carrying the president of Botswana was accidentally attacked by an

Angolan MiG-21, which fired two R-60s. One missile struck the right engine pod, blowing it off. However, the damage was not sufficient to cripple the aircraft, which landed safely.

Details of the newer R-72 are lacking. The missile comes in both radar-guided and infrared-guided versions. It is more comparable to the American AIM-7 Sparrow and offers longer range (and a bigger warhead) than the R-60. The problem with the R-72 and other semiactive radar-guided missiles, is that the aircraft must continue to illuminate the target with its radar until the missile impacts. This is difficult to do in high-speed dogfights, as a wildly jinking enemy aircraft can break radar lock if it can escape the limited cone of the radar's emissions.

Radar missiles are not really intended for dogfighting; they are intended for long-range engagements beyond visual range. They favor aircraft with big, powerful radars that can locate an enemy aircraft before they themselves are detected. In the fictional scenario, the Canadian CF-18 Hornets discover the attacking Soviet flight first and engage them with Sparrow missiles. The Soviets do not see the Canadians, since the Canadians are attacking off axis, from the side where the Soviet's radar cannot see them. The MiG-29's radar warning receivers (RWR) do pick up signals. But RWRs are notoriously fickle and a regular source of false alarms.

The new generation of radar-guided missiles, like the U.S. Air Force's AMRAAM, will mark a revolution in fighter weapons. The AMRAAM contains its own little radar in the nose. The fighter no longer has to continue to use its radar to guide the missile to its target. This will enable small fighters, like the F-16, to fire multiple radar-guided missiles at different targets nearly simultaneously. The AMRAAM represents a growing trend to extend the range of dogfights and the lethal envelope of the fighter plane.

By the time of the Vietnam War, most aviators were expecting that dogfights would take place primarily with missiles. However, the early generation Sidewinders and Sparrows were fickle. Their electronics took a beating, and they often worked poorly as a result. Missiles accounted for the majority of air-to-air kills in the Vietnam fighting, but they were expended at far higher rates than expected. As a result, there was a backlash against all-missile armament, and renewed interest in air combat maneuvering with a gun. The best evidence of the revival of classic dogfighting is the establishment of special air combat maneuver courses such as the well-known "Top Gun" program.

In spite of the backlash against missiles due to the Vietnam experience, newer generations of missiles have overcome many of the reliability problems. During the Falklands War, British Harriers shot down eighteen Argentinian fighters, using twenty-seven AIM-9L Sidewinder missiles. Israeli F-16s during the 1982 Lebanon war shot down thirty-five Syrian fighters with forty-seven AIM-9L or AIM-9P missiles, and five more with 20mm guns. These recent conflicts suggest that missiles will remain the primary weapon in air-to-air combat, although the gun will remain an important supplement. New weapons like AMRAAM will continue to extend the range of dogfights. The majority of dogfights in past wars have been within visual range. The availability of weapons like AMRAAM will increase the percentage of engagements that occur beyond visual range.

## The Soviet Pilot

Besides the aircraft and missiles, the other key ingredient in fighter combat is the pilot. Indeed, a good many pilots would argue that the pilot is *the* key ingredient in dogfighting. How do Soviet pilots stack up against NATO pilots? This question is nearly impossible to answer due to the lack of information and lack of evidence of Soviet pilots in actions.

NATO judgment of Soviet piloting skill has been influenced by Soviet performance in World War II and, indirectly, by the performance of Soviet-trained pilots in the Mideast and Asia. Soviet pilots in World War II, on average, were not very good. German pilots were so contemptuous of Soviet pilots that high scores won by German aces on the Eastern Front were considered equal to scores only a fraction as large won fighting against the better trained British or American pilots in Western Europe or the North African campaign. And Soviet-trained pilots in Korea and the Mideast have not done well. The embarrassing performance of the Syrians in Lebanon in 1982, when they lost more than seventy aircraft to the Israelis without extracting a single loss from their opponents, rebounded on the Soviets, staining them with the taint of Syrian ineptitude. Western views of Soviet pilot quality are further soured by negative judgments about Soviet tactics. The Soviets have favored ground control of fighters, particularly when they are used in an air defense role. NATO fighter tactics place greater emphasis on individual pilot initiative.

This combination of historical factors and recent experience with Soviet-trained pilots has created many myths about contemporary Soviet pilots. Here are some of them: Soviet wingmen are helpless without their leader. Soviet pilots are good at interception, but they are totally dependent on ground control and do not train for maneuvering engagements. Soviet training is so rigid that pilots will not display initiative in combat.

The myths about Soviet pilots contain a grain of truth, but miss several key points. Some pilots, especially Soviet PVO air defense pilots and foreign pilots trained by the PVO (like the North Vietnamese), tend to place the accent on interception and ground control. This is natural, since their main role is strategic bomber interception, not tactical fighter combat. It is often forgotten that there are two Soviet Air Forces, the PVO, which controls air defense missiles and air defense interceptor fighters, and the VVS (Air Force), which controls tactical fighters (such as the MiG-29) as part of their Frontal Aviation branch.

Soviet writing in their air force magazines suggests that they have appreciated many of the shortcomings attributed to them by NATO. They mouth all the right words about requiring greater pilot initiative, and the need for more attention to "free-lance" or "free-hunt" offensive fighter sweeps. It is not clear if Soviet tactical training is yet up to the task of preparing Soviet pilots for these roles. As in other branches of the armed forces, Soviet aviation training leans toward the staged and the stereotyped. Missions, even training missions, are meticulously planned without much accent on dynamic tactical environments and the unexpected. Soviet air combat maneuver training does not appear to be comparable to American Top Gun-style training. A study prepared by a fighter pilot at General Dynamics suggests that Soviet pilots display good basic airmanship, but are not as well trained as American pilots in adapting to the changing environment in tactical situations.

The Soviets have often tried to overcome qualitative disadvantages in men and machines with greater numbers. This is true of aircraft as well. In the NATO environment, the Soviets are likely to have some numerical superiority in fighters and tactical aircraft over NATO. But these advantages are not as great as in many areas of ground equipment. It is not as easy to translate numerical superiority in aircraft into superior combat power; the key link would be the ability to sustain air operations. Maintenance is absolutely critical. In Korea, the Chinese and Korean air forces had marked superiority in overall numbers. But American fighters displayed sustained combat power because they were well maintained and could be sent on missions more often than their adversaries.

The Soviets appear to have shortcomings in sustaining air operations. Their ground maintenance force suffers the endemic problems brought about by a reliance on a conscript force without an adequate middle level of professional, nonofficer technical personnel. Maintenance is slow because the officers must closely supervise the handling performed on the aircraft. This problem may be addressed in new reforms, but it is likely to linger well into the 1990s.

Like the Soviet Union itself, the Soviet Air Force is a curious blend. The most advanced technology coexists with outdated technology, advanced tactical thinking with outdated training. The capabilities of the Soviet Air Force can be exaggerated by concentrating on one aspect, or underestimated by concentrating on the other. Soviet pilots are well trained and courageous; their planes among the world's best. But in the arena of air combat, a little bit better training and a little bit better technology often make the critical difference between victory and defeat.

# CHAPTER 8

## Chemical Warfare:
## Gas Attack at Geiselhoring

1700, 8 October, Geiselhoring, FRG

Senior Lieutenant Pyotr Chazov surveyed the field where his motor rifle company was bedding down for the night. His troops had done a good job concealing their armored vehicles along the edge of a neat Bavarian pine forest. The sun was setting, and you could hardly see the silhouettes of their BMP armored vehicles against the dark pines. His troops weren't as sharp as the platoon he had had under him in the Panshir Valley fighting in Afghanistan back in 1988. But they had become remarkably battle hardened in only a week of war. They had overrun a German mechanized infantry unit during the forest fighting on the third day, which had given them a lot of needed confidence. Some of them were even becoming a bit cocky. His company had been pretty lucky so far — no air attacks. Still, he hollered over to Sergeant Aksai to get his two Igla[1] antiaircraft missile teams into position in case any NATO attack helicopters did show up.

Chazov's company had seen hard fighting. They had lost a third of their vehicles during the forest fighting along the Czechoslovak border. Two BMPs were blown up near the border by mines, and a third was lost in an ambush to a German Milan antitank missile. They had crossed the Danube two days before without too much trouble, and had been assigned

---

1. *Igla*, meaning "needle" in Russian, is the name for a small, man-portable antiaircraft missile. It is fired from a tube, like a bazooka, and homes in on the heat of an airplane's or helicopter's exhaust. NATO calls the Igla the SA-14 Gremlin. The most comparable NATO weapon is the American Stinger missile.

to the western flank of the Straubing bridgehead. The neighboring BMP company under Lieutenant Dudkov had been roughed up far worse. Earlier in the day, they had been ambushed by a German Leopard 2 tank unit, losing most of their vehicles. The remnants of Dudkov's company were put under Chazov's command. This brought it back up to its normal full strength of ten BMP armored infantry vehicles.

His company had started the war with a full complement of the newer BMP-2 Yozh. The Yozh was well armed, but it had real limits when faced with enemy tanks. Chazov hoped that if he ever ran into Leopards he would have some T-80 tanks to help. His regiment had a single tank battalion with T-80s to support the three BMP battalions.

Chazov's 3d Platoon was equipped with older BMP-1M Korshun-Ms[2] from Dudkov's company. The old Korshun-Ms had a low-pressure gun in the turret instead of the 30mm woodpecker autocannon on the Yozh. It was derisively called a "sparrow shooter" by the troops. It was slow to fire, maybe three rounds a minute if everything worked right. But the autoloader in the turret was finicky, and if the gunner wasn't careful, it would catch on this clothing and mash him up against the gun breech. The Korshun's gun fired a little PG-9 rocket-powered grenade, much like the RPG-7 antitank rocket launcher, which was supposed to be able to destroy a tank. But NATO tanks now had reactive armor and Chobham armor, so it didn't work worth a damn. Its warhead just wasn't big enough to get through the new armors. To give the old BMP-1 some tank-killing power, a Fagot[3] missile launcher had been lashed on the roof. This was a smaller cousin of the Konkurs missile on the BMP-2. The Konkurs missile could be fired from within the turret, however; with the Fagot, the gunner had to open up his hatch and aim the missile from outside. Needless to say, the old Korshun-Ms weren't too handy when facing tanks.

Dudkov's company had found this out the hard way earlier in the day. His company was moving through some hilly pastures outside the village of Mitterharthausen in support of the day's regimental attack. They were separated from the regiment's T-80 tank battalion by a small woods on

2. *Korshun* is the Russian word for "kite," a type of bird.
3. *Fagot* is the Russian word for "bassoon," a musical instrument. The Fagot is better known by its NATO code name, the AT-4 Spiral. It has a range of about 2,000 meters and is wire guided. It is comparable to the Franco-German Milan; however, the later-model Milan missiles, like the Milan 3, have much better performance.

their right flank. Pyotr Chazov's company was to their left behind some low hills. Before Dudkov had even reached his objective, about four German Leopard 2 tanks came spewing out of the woods, going full tilt. It was a fearsome sight. The Leopards could move at nearly forty miles an hour, even on rough ground. And they could fire on the move. Dudkov's old BMP-1s had to stop to fire. It was a completely unequal contest. Dudkov's BMPs outnumbered the tanks two to one, but the tanks could open fire from 2,000 meters, far outside the range of the BMP's little "sparrow shooter." At that range, only the Fagot missile could be used. Two BMPs from the 1st Platoon stopped to fire their Fagots. They managed to launch them all right, but the Fagot missile takes nearly fifteen seconds to travel 2,000 meters. The Leopard 2 crews were well trained and they saw the white puff of smoke when the Fagots were launched. They swung their boxy turrets at the two offending Korshuns and fired. The 120mm gun projectiles took only two seconds to travel 2,000 meters, long before the Fagot missiles arrived. The high-explosive rounds hit the Korshuns squarely on the sides. The explosions blew the turrets high in the air and ignited the ammunition and fuel. The Korshuns went up in fireballs. None of the eleven crew in either vehicle survived.

The remaining eight Korshuns tried to hide behind small hills until the German Leopards were close enough to be in range of their sparrow shooters. Dudkov knew he was supposed to keep radio silence before the attack and use flag signals. In the confusion, he violated orders and radioed the surviving vehicles to dismount their infantry. Only one platoon seemed to hear the orders. The Leopards closed to about 500 meters and the Korshuns started firing. Two of the Leopards were hit almost immediately. There was a big flash on the front of their turrets and for a moment, it seemed like they might have been stopped. But then their turrets started traversing, looking for new victims. The lousy little PG-9 rounds had only scorched their laminate armor. The Leopards waded into the Korshuns, firing the whole time. Each time the 120mm gun fired, the ground shook. The tanks were engulfed in a cloud of flash and dust, kicked up by the guns' blasts. But the Leopards had an uncanny ability to see through all this smoke and debris, and still were able to hit the Korshuns with precision. It was a massacre. One after another, five more Korshuns were blown to bits.

Dudkov had managed to reach the regimental tank battalion on radio moments before his own Korshun was gutted. The tank battalion commander, Major Gaipov, responded by sending a platoon of three T-80s to rescue Dudkov's company. They surprised the Leopards and managed to hit two of them in the rear. The surviving infantry watched with glee as two Leopards were left smashed and burning. The other two turned away from the remaining Korshuns and began a losing battle with the Soviet tanks.

Chazov heard Dudkov's radio calls. He sounded frantic. Moments later, he saw the smudges of oily fires over the rise to his right. He continued forward with his company, but a few minutes later his battalion commander, Major Barchuk, radioed him to halt his attack. The ambush had badly disrupted the attack, and one of the other companies had taken stiff losses as well. He was to take his company back to the site of Dudkov's ambush and pick up the survivors.

Chazov left one platoon facing toward the German positions in Geiselhoring and led the other three vehicles back to Dudkov's company. It was easy enough to find the site of the ambush from the billowing plumes of sooty black smoke. Chazov raised Senior Sergeant Vasilev on his radio. Vasilev, the highest ranking survivor from Dudkov's company, was badly shaken up and incoherent. Chazov realized that Vasilev was incapable of leading the survivors. He ordered one of his sergeants to take over command of the remnants of the unit. A couple minutes later, the three surviving Korshuns came up the hill with several soldiers clinging to the rear deck of each. The Korshun was too cramped inside to carry anybody except its own crew. Survivors from the knocked-out vehicles had to be carried on the outside.

The attack on Geiselhoring on 7 October had been a failure. The attack had continued, minus Barchuk's battalion on the left flank. The two remaining BMP battalions, supported by some of the tanks, didn't have the strength to overcome the well-entrenched German defenders. Chazov's company was ordered to take up night defensive positions near a woods five kilometers from Geiselhoring. He was told over the regimental radio net to expect orders at about 1900.

Chazov had his hands full. His company was well positioned for the night, but the morale of the men hadn't been helped by the day's fighting. His own two platoons were in good enough spirits, but the remnants of Dudkov's company were another matter. Chazov called the company zampolit, Junior Lieutenant Sudro, to his vehicles and ordered him to take over the battered Korshun company. Because one of Dudkov's companies had managed to dismount before their BMPs were destroyed, there were more troops in the company than spaces in the BMPs. Sudro was ordered to sort through the survivors and cull out those who were most obviously shell-shocked. Chazov would worry about them later. He didn't expect the Germans to launch a night counterattack, but he had to keep his men on their toes for such an eventuality. At about 1800, a villiys came down to pick him up for a regimental officers' meeting. He left Lieutenant Sudro in charge.

In the jeep was the commander of the 1st Motor Rifle Battalion, Major Barchuk, and the other surviving company commander, Captain Glebov. Glebov's company had lost four vehicles in the afternoon fighting, mostly to missiles. That left the whole battalion at only half strength, with Chazov's company in the best shape. Major Barchuk said that he expected the attack to be repeated the next morning.

When the officers from Barchuk's battalion arrived at the regimental command post, they saw the usual faces, with a few conspicuous absences. The battalion had suffered heavy losses in the past few days of fighting. The men looked exhausted. They had little chance to bathe or shave, and looked like they could care less. Few had gotten more than a few hours of sleep each night for the past week. There were three officers Chazov didn't recognize. They stuck out due to their clean uniforms. He noticed that one was wearing the branch-of-service collar insignia of the Chemical Warfare Forces. After a bit of milling about, the regimental commander, Colonel Rusak, ordered the men to sit down and he proceeded with his briefing.

"Comrade officers. As you are well aware, the attack against Geiselhoring was not successful. It is the most essential road junction in our divisional sector. The divisional commander is insistent that we take that village by tomorrow afternoon, at all costs. We cannot expect any rein-

# 15th Komorovskiy Motor Rifle Regiment

| Regimental Commander<br>Col. Ye. A. Rusak | | | |
|---|---|---|---|

| 1st Motor Rifle<br>Battalion<br>Maj. Barchuk | 2nd Motor Rifle<br>Battalion<br>Maj. Charnov | 3rd Motor Rifle<br>Battalion<br>Maj. Karskly | 1st Tank<br>Battalion<br>Maj. Galpov |
|---|---|---|---|
| 1st Co: Lt. Chazov<br>2nd Co: Lt. Dudkov<br>3rd Co: Capt. Glebov | | | |

forcements. We are not the only ones who have had problems on this front. Several of our neighboring divisions have not kept their schedules either. Our artillery preparations have not been as effective as we expected."

There was a murmur of assent from the assembled officers. The artillery preparation against Geiselhoring had been piss poor. It did little more than bounce around the rubble.

"The front commander has ordered the use of chemical weapons to soften up the resistance to our advance."

At the mention of chemical weapons, the officers began to fidget. Rusak then turned to the visiting officers. "Captain Kasparov from division headquarters will continue this briefing."

Kasparov went up to a covered map board and lifted off its canvas cover. It was the normal 1:50,000 scale map of the local area. It was covered with the usual bewildering assortment of colored pencil symbols. Kasparov began.

"Comrade officers. Our artillery preparations have not proven effective in routing out the German troops in Geiselhoring. The Germans are well entrenched in the rubble. We believe they will receive reinforcements tonight. There are about three companies of infantry, supported by about ten Milan antitank missile launchers."

Ten entrenched launchers. Great! Chazov figured that meant two or three in his sector, or one for every three BMPs – not good odds for his men.

"We are planning a gas attack at 0515, followed by your attack at 0530. We will be using Agent AC. Do you remember what AC is?" Kasparov looked around the room. From the sheepish looks he encountered, he knew the answer. "Agent AC is a hydrogen cyanide gas, a nonpersistent blood agent. You inhale it, you die. Two good whiffs in a heavy concentration and you'll immediately become unconscious. You'll be dead in three to five minutes. It acts through the lungs and the bloodstream, not through the skin. So all your troops need to wear is their protective masks, not their slime suits."

There was a sigh of relief among the officers. The slime suits, officially designated "OP-1 chemical protective suits," were a real horror to wear. The chemical masks weren't so bad. At almost the same instant, there was a collective reflex by the officers to check their gas masks. Several of the officers patted the bag on their left thigh. But most of the officers realized they had left their gas mask bags behind in their vehicles. Lousy gas discipline, they thought. Most of the officers began to worry that their men might have lost or thrown away their chemical gear.

The Soviets have long favored multiple rocket launchers to supplement conventional artillery. The most common type now in service is the BM-21 Grad (Hail), which consists of a 40-tube launcher for 122mm rockets, mounted on a Ural 375 heavy truck. The BM-21 can deliver a massive salvo of high explosives and metal in a single blast, but such rockets are not as accurate as conventional artillery.

The MiG-29 Fulcrum is a sophisticated all-weather fighter comparable to the best NATO aircraft. It is similar in size to the US Navy's F-18 Hornet fighter, and larger than the US Air Force's F-16. Although the original versions did not use fly-by-wire flight controls, the MiG-29 is still a remarkably responsive and maneuverable aircraft in the dogfight arena. Steven Zaloga.

*A pilot's eye view of the MiG-29's cockpit. Toward the upper center of the photo is the heads-up-display, which provides the basic flight data to the pilot during combat maneuvering. To the upper left is the small shielded screen for the radar. In general, the cockpit features are less sophisticated than those on contemporary American fighters, and place greater demands on the Soviet pilot. USAF.*

*The workhorse of Soviet ground attack units has been the Su-17/Su-22 Fitter family of fighter bombers. These supersonic aircraft are used for close-support missions, while the more sophisticated Su-24 Fencer is reserved for deep attack missions.*

*The Soviet OP-1 chemical protective suit is sometimes nicknamed the "slime suit" due to its texture when decontaminated with special soaps. This type of non-permeable suit can protect the wearer from most chemical weapons, but can itself become dangerous in hot weather; because the soldier's sweat cannot properly evaporate, heat prostration can result.* Beryl Barnett.

*The Su-25K Grach, known in NATO as the Frogfoot, is a new ground attack aircraft. It first saw service in Afghanistan in 1980–81. Comparable to the American A-10 Warthog, the Su-25K is designed to carry a wide variety of bombs and guided missiles, and its pilot is protected in an armored cockpit.* Steven Zaloga.

Kasparov continued: "I said that you didn't have to wear the OP-1 suits. But you had damn well better have them ready. If we use gas, NATO may use gas. You should make certain to refresh your memory about gas procedures. Are there any questions so far?"

Captain Savin from the 2d Motor Rifle Battalion started with a question that was on everyone's mind: "What if our troops have lost their chemical defense gear?"

Chazov remembered seeing a number of chemical defense bags left behind at one of the other battalions' bivouac sites two nights before. He had cautioned his own platoon leaders about this, but he wasn't certain how much good it had done.

Chemical defense gear is a prominent part of a Soviet soldier's kit. The Soviet infantryman has far less equipment than the average NATO soldier: no sleeping bag, a very small rucksack, and only one cartridge belt. He is issued a chemical defense mask in a canvas bag to be worn over his left hip. The ammunition pouch is worn on the right hip. The OP-1 chemical defense suit is rolled up and carried on his back under the rucksack. These are a real nuisance when riding and fighting in a BMP. The interior of the vehicle is so cramped that the soldier can't leave his rucksack or slime suit on his back. And there's no space on the floor. There's a bit of space behind, on a ledge formed by the fuel tank and the back of the two rows of seats. But this is supposed to be reserved for the Igla air defense missile launcher. There is a space in front, on the ledge over the tracks, but if the kit is put there, the vehicle firing ports can't be used. There are no provisions for stowing the kit on the outside of the vehicle. There is a rolled tarp around the back of the turret, but that isn't big enough for the whole squad's gear. If the tarp is filled up with rucksacks and chemical masks, it blocks the two top roof hatches. In peacetime this doesn't really matter. The men are seldom in the BMP for more than a few hours at a stretch, and they seldom use the firing ports. But in war, extra belongings and spare parts accumulate and fill up the vehicle.

Most of Chazov's squads had loaded a lot of the more useless kits (meaning the gas masks and suits) into the tarp and put it on the rear roof. This wasn't the safest thing to do, but it got the junk out of the way. In some of the other companies, the chemical gear had been thrown away.

Kasparov had anticipated this problem. "You know as well as I how often we've drilled chemical defense into those blockheads! Those troops know that discarding state property is a punishable offense!"

Captain Savin interrupted: "Comrade Captain, I know that, and you know that. But we are at war. The troops have other concerns. What am I going to do? I can't send my company into action without masks. I mean if they stay in the BMPs they are all right. But those fucking nyemtsi have been fighting like bastards and we'll have to fight this one dismounted!"

Kasparov calmed down a bit. "Look, if the agent works as the front leadership expects, you ought to be able to roll into that town mounted up." Several of the officers looked very agitated. Chazov stood up.

"Comrade Captain, the front commanders haven't seen what those towns look like after our artillery finishes with them. The streets are all full of rubble. The nyemtsi are down in the cellars or in bunkers. We can't drive our BMPs over all that crap. It'll rip the tracks off. Besides, in close quarters the nyemtsi will start shooting at us with those damn *panzerfaust*. Have you seen what a panzerfaust does to an infantry squad shut up in a BMP? Burnt strawberry jam splattered all over the insides! Even if the gas works, we'll have to fight this one dismounted!"

The regimental commander, Colonel Rusak, was surprised by Chazov's outburst and by the surly attitude of his company commanders to the divisional staff officers. In peacetime this wouldn't be tolerated. But it wasn't peacetime. Rusak knew that several of these company commanders were decorated veterans of Afghanistan and had little patience for book-learned tactics.

Colonel Rusak got up. "OK, look boys, let's calm down. Comrade captain is here to get you prepared for the attack, not to instruct you *veterani* on tactics. We'll discuss the tactics for tomorrow's attack once he's finished briefing us on the chemical aspects of the attack."

Captain Kasparov returned to the center. "Look, Agent AC is nonpersistent. It evaporates really fast. It's lethal only in thick clouds. We're going to really have to plaster that town with bug spray to build up concentrations high enough to gas those nyemtsi. By the time you get into the town, the concentrations will be really low. You shouldn't have any problems. Watch out in the cellars. The gas will not disperse in confined areas. But it won't be bad up on the surface."

Savin interrupted again: "Can we count on a napalm strike before we go in, like we used to do in Afghanistan?"

Kasparov looked over to the two other officers who had accompanied him from headquarters. One of them, a stocky KGB security officer named Kaminskiy, nodded negatively: "You know as well as I do that getting tactical air support is very difficult." Everyone nodded in agreement. "Besides, we used to use a napalm strike to burn off persistent agents, not blood agents like AC. We really don't need it. As long as you don't breathe this stuff, you'll be all right. We'll have a medical team at regimental headquarters for any of our own casualties."

"What about NATO? If we use this stuff, won't they?" asked Savin. Kasparov looked back at the KGB major, who got up and walked to the center of the room.

"Comrade officers, we at front headquarters feel that gas will give us a critical advantage in tomorrow's attack. You know we are behind schedule. This situation is the same along much of the battle line. We feel that the shock of the gas attack will help us breach the main enemy defensive belt. I am not supposed to mention this. It is very secret and you should tell no one. We will be using other secret weapons tomorrow as well. Also, if you manage to secure your objectives, we plan to push a divisional mobile group through your sector to exploit our success. You can see how much depends on you. Overcome the resistance at Geiselhoring, and gain your objectives. The lead will then be taken by a fresh unit. You must keep these details in confidence from your men. But I thought you deserved to know. We at Front HQ expect that tomorrow will give us the breakthrough we've all been waiting for. The enemy is badly weakened. And tomorrow you will see a real demonstration of the power of the Soviet Army!"

The officers felt a bit cheered by the major's pep talk. Doubts would creep back in later. But for now, it was the matter of planning the details of tomorrow's attack with Colonel Rusak.

Chazov returned to his company at about 2100. It was already dark. The sentry was alert and issued the proper challenge. He was a soldier from Dudkov's old company who Chazov didn't recognize. He looked like a Tatar. "Is everything all right, soldier?"

"Yes, exactly so, Comrade Lieutenant!" the sentry replied.

"Soldier, let me see your gas-mask bag." The young soldier looked sheepishly at the sack and reluctantly unslung it from his shoulder. Chazov took it, and was surprised by its weight. Much too heavy for a gas mask! And a bit too much clanking noise for a gas-mask bag. Chazov unfastened the strap and spilled the contents out onto the ground. From the dim light of his flashlight he could see at least four RGN concussion grenades and two more RGO fragmentation grenades. There were four 30mm BG-15 grenades for the squad grenadiers, an extra clip of 5.45mm ammunition for the private's AKS-74 assault rifle, and a couple of boxes of 5.45mm ammunition. The tools of a good infantryman. But no gas mask.

"Soldier, where is your gas mask?"

"I lost it, Comrade Captain, when our BMP burned."

Probably a lie, thought Chazov. "Soldier, you know you must keep your chemical protective gear with you at all times!"

"Yes, exactly so, Comrade Captain!" Chazov didn't see any more point in berating the private. Maybe he did lose it in the BMP fire.

Chazov returned to his BMP-2. His two platoon commanders, Lieutenant Shepel and Lieutenant Khalkin, were there waiting for him along with his zampolit, Lieutenant Sudro. "Well, gentlemen, how's Dudkov's bunch doing?"

Pavel Sudro, the senior of the trio, answered. "Well, they've lost all three platoon commanders. The highest ranking trooper left is Senior Sergeant Vasilev. You know, that guy you talked to on the radio. He's a real *makaroniki*.[4] He's completely gone . . . useless. There's a young squad leader, a Ukrainian kid named Burak, who seems pretty decent. He took charge of the platoon that dismounted during the fighting and he kept them together. The other soldiers seem to have confidence in him. There's about fifty of them, so I gave some of the extras to the 1st and 2d platoons."

Chazov asked, "Can't we shift one of our sergeants over there?"

"Pyotr, we need our guys," Khalkin replied. "I really don't think we can spare anyone, especially with Dudkov's leftovers. A lot of those guys are really demoralized. Our sergeants are going to have to sit on them. Besides, there's no real hotshots in our platoons. You know what they're like. They're not a bad bunch, but taking care of a new platoon? No chance. We have our hands full as it is."

Chazov nodded in agreement. "Sorry, Pavel Aleksandrovich. You're stuck with them." Sudro shook his head.

"Now listen," said Chazov. "The brass from Front HQ are planning to gas those fucking nyemtsi tomorrow before we attack. They're going to dump a big load of insecticide on the town using a few salvos of Grads. They want to soften them up. This isn't going to be like fighting the

---

4. *Makaroniki* is Russian slang for "macaroni men." It refers to professional senior sergeants who remain in the service to collect additional service stripes (called "macaroni") and the benefits that accrue with seniority. They are mostly men from rural areas, usually in the Ukraine, with little prospect in civilian life. They are often hated by the lower ranking soldiers due to their abusive behavior, and are looked on with disdain by the officers as mere ticket-punchers and not real soldiers. There is a certain amount of class and ethnic conflict involved as well, since the officers are generally well-educated Russians from towns or cities.

*dushmani*[5] with gas. The nyemtsi probably have gas masks. If we catch them by surprise, we might panic them. That'll make our job easier. The main trick is to keep our troops calm. We'll be using Agent AC. It's not persistent. It's only lethal if you breathe it in. The gas boys tell us most of it will be gone by the time we reach the town. So we only need masks. You two, check out your platoons and make sure everybody has a mask. I'll go with Sudro and check the situation with Dudkov's old bunch. Also check on the slime suits. We'll meet back here in an hour."

As Chazov had feared, a lot of Dudkov's troopers had thrown away their gas masks. Fortunately, one of the platoons had thrown most of the masks into the compartment behind the engine in their BMPs where spare Fagot missiles are carried. Out of the fifty-four troops, Chazov counted forty-four gas masks and only twenty OP-1 protective suits. The divisional chemical officers had told him earlier in the evening that he could expect no additional gear from them. All the units had the same problem. But he had scrounged a half-dozen masks and some slime suits from one of the divisional artillery units. Khalkin's and Shepel's platoons were in much better shape. Both had a full load of gas masks and about ninety percent of their OP-1 suits.

The three officers met near Chazov's BMP at about 2200 to plan the attack. The BMP has a chemical filtration system to protect troops inside from chemical weapons. Chazov decided that the squad without gas masks would remain inside the BMPs during the attack. The extra two squads of men from Dudkov's old outfit would ride to the dismount point up on the roof of the BMP, wearing their masks. It was risky, but better than leaving the extra troops behind. It was going to be a tough fight, and Chazov needed all the men he could get. He decided against having his troops don the OP-1 suits. There were not enough to go around, and he didn't want any trouble over that. The troops without the suits might act gun-shy of entering the town. Besides, the OP-1 suits would make the attack very difficult to carry out.

The OP-1 slime suit consists of a chemically impregnated set of long johns, which is worn under the normal uniform. On top of this is worn a coverall made of rubberized fabric. It's called a slime suit because when you decontaminate it with caustic soaps, it feels slimy to the touch. There

---

5. *Dushmani* is Russian military slang for "bandits." It refers to the Afghani guerrilla fighters.

are also clumsy rubber mittens for the hands and a hood to go over the helmet. The suit works well to keep out chemicals, but the outer rubber coverall is impenetrable to moisture, so sweat does not evaporate. This is acceptable for an hour or so if the troops are riding in vehicles. But strenuous activity can lead to rapid heat exhaustion and unconsciousness. Troops wearing the OP-1 suit would have a hard time carrying out an attack on foot on a hot day. The face masks would soon steam up, and the men would have a hard time seeing. Heat prostration would set in rapidly, and the soldiers would be useless in forty minutes.

It was risky either way. Wearing the suits would cause all sorts of problems. Not wearing the suits would cause problems only if the Germans retaliated with gas at some point during the fighting. Chazov hoped that his company would be warned by division HQ if such a retaliatory gas attack was expected, so he'd have time to get his troops into protective suits or into the BMPs. There's damn little certainty in war.

The attack on Geiselhoring was scheduled to begin at 0530. In the autumn, the area has early morning mists, which would help hide the attacking Soviet forces. The gas attack would not be preceded by normal artillery fire. The artillery officers hoped to catch a lot of German troops in their sleep, not wearing protective gear.

In Geiselhoring, at least, this was not to be. The first salvo of BM-21 Grad rocket projectiles began slamming into the town at 0515. Or at least near the town. Multiple rocket launchers like the BM-21 Grad have bad dispersion problems at long ranges, and this attack was no exception. Many of the rounds fell to the south of the town, where they killed a lot of the livestock abandoned when the civilians fled two days before. As soon as the first rounds struck Geiselhoring, Chazov started to move his company out of the woods and toward the town, five kilometers away. The plan called for the regiment's tanks to lead the attack, about 1,000 meters in front of the BMPs. There would be one tank company attached to each BMP battalion. If resistance was light, the BMPs were to proceed right up to the edge of town and dismount their troops. If any heavy antitank fire was encountered, the BMPs would dismount their troops 2,000 meters from the town, outside the range of the Milan antitank missiles. The tanks would suppress the Milan sites with gunfire, supported by the woodpeckers on the BMPs.

Major Barchuk's BMP battalion, to which Chazov's company belonged, had only two companies left. Chazov's company was the best equipped, so it was directed toward a built-up area at the southern edge of the town. Captain Savin's understrength company was to his left, aiming for the road on the southern edge of the town. An understrength company of six T-80M tanks was right in front of Chazov's company. He warned his troops to stay away from these tanks during the fighting. The T-80Ms were covered with reactive armor, and if the reactive armor went off near infantry, it could kill unprotected foot soldiers nearby (see Chapter 3). To his right, Chazov could see the other battalions forming up for the attack. The area in front of the town consisted of fairly flat farm fields, and there was little cover for the infantry except for a few irrigation ditches. The main German positions were in the rubble at the edge of town. More troops could be expected inside. The day before, they had knocked out the four Leopard tanks supporting the infantry company in the town, but who knew what reinforcements the Germans had managed to scrape up the night before. Maybe they had even abandoned the town last night! Fat chance.

The tanks moved forward at a top speed of about thirty-five miles per hour, with the BMPs bouncing a thousand meters behind. The BMP-2 could easily keep up with the T-80s, but it was a rough ride. The torsion bar suspension was stiff, and every time a bump was hit, the soldiers' heads slammed against the low steel roof. The rough ride, the stench of diesel fumes, and the smell of the rubber chemical masks made many of the soldiers nauseous. They each had a small periscope in front of them to see outside. But the ride was so rough it was hard to keep an eye on the periscope long enough to see what was happening. The soldiers were bunched up in the back of the vehicle with no room to move. It was dark except for a small electric light bulb at one end of the compartment, which did little more than create strange shadows. The inside of a BMP on an attack run was no place for someone prone to claustrophobia.

An element of fear was added by nagging memories of the BMPs that had been destroyed in previous skirmishes. The soldiers knew that at any moment a Milan antitank missile might come slamming into the vehicle, incinerating the crew. In four days of fighting, they had seen plenty of examples of what happens when a BMP is hit with an antiarmor missile. The BMP is so full of ammunition and fuel that a solid hit nearly anywhere leads to a catastrophic fire or explosion. Seldom does any of the crew survive. The German troops had begun calling the vehicles "Ivan cookers." After a few kilometers, the troops were very anxious to get out of the

BMPs into the open air. It was hard to keep the men calm. Chazov realized that it would be especially difficult to control the troops with the added fear of gas mixed in.

The men from Dudkov's old company were riding on the back roof of the BMPs behind the turret. They were very vulnerable to artillery, but it was better than walking the five kilometers. It was a real adventure trying to hold on with the BMPs going thirty-five miles an hour. But in a way, the ride was less draining for the troops on the roofs than it was for those canned up inside. They could clearly see the ruins of the town in the front of them and the waves of BMPs and T-80 tanks advancing to either side. Reality was far less frightening than the frenzied imaginings of the troops cramped together inside. The town was obscured by mist and by a cloud of smoke from the gas attack. No German positions were visible. If they were still alive, they were holding their fire.

When the first wave of tanks got about 1,500 meters from the town, eerie flickers of Milan missiles could be seen racing through the mist. If the Milan was coming right in your direction, the small tail flare was nearly impossible to see. But the missiles fired at neighboring units could be seen skimming a few feet over the ground. At least two T-80Ms in front of Chazov's company were hit. There was a big flash as the missile and reactive armor went off almost simultaneously. At first it was hard to tell the results. Some German units still had the old Milan 2 missiles. These couldn't get through reactive armor. But some had the improved Milan 2T, which had a fifty-fifty chance of burning through reactive armor. So much flame and dust were thrown up when the missile hit, it was difficult to tell if the tanks had survived. As the smoke cleared, Chazov could see that the crew of one tank was bailing out. Their coveralls were on fire. The tank erupted as an internal fire reached the ammunition under the turret and cooked off. Chazov watched in horror as the turret flew up in the air, somersaulting like a carelessly tossed skillet. He hoped his men hadn't seen it. Obviously, there was going to be a fight for this town.

Chazov ordered his company to prepare to dismount. They were still more than two kilometers from the town, but he didn't want to risk losing any BMPs to the missiles. The mist would cover the advance of his infantry. He warned the BMP-2 gunners to be careful not to fire too low, for fear of hitting their own men. While climbing out of his BMP-2, Chazov noticed that the neighboring BMP companies on either side were following suit.

His troops were deployed in a standard skirmish line, as they had practiced so often in peacetime training. They advanced at a slight crouch, Kalashnikovs at the hip. The line was a bit ragged, but then this was no parade ground. German small arms fire could be expected in another 500 meters. There was one real advantage to the Soviet style of training: It was very simple. Even troops scared witless could remember the basic drill. Chazov's men seemed relieved to be outside of the BMPs. They were moving forward without hesitation.

Chazov heard the whine of incoming artillery rockets overhead. He instinctively hit the ground. Afghanistan had taught him the sound of artillery rockets. The dushmani loved those Chinese artillery rockets! The rounds must have passed overhead, but he did not hear the usual ground-shaking crunch of their impact. Instead there was a series of loud bangs, more like grenades than normal artillery. It suddenly occurred to him why. The Germans were firing gas rounds back. Shit!

Chazov couldn't have known it, but NATO intelligence had expected a Soviet gas attack along this front. The day before, several reconnaissance drones had spotted Soviet chemical troops preparing decontamination facilities in the rear. Soviet communication nets started behaving in a peculiar fashion, and Soviet artillery units were obviously receiving an unusual munition. Soviet deceptive measures, maskirovka, had failed them. Local German and American artillery units were supplied with chemical munitions and authorized to use them if the Soviets attacked first. Troops along the front were instructed to don their protective gear at the first signs of a Soviet attack. The German garrison in Geiselhoring expected the early morning attack and had donned their suits at 0300. The NATO forces decided to use a nerve gas in hope of forcing the Soviets to don full protective suits as well. This would slow them down a bit.

The first salvo of gas projectiles burst among the BMPs behind the advancing wave of infantry. A few also seemed to hit in front. But in the mist it was hard to tell. One soldier in the company carried a small gas testing kit. But it was manual, and you had to be inside the cloud of gas to tell what type it was. By that time, it would be too late. Chazov was a bit confused. The troops had stopped moving forward and were crouched near the ground, looking around aimlessly.

Chazov signaled to his radioman to bring the manpack radio over to him. He called back to Sergeant Aksai in the command BMP. "Any word from division about a German gas attack?" There was a lot of static on the line, probably NATO jamming. He could barely hear Aksai even though he was only 500 meters away.

"Comrade Lieutenant, the divisional warning net said they've been hit by a nerve agent attack. They instruct all units to don protective gear immediately." Nerve gas!

Chazov instructed Sergeant Aksai to warn the other platoons. "Everyone with OP-1 suits, don them immediately and withdraw to the BMPs for further instruction. Everyone without suits, back to the BMPs immediately and get inside. BMPs to start up vehicle overpressure and filtration systems. Keep all doors and hatches closed except in absolute emergencies."

A second salvo of artillery rockets struck the regiment. A few landed right in the midst of the BMPs, some of the others nearer to the troops. There was panic everywhere he looked. Some of the soldiers broke and ran with no regard for their equipment. The worst affected were those without chemical suits. A few from Sudro's platoon got about halfway back to the BMPs when they encountered the first mists of nerve gas. After a few gulps they collapsed to the ground, shuddering with uncontrollable twitches as the gas attacked their nervous system. Some troops kept calm and hurriedly put on the outer OP-1 coveralls. There was no time to strip, and don the undergarment and then the coveralls. The outer coveralls would have to do. Pretty soon, Chazov was surrounded by a platoon of bug-eyed Martians. The slime suits came in a pea green and rusty orange color, not the usual drab khaki of Soviet military uniforms. Chazov led his remaining men back to the BMPs at a slow pace to prevent premature exhaustion. It took a lot of courage to do this under the circumstances. Some soldiers tried to run ahead, but the exertion soon forced them to stop.

About a hundred meters to the north, Chazov could see the effects of the gas. A squad from Sudro's platoon had been very near to one of the first nerve gas rockets that exploded. Many of them didn't have suits, but they probably wouldn't have done them much good anyway. The concentrations were so high that their exposed skin absorbed fatal doses. The nerve agent acted as an extreme nerve stimulant, causing convulsions and difficulty breathing. Most of the squad had fallen on the ground, where contamination by the aerosol was even worse. Some soldiers threw off their gas masks in panic, and inhalation of the nerve agent brought death even quicker. The screams, twitching, and convulsions scared the surviving soldiers. Even the units in suits were near panic when they arrived back at the BMPs.

A few soldiers without suits had gotten back to the BMPs before the main group. They had quickly climbed into two of the BMPs, where the overpressure and filtration system could protect them. Lieutenant Khalkin was at the fore of the main group and had seen this. Now he was in a quandary. Since the soldiers with OP-1 suits had walked through areas contaminated by the nerve agent, there was probably agent on their boots and on the protective suits. If these exposed troops entered the BMPs, they would contaminate the unprotected soldiers. Khalkin blocked the entrance to one of the BMPs and tried to direct the contaminated troops to those BMPs without unprotected soldiers inside. The voice emitter on his gas mask made it very difficult for him to communicate with the troops. There was some pushing and shoving. The soldiers were in a near panic and, with their suits on, could barely hear Khalkin. Enemy artillery soon settled the matter.

The nerve gas attack was followed by a conventional artillery barrage. It wasn't particularly heavy, only a few dozen rounds in the battalion sector. But the enemy artillerymen had chosen the worst (or best) possible moment to strike. With most of the Soviet infantry still out of the BMPs, the battalion was hit by a barrage of antipersonnel ICMs. Dozens of small explosions began going off all around.

The fireworks caused by the burst of the ICMs finally broke the last vestiges of control that Chazov had over his men. Those who survived the ICM attack packed into the BMPs, the unprotected soldiers be damned! There was a mad scramble to get in as fast as possible. Chazov managed to climb onto the roof of his BMP-2 command vehicle and enter through the turret hatch.

Once inside, many of the men began to calm down. But there was a hellish scene inside two of the BMPs. BMP 412 had four soldiers of the 3d Platoon inside without OP-1 suits. When seven soldiers with suits came charging in during the artillery barrage, these four soldiers were pushed into the left tunnel leading to the driver's station. The nerve agent on the suits and in the outside air began to affect the unprotected soldiers. The vehicle had a medical kit with atropine injectors as nerve agent antidotes, but the troops were in such a panic that no one thought to use it. Two of the soldiers began to vomit and suffer convulsions. They were forcibly shoved away from the back compartment, where the protected troops were sitting. After a few minutes, one of the sergeants remembered the atropine kits and injected the contaminated soldiers. They were unconscious but still alive. A measure of calm was finally restored. In BMP 417 the driver and gunner were without suits, and they suffered much the same fate as the four soldiers in BMP 412.

Chazov's command vehicle, BMP 410, was crowded, but everyone had suits. He began making radio calls to the neighboring BMPs to check their status. The gas masks used by officers and radiomen have small voice devices to permit them to issue commands and to use radio equipment. But the sound quality is lousy. Of the ten BMPs, two were unresponsive. Through the periscope, Chazov could see that their rear doors were open. They were probably contaminated. They were near the impact point of some of the nerve gas rockets, and their crews had probably been killed by gas before they could get their suits on. Once the artillery fire stopped, Chazov sent two sergeants from the command vehicle to check them out. The eight other vehicles were in varying states. The two nearest BMP-2s were fairly intact, with nineteen troops between them. Three more vehicles had only six men each. BMPs 412 and 417 had a total of twenty-two soldiers, of whom six were contaminated. This added up to sixty-six of the one hundred twenty men who had started the attack. At least two squads, about twenty men, had been killed outright by the gas. About twenty-five more had been wounded in the subsequent artillery barrage. Left in the open with nerve gas on the ground and in the air, they soon became comatose. The other men were missing and presumed dead. Chazov tried to get the BMPs to send out parties to help the wounded, but the troops were in no mood to budge from the security of their armored vehicles. And Chazov was in no mood to threaten them. As the sun came up, the insides of the vehicles started to bake. The suits became unbearably warm, and it became tiring to move.

Chazov was unable to raise the other battalions on his radio. The frequencies were being jammed, or the sets were inoperable. He used the telescopic sight of the woodpecker autocannon to try to find out about neighboring units. There was no evidence of any Soviet vehicles to his immediate right except for some burning tanks and BMPs. There were several BMPs to his left, but little sign of action. Fortunately, the German's Milan missiles were out of range. Sergeant Vrobel volunteered to walk over to the neighboring company. Chazov told him to take it easy and walk slowly. There was no sense getting heat stress.

Chazov realized that his unit wasn't fit for further action. The vehicles would have to be pulled back soon and decontaminated. The troops inside would eventually be overcome by the heat, even just sitting and waiting. They might become uncontrollable and do stupid things like try to take off their masks to cool down. It was imperative to reach regimental or divisional command and find out what provisions were being made for decontamination.

Chazov tried raising regimental HQ on the radio, but there was too much jamming. He finally managed to get through on one of the alternate nets. The radioman on the other end told him to keep his unit in place and await further orders. Chazov asked about provisions for decontamination. They were cut off by another burst of jamming before he got a reply. He started to think about sending one of the vehicles back to HQ for further information. Before he could decide, the Germans started getting active.

It was a sight Chazov dreaded. From over the town he saw the glint of helicopter rotors. It wasn't clear if it was just a scout helicopter or an attack helicopter. He let the gunner get back into his seat, and moved over to the commander's seat in the turret. His gunner took the helicopter in aim but it was a bit too far to engage. From the corner of his eye Chazov caught the bright flash of a missile tracing flare. A HOT antitank missile, fired by an unseen second helicopter, hit BMP 412. It exploded against the turret, causing a gaping hole. Secondary explosions started from burning 30mm autocannon ammunition. The fire licked up against three stowed Konkurs missiles, which blew up, igniting the fuel tank in the back. In seconds, the whole vehicle was engulfed in flames. No one could have survived. These damn BMPs burned like torches!

The BMP-2 on the right caught sight of the helicopter. It was a tiny German PAH-1, armed with six HOT missiles. The woodpecker on BMP 416 began hammering away at the chopper, but it scooted out of range to the safety of the town. If the situation wasn't bad enough, Chazov spotted some German infantry sneaking out of the town toward the Soviet lines. The Germans had the luxury of modern chemical suits. They were charcoal coated, with permeable surfaces that permitted sweat to evaporate. It was no picnic to run with heavy weapons in such a suit, but it was a lot more practical than the Soviet rubber suits.

Chazov decided it was pointless to keep his vehicles here. There was no evidence that the rest of the regiment was continuing the attack. His BMPs were waiting like sitting ducks for more helicopter attacks. Those damn PAH-1s could wipe out his company without even needing to reload. And the German infantry were probably tank-hunter teams, armed with panzerfaust antitank rockets.

Ignoring his previous orders, Chazov signaled to his troops to begin a staggered pullback to the woods they had occupied the night before. The company was useless as a combat force. It was down to seven BMPs and less than fifty men. The vehicles were too badly contaminated to permit normal combat operations. The troops were too frightened and exhausted to fight.

Sergeant Dobrovolskiy's BMP led the way and continued on to regimental HQ to check on the matter of decontamination equipment. The company waited in the woods for nearly an hour before Dobrovolskiy returned, bringing back three decontamination kits. One kit contained soap and bleach to clean up the troops. In peacetime practice, personnel cleanup had always been done in a prepared facility, with showers. Here, there wasn't enough water or equipment. It all had to be done laboriously by hand. At least once out of the vehicles, it was a bit easier to cool down.

Chazov still found it very difficult to control the men. Ignoring the usual precautions, some of the soldiers simply removed their OP-1 suits without rinsing first. It was dangerous, although by then most of the nerve agent had evaporated. Everything was done in such a hurry that it wasn't clear which suits had been cleaned and which ones had not. There were two canisters of a special caustic agent to wash down the BMPs. But to wash out the insides, it would be necessary to get back into the suits, which were now in heaps scattered along the edge of the forest floor. No one dared touch them for fear they were still coated with nerve agent. Chazov, Dobrovolskiy, and Khalkin had taken the trouble to scrub their suits before removing them. So the three men were given their suits and assigned the laborious task of cleaning out the insides of the BMPs. They managed to clean two of them before water and caustic agent ran out. The rest of the troops were sent to dig in and prepare defensive positions at the edge of the woods. He hoped that the woods hadn't been hit by chemicals. If the Germans decided to use chemicals again, they were done for.

# Analysis

This fictional account of the attack on Geiselhoring highlights the temptations for the Soviets to use chemical weapons, as well as the enormous risks. This scenario shows the most likely conditions for the use of chemical weapons. The tempo of a vital operation has been thrown off by determined resistance. Conventional means to smash the resistance in built-up areas has proven to be a failure. Something out of the ordinary seems necessary. Chemical weapons are seen as a panacea in such a situation. They hold the allure of providing the shock needed to break a stalemate.

The first use of chemical weapons could be expected to have enormous psychological impact on unprepared defenders. Soldiers who have proven very resistant to conventional weapons might break and run when the added horror of chemical weapons is unleashed on them. It is not inconceivable that this could have a decisive effect on the outcome of a war. Such an expectation would be the main reason for employing chemical weapons.

Other factors support such a decision. Soviet troops train regularly with chemical weapons and simulated chemical weapons. Soviet military leaders might expect that their troops would perform well in chemical warfare conditions since they are familiar with it, better than NATO troops would perform under these conditions. Soviet officers could harbor the illusion that they have a decided edge on the chemical battlefield. The Soviet Army has substantial stockpiles of a wide variety of chemical weapons, allowing the front commander to choose chemicals tailored to a particular task. But the main attraction is the surprise effect.

As the scenario of the attack on Geiselhoring suggests, many of these expectations may prove to be dead wrong. Indeed, the use of chemical weapons could prove to be a major mistake for an attacking force. The use of chemical weapons forces both sides to engage in time-consuming and complicated chemical protective measures. Troops have to be adequately supplied with chemical suits, decontamination equipment, and additional medical support. Tasks that normally take thirty minutes would take hours in a contaminated environment. Chemical contamination is a glue that slows down the tempo of operations. If it does not have an immediate and decisive effect on its first use, then it backfires on the attacker. The Soviets as the aggressor would be far more dependent on the speed and tempo of operations than NATO would be as the defender. These points are worth examining in detail.

## Soviet Preparations for Chemical Warfare

The Soviet Army, like most modern armies, has been interested in chemical warfare since World War I. The Tsarist army suffered monstrous casualties in World War I, largely because it was technically unprepared.

In the wake of these horrors, the new Red Army of the 1920s made a determined effort to prepare for the use of chemical weapons. It has maintained this interest through the present.

Although chemical weapons did not have a decisive impact on the Western Front in World War I, they proved more effective in the East. Russian troops were so ill prepared that gas attacks by the Germans were far more successful than comparable attacks against French or British troops. The Russians suffered at least 50,000 dead and more than a half million injured from German gas attacks in World War I. Chemical weapons had not changed greatly by the time of World War II. The main types of chemicals were blister agents like mustard gas, which burn out the inside of the lung and can cause severe skin burns and blinding. Neither the Allied nor Axis forces used chemical weapons during World War II. Blister agents were not suitable for the more mobile style of war waged in Europe. In addition, both sides were deterred from using chemicals since both were well stocked with such agents. The trigger for their use in World War I had been the expectation that they would be a major surprise and have a decisive effect. In World War II, surprise could not be expected, greatly diminishing the incentive for first use.

Although World War II did not see the use of chemical weapons, it did see the development of several revolutionary new chemical agents. The most lethal of these were the new nerve gases. Blister agents like mustard gas require heavy contact to have any effect. Simple precautions like a gas mask and adequate clothing can prevent most detrimental effects. But nerve gases can attack through the skin as well as the respiratory system. A gas mask alone is inadequate. Full body protection is needed, with no skin exposed to the air. The amounts of agent needed to kill are far smaller, only seventy to one hundred milligrams—a small drop of liquid. It took decades to develop medical treatment for these agents and to devise protective equipment. Without these, nerve gas would be as dangerous to the side that used it as to its opponents. By the 1960s, chemical protective suits and medical treatments were available.

The Soviet Army began a major program of chemical warfare modernization beginning in the mid-1960s. Soviet units are amply provided for waging chemical warfare, with both the weapons and the protective equipment. And there is strong evidence that they have experimented with chemical weapons in a number of circumstances, notably in Afghanistan.

Soviet motor rifle and tank divisions have an extensive infrastructure for chemical defense. Each division has a chemical defense battalion, and each of its four component regiments has its own chemical company. In total, about 500 soldiers in each division, about 4 percent, are devoted to chemical defense tasks. The division has a wide range of equipment for chemical defense, ranging from mobile decontamination facilities to individual protective suits.

Soviet equipment since the 1960s has been designed to fight in a chemically contaminated environment. All the standard combat vehicles are fitted with chemical protective equipment. Armored vehicles have a system of air filtration to remove chemical contaminants from the air breathed by the crew. The vehicles are also fitted with an overpressure system to keep contaminants out of the vehicle. Soviet tanks have had this feature since the mid-1960s. In contrast, American tanks did not have such a system until the mid-1980s, and only a tiny fraction of American armored vehicles have been equipped.

The Soviet Army has a number of specialized vehicles to operate in chemically contaminated areas. In the mid-1960s, they introduced the first chemical scout vehicles. These armored vehicles are sent into contaminated areas to conduct surveys of the type of chemical agent present and the degree of contamination. They are equipped with sensors that can detect all common chemical warfare agents. Each Soviet regiment has four of these, and there are more at divisional level. There have been three generations of these vehicles since the 1960s, the most recent being the RKhM tracked chemical scout vehicle that is fully amphibious. The Soviets also use a full range of manual testing equipment. By themselves, these chemical scout vehicles are not very threatening. But they are indicative of the sophistication and breadth of the Soviet chemical effort. In contrast, the U.S. Army has been talking about such a vehicle for the past few years, but has none in service. At the moment, the U.S. Army relies entirely on manual chemical testing kits.

The individual Soviet soldier is provided with a chemical protective suit and a chemical mask. As the scenario has depicted, the standard Soviet suit, the OP-1, is no joy to use. It is clumsy, slow to don, and dangerous to the user in many circumstances. But it is better than nothing. This is one area where NATO has a clear advantage. In the mid-1970s, the British Army came up with a new semipermeable material for chemical suits. It allows sweat to evaporate, but does not allow chemical agents to enter. This is a major breakthrough, since it means that the soldiers can operate in a more normal fashion. The Soviets' rubberized suits can be debilitating in hot weather, or even in cold weather if a lot of exertion is called for, although they are reusable once they have been washed. The main disadvantage of the new NATO suits is that they must be replaced fairly often, since certain chemicals can break down their filtering abilities. The Soviets have continued to use washable, rubberized fabric for the time being, in spite of its disadvantages. They have shown little interest in the NATO permeable suits, probably due to the high cost of the NATO-style suits, as well as a certain backwardness in Soviet textile technology.

The same applies to chemical masks. The no-frills approach reigns here as well. The Soviets rely on cheap masks with replaceable filters. There are none of the clever features used on NATO face masks. For example, certain NATO face masks have a small opening that permits the soldier to drink water from his canteen. While this may seem to be a luxury, the main problem of all suits, even the permeable ones, is that they invariably lead to the soldier heating up and sweating. Combine the normal stress of combat, sweating, and the resultant dehydration, and you get a debilitating heat exhaustion. A few mouthfuls of water become a medical necessity, not a luxury. Also, Soviet officers and radiomen receive face masks with voice emitters, but the rest of the troops receive chemical face masks without emitters since they are cheaper to manufacture. As a result, under chemical warfare conditions, it is virtually impossible for the troops to communicate with one another. This is another impediment to the smooth functioning of a combat unit.

The problem faced by the Soviets is that their army is so enormous, all these little economies are necessary if everyone is to be provided with equipment. They feel that mediocre protection is better than none at all.

In the area of chemical weapons, the Soviets probably have the world's largest stockpile. The U.S. estimates that the Soviet military has on the order of 500,000 tons of chemical agents, ranging from simple blood agents, like the Agent AC previously described, to sophisticated nerve gases. Delivery methods are ample, ranging from chemical hand grenades to large bombs capable of carrying more than a ton of nerve gas. The usual Soviet method for delivering chemical agents on the battlefield is artillery. This includes conventional artillery cannon, as well as artillery rockets and missiles. The cannon would be used to attack targets up to 30 miles from the battle line; the missiles could be used to attack vital targets like airfields and command posts up to 250 miles from the battle line.

## Soviet Intentions and Chemical Warfare

It can be argued that much of this Soviet equipment simply points to a prudent concern about defending Soviet troops in the event of chemical attacks. This is not plausible for a variety of reasons. The Soviet buildup in chemical weapons and the related protective equipment came at a time when NATO showed very little interest in chemical warfare. If NATO had had any serious interest in chemical weapons between the 1950s and 1960s, this would have been manifest in defensive measures like chemical defense suites on armored vehicles.

Soviet interest in chemical warfare has been long-standing, but the surge of effort in the mid-1960s is probably due to refinements in Soviet doctrine. At that time Soviet military planners were making revolutionary changes in their war plans. The Soviet military leadership had previously assumed that all wars with NATO would inevitably turn nuclear. Compared to tactical nuclear weapons, chemical weapons were little more than an interesting curiosity. Soviet strategists began arguing that the enormous strategic nuclear arsenals created a stalemate. Neither the U.S. nor the USSR would dare use tactical nuclear weapons on a European battlefield, since there was the risk that it would escalate to strategic nuclear exchanges against the American and Soviet homelands. Because of this stalemate, a war in Europe would likely be nonnuclear.

Due to this radical rethinking of Soviet military doctrine, weapons planners began looking afresh at chemical weapons. Chemical weapons have certain attractive features to an invading force, primarily an enormous psychological advantage against an unprepared defender. And in the early 1970s, NATO was certainly unprepared. The Soviet Army began an extensive training program for its troops. Soviet soldiers became accustomed to using chemical weapons and working in chemically contaminated environments. They began training with chemical decontamination gear to an extent unprecedented in NATO. And the Soviet Union began acquiring new chemical weapons and chemical warfare systems.

The presumption that chemicals would be used on a conventional battlefield became so prevalent that it seeped into the marrow of Soviet tactics. This is manifest in many small ways. Soviet books and magazines aimed at officers provide guidelines for operating in a chemical environment. To take but a single example, Soviet publications instructing Soviet officers on the standard methods of notating tactical battle maps provide extensive details about how to mark up different types of chemical contamination.

Soviet Army defectors have made it clear that the Soviet Army regularly includes in its war games and staff exercises plans to use chemical weapons against NATO. This is not particularly surprising in view of Soviet force structure, tactical doctrine, and training.

## The Likelihood of Soviet Use of Chemical Weapons

In spite of the enormous scale of Soviet preparations for the use of chemical weapons in a conventional war, doubts must still linger in the minds of Soviet planners. Chemical warfare seems like an intriguing technical solution to battlefield requirements in the calm of peacetime. But in the confusion of war, it threatens to unleash a host of devilish problems.

The scenario of the attack on Geiselhoring highlights some of these. To begin with, peacetime preparations do not always prove adequate in war. The Soviet Army might start a war with chemical defensive measures in place. But a few days of war would disrupt these. Unless chemicals were used from the outset, chemical defense preparations might begin to dissolve. Soldiers would lose or misplace their chemical protective gear. Chemical defense companies would be stripped of their personnel to serve as replacements in more critical combat functions. Decontamination trucks would be given less priority for fuel or rail transport in favor of ammunition and other essentials.

Some of these problems could be avoided by the use of chemical weapons right from the outset of the fighting. In such a case, the carefully prepared chemical defense equipment would be in place and ready to go. However, this would come at an enormous cost.

That cost would not be borne by the troops of either NATO or the Warsaw Pact, but by the civilian populations near the battlefield. Modern chemical agents are so lethal that full protective equipment is essential. It would be impossibly expensive to equip the population along the German border with this type of equipment. As a result, any chemical attack would cause massive civilian losses of a magnitude that might prompt the NATO countries to respond in kind against East German or other Warsaw Pact cities, and could very well lead to a cycle of escalation eventually culminating in a nuclear exchange. The basic premise of any Soviet attack on NATO would be to limit it to the conventional level. Any action that might eventually trigger the use of nuclear weapons would have to be avoided.

For this reason, it seems likely that the use of chemical weapons would be curtailed until their effects would fall mainly on military targets. Chemical weapons are too indiscriminate to use when military and civilian targets are mingled, as they would be at the outset of a war. Once the war broke out, however, it is likely that the civilian population would soon flee, which would remove a major constraint in the Soviet use of chemical weapons.

Another major constraint on Soviet use of chemical weapons would be concern about the performance of Soviet troops in a chemical environment. It is one thing to practice chemical warfare in peacetime; it is quite a different matter to actually use it in wartime.

Soviet peacetime training is notoriously contrived. Their war maneuvers smack more of military choreography than military training. Simple drills, like donning a chemical suit or scrubbing down a vehicle, are realistically rehearsed, and rehearsed quite often. But more elaborate exercises are needed to simulate the real pressures of war. Such exercises would include an attack under simulated chemical conditions, followed by prolonged exercises while still in chemical gear, culminating in the decontamination of the men and equipment some hours later. Full-blown exercises of this kind do take place. But the results often give Soviet officers reason to pause before using chemical weapons.

Soviet protective gear is so uncomfortable that troops have discovered ways to circumvent it during peacetime practice. According to former Soviet soldiers, it is common for them to detach the air hose leading to the filter can. This would render the mask useless in wartime, but in a peacetime exercise where no real gas is present, it makes it easier to breathe. Decontamination exercises are similarly unrealistic. The drill is often practiced on old worn-out vehicles. Usually only the outside is scrubbed down, ignoring the difficulties and dangers involved in cleaning out the interior of a contaminated vehicle. Soviet officers are undoubtedly aware of the problems with these staged exercises. The more professional officers must have doubts about how these procedures would be carried out in a real war.

As unrealistic as these peacetime war games may be, they do impress the average Soviet officer with the exhausting and time-consuming nature of chemical defense. This could be a major disincentive to the Soviet use of chemical weapons. Any Soviet attack against NATO must be based on the idea of a rapid offensive across the German plains before NATO could adequately mobilize. The use of chemical weapons would slow the pace of the Soviet advance by obligating the use of protective gear. After an attack was made, the vehicles and troops would have to be arduously decontaminated before another attack would be possible. This would disrupt the momentum of the attack and slow the pace of the advance, which is extremely undesirable from the Soviet perspective.

The Achilles' heel of the Soviet Army is its rear areas. The troops at the front may be well provided with chemical protection gear, but many of the rear area troops are not. Support troops who bring forward critical supplies, ammunition, and food are not as well prepared for chemical warfare as the fighting branches. The Soviets do not appear to have developed protective shelters that would enable command facilities to function if NATO retaliated with chemicals. Soviet command vans are usually provided with filtration systems. But the vans cannot sustain the command elements in the presence of persistent chemical agents like certain nerve gases. They have no beds, toilet facilities, or decontamination features. Chemical attack of their rear support areas would be a nightmare for Soviet military leaders. Tanks without frequent resupplies of gas and ammunition are useless scrap metal. Infantry without food and ammunition has no attacking power.

An essential element in any Soviet plans to use chemical weapons is an assessment of NATO's reaction. In the 1970s, NATO was ill prepared to handle a Soviet attack. By the 1980s, NATO had managed to make important strides in chemical defense. The permeable suit developed by Britain is one of the best examples. But there are a host of other examples as well. The U.S. Army has developed and fielded a number of protective shelters for command centers that could be used in a chemical environment. This shows a much more realistic appreciation for the difficulties of operating in chemical contamination than the Warsaw Pact has demonstrated. NATO planning for chemical warfare in many ways has concentrated on its more mundane aspects, such as logistics and command and control. This must force the Soviets to wonder whether NATO is better prepared to fight a protracted war in chemical conditions. The Soviets might do pretty well in a short war in which chemicals are used primarily against fighting troops, but in prolonged warfare, chemical weapons could threaten many of their support troops and their logistics network.

## Chemical Weapons and Arms Control

Soviet military leaders are not unaware of the many problems associated with chemical warfare. In the mid-1980s, these anxieties became more manifest. The Soviets again began to talk seriously about arms controls to limit chemical weapons. In an unprecedented move in 1987, they permitted NATO observers to tour a portion of their main Chemical Weapons Proving Grounds at Shikany. The officials were permitted to see a selection of Soviet chemical weapons and were given limited details of the types of weapons the Soviet Army possesses.

Some NATO hard-liners have argued that this was nothing more than a small concession by the Soviets in hopes of putting NATO off guard. The NATO democracies are subject to public pressures. If there is a popular consensus that chemical weapons should be banned, then there will be little incentive to continue funding NATO chemical defense modernization. The Soviets used this type of maneuver to influence American efforts to deploy a new generation of chemical weapons in the early 1980s, with considerable success. Nevertheless, the Soviets may have come to realize that chemical weapons are more trouble than they are worth. It is questionable whether they could have a significant effect on a conventional battlefield so long as both sides are prepared.

Arms control agreements on chemical weapons, however, are extremely unlikely at the present. Verification would be next to impossible, short of a radical change in Soviet attitudes toward secrecy. Unlike nuclear weapons or missiles, chemicals are easy to conceal. Chemical projectiles look no different from other projectiles. They differ only in their contents. For NATO to verify that all chemical weapons had been destroyed, it would be necessary to allow inspection of virtually every Soviet military facility and every artillery and bomb stockpile. Important strides have been made in getting the USSR to accept intrusive verification, notably the 1987 INF Treaty. This is the first treaty to contain significant verification provisions, allowing American officials to inspect Soviet facilities for treaty violations. It allows the U.S. to visit several dozen facilities in the USSR and other Warsaw Pact countries. But a chemical arms control treaty would require inspections at virtually all Soviet military bases. It seems doubtful that the Kremlin or the KGB would stomach that, at least for now.

## Other Shock Weapons

Although the fictional scenario presented here depicts the use of chemical weapons, other shock weapons might appear on the battlefield in the not-too-distant future. One of the more likely is laser weapons. They have received a lot of attention in the context of strategic defense and "Star Wars." But whereas the technology for Star Wars is probably a decade in the future, tactical laser weapons are practical today.

Lasers emit a beam of intense, coherent light. At the moment, they are used mainly for range finders and weapons designators. Current laser range finders and designators can blind a person if they happen to hit him in the eyes while the laser is operating. Armies are very careful with lasers during peacetime training.

It does not take a lot of imagination to calculate that lasers could be turned into weapons capable of blinding enemy troops. The existing lasers use very modest power sources. More powerful lasers could be expected to cause considerably more optical damage, and could be powerful enough to damage optical sights like the FLIR and passive night vision sights on tanks.

No army presently talks about developing weapons to blind enemy troops. The outcry from the public would be intense. But such weapons have been under development for at least fifteen years. Although the U.S. Army refuses to talk about laser weapons in any detail, some information on laser protective measures is available. The U.S. Army obviously expects the Soviet Union to be developing laser weapons, and has already begun developing countermeasures. The U.S. Army has spent about $30 million on research and $120 million on laser defensive systems, according to public testimony to the U.S. Congress in 1988. For example, the Stingray program is developing optical filtration and other systems to protect the M2 Bradley infantry fighting vehicle from enemy lasers. For individual protection, filtered eyeglasses are being developed. Special laser hardening techniques are being developed for optical sights.

There may be the same inhibitions against using laser blinding weapons as against using chemical weapons. Both the NATO and the Warsaw Pact countries may be unwilling to be the first to use such systems, since they will inevitably result in the other side retaliating. But there are also the same attractions in using laser weapons as there are in using chemical weapons. Lasers, like chemicals, are shock weapons. The first combat use of such a weapon would probably cause considerable panic among the troops. The affected troops would be defenseless. Lasers are likely to add a new horror to the already lethal modern battlefield.

# CONCLUSION

The introduction to this book raised the question "How good is the Soviet Army?" The question has been addressed indirectly by depicting how Soviet units might perform in a future war in Europe. In the fictional scenario, Soviet units have managed to seize objectives significantly behind schedule, and have suffered losses much more severe than anticipated. But the important point is, they have seized their objectives.

Could the Soviet Army triumph in such a contest? This book has not attempted to answer such a difficult question. The fictional scenarios cover only the first week of fighting, with the outcome still very much uncertain. Since they have focused on the Soviet side, the deficiencies in the Soviet armed forces have been accented. A similar examination of the NATO side also would reveal deficiencies, though of a very different nature. It has not been the intention of this book to suggest which side holds the ultimate advantages in a future war, but rather to depict how one side is likely to fight. While there is no sufficient reason to conclude that the Soviets could not prevail, neither is there much certainty that their superior numbers would ensure a quick victory.

The Soviets pattern their tactics on lessons learned from World War II. They have meticulously studied the experience of the war and tried to draw scientific conclusions. Their planning for war often reflects the campaigns of 1944–45, when the Red Army stormed victoriously through Central Europe and smashed into Berlin. But NATO is not the emaciated Wehrmacht of 1945, nor is the current peacetime Soviet Army the battle-hardened Red Army, honed by four grueling years of warfare. Soviet estimates of attrition rates, rates of advance, rates of ammunition usage, and other assessments seem optimistic compared to more recent wars, like those in the Middle East.

All other things being equal, modern warfare tends to favor the defender. Offensive forces, unless they have significant advantages in technology, training, and operational skill, usually require two or three times the forces to overcome a stubborn defender. The question is not whether the Soviets are as good as NATO tank for tank, or rifleman for rifleman, but whether they have the skill to use their numerical advantages to overcome NATO defenses. Soviet operational planning accepts that their performance at the tactical level may not be up to par with opponents like NATO. But there is the conviction that at the operational level, Soviet numerical advantages and command skills will make tactical deficiencies less meaningful, as they did in the last year of fighting in World War II.

The conclusion of this book is that deficiencies at the tactical level have significant influence on the operational conduct of war. The Soviets have enough shortcomings at the tactical level that their operational plans could be seriously jeopardized. The Soviets have strapped themselves into a straitjacket with their enormous force structure. This oversized force may have value for intimidation, but it undercuts efforts at reform and modernization. The MiG-29 is a very good fighter, but its designers have been forced to adopt lower cost features, which compromise the interface between pilot and plane, and undercut its combat power. The T-80 is an excellent design, but too many tanks are needed to permit each T-80 to be fitted with a thermal imaging sight and advanced armor like their NATO counterparts. Soviet officer training is thorough and professional, but the Soviet Army neglects development of an adequate infrastructure of squad leaders such as sergeants.

This straitjacket is one of the lingering remnants of the Stalin era. World War II was horribly costly to the Soviet Union. More than twenty million Soviet citizens died, probably more than the combined total of all the other European and American victims of the war. Defense and military power had always been a preoccupation with the Soviets; after the war it became an obsession. To Americans and Western Europeans, the massive peacetime Soviet Army was seen primarily as a means to impose Soviet control over its Eastern European satellites and to intimidate NATO. From the Soviet perspective, size meant security.

A maxim attributed to Lenin sums up the Soviet view of military strength: "Quantity has a quality all its own." The size of the Soviet Army hides the country's insecurity about its capabilities facing European or American adversaries. The Red Army of 1941 was trounced by a German army many times smaller than itself. It took the Soviets four years of savage fighting to defeat the German armed forces. Throughout the war, the German armed forces were smaller than their Soviet adversary. And

Soviet victory didn't come until after the British and American forces began tying down large elements of the German armed forces by their bombing campaign and their belated invasion of the European continent. The Red Army was never able to deal with the Wehrmacht on an even footing; it always needed numerically superior forces to prevail. In 1946, they faced a combination of opponents, including the United States, with far greater military mobilization potential than Germany's. Stalin's paranoid fear of hostile conspiracies, combined with deep-rooted Russian sentiment to avoid a repeat of 1941, led to an enormous peacetime army.

To Stalin, and to the generals of Stalin's generation, numbers meant strength. Lacking confidence in their ability to equal or surpass the Western armies in tactical skill and military technology, the Soviet Army embraced numerical superiority. If one Soviet tank wasn't as good as one German tank, well, three Soviet tanks were surely as good as one NATO tank. Eight Soviet howitzers were surely as good as one NATO howitzer. Numerical superiority was the Soviet shield to dissuade NATO action against the USSR, and to calm their own fears.

This viewpoint backfired on the Soviets. To NATO, the massive Soviet numbers meant hostile intent, not defensive cautiousness. In trying to ensure their own security, the Soviets provoked NATO into continuous force modernization. The NATO commanders realized that their governments would never consent to matching the Soviets man for man, tank for tank, so they attempted to exploit NATO's industrial and technological advantages, and Soviet disadvantages. In turn these NATO efforts undermined Soviet confidence in their security and reinforced their conviction of the need to maintain a large and powerful army.

In the early 1960s, Khrushchev tried to break out of this vicious circle. He appreciated that the large armed forces were an excessive drain on the weak Soviet economy. He attempted to cut back on the conventional armed forces, especially the army, and reorient Soviet doctrine by placing more emphasis on the small and potent strategic missile force. But he made crucial mistakes. The Soviet Union in the early 1960s wasn't yet ready to challenge the United States' technological edge in strategic weapons. Impatience and rash decisions led Khrushchev to try to overcome the technological problems by sly tactics. If sufficient Soviet missiles couldn't threaten the U.S. from Soviet soil, they could from Cuban soil. Khrushchev deployed medium-range nuclear missiles in Cuba, leading to a prompt American reaction. The result was a humiliating defeat when the U.S. forced the Soviets to remove the missiles from Cuba in the face of military threats. To make matters worse, Khrushchev's heavy cuts in the conventional forces alienated the military leadership. Khrushchev was finally ousted from power, his reforms evaporating as Brezhnev coddled the military.

Gorbachev inherits Khrushchev's problems, but also inherits his lessons. The average Soviet citizen is growing weary of nearly sixty years of "*skoro budyet*": Everything will be wonderful tomorrow. Economic progress is not possible when the weak economy is saddled with constant, heavy levels of military expenditures. Gorbachev is the first Soviet leader of the postwar generation. He was too young to have served in World War II. His outlook is shaped less by the insecurity and paranoia of the Stalin years than the promise of the 1960s. The Soviets put the first satellite in space, and it was a Soviet *kosmonaut*, not an American astronaut, who first orbited the world. The Soviet Union should be able to take pride in something beyond its military might. Seventy years of empty promises have demoralized Soviet society.

Gorbachev has learned Khrushchev's lesson and, so far, has not made any rash moves that would excessively alienate the military. Nor has he accepted their every demand, as was the case in the Brezhnev years. The Soviet military press often carries articles by military officers complaining about the change in the popular press—the gradual disappearance of the adulation of the army in Soviet newspapers and magazines. There is undoubtedly some discontent over elements of Gorbachev's reforms, but at the same time, many of the more astute officers realize that efforts to improve the economy will ultimately aid the Soviet armed forces. Gorbachev also has forced the retirement of many of the overaged dinosaurs in the army's upper ranks, replacing them with younger leaders like himself who grew up in the 1950s and early 1960s.

The unilateral cuts in the Soviet military announced in December 1988 suggest a reassessment of the defense needs of the USSR. The Soviets appear to be turning to the belief that a "leaner and meaner" armed forces is more cost effective, and more combat effective, than the current force. It is easy to make the armed forces leaner. The military leadership will undoubtedly keep an eye on the reforms to ensure they get the "meaner" part too. It will be Gorbachev's dilemma to transfer scarce funding from the military to the civilian sector without undermining essential elements of the Soviet armed forces.

The Gorbachev policies may lessen the likelihood of a NATO and Warsaw Pact confrontation in Europe. The Soviet Union in the late 1980s has begun to turn in on itself, shifting focus to internal reforms and away from the superpower posturing of the Brezhnev years. For Gorbachev's economic policies to succeed, Western trade and credits could prove useful, but a slackening in military tensions and competition is essential. These revolutionary changes will not be easy. Reforms in Eastern Europe are likely to lead to more instability in Poland, East Germany, and Czechoslovakia, undoubtedly causing anxiety to the military leadership. It will be a difficult balancing act to keep the lid on political ferment without using ham-fisted police repression that will alienate the West. At the same time, relaxation of police repression in the USSR and in its satellite countries, combined with force reductions and budget cuts in the military sector, will undoubtedly be very troubling to the Soviet military leadership. Russian society, whether Tsarist or Soviet, has feared the anarchy that political change may bring, especially those elements of Russian society assigned to the maintenance of state security.

It remains a question whether the Gorbachev reforms are a temporary respite in world tensions, or a harbinger of long-term change in East-West relations. Some military analysts are convinced that Gorbachev's talk of peace and harmony are nothing more than deceitful tactics meant to buy time for the Soviet economy to strengthen itself sufficiently for some future round of military competition. Others feel that it is a genuine attempt to finally calm the animosities and suspicions lingering since the end of World War II.

Do these reforms reduce the likelihood of a conventional war in Europe like the one pictured in the fictional scenario? This can be argued in either direction. On the one hand, Gorbachev's reforms contain the risk of increasing social and political tensions in the Warsaw Pact satellite countries like the fictional German crisis portrayed here. Such a crisis is one of the more likely events to precipitate a war in Europe. On the other hand, Soviet unilateral arms reductions, although far from bringing both sides to parity in combat power, do reduce the probability for Soviet success in a conventional war with NATO. Soviet anxieties over the combat potential of their forces at a tactical level, as well as real reductions in the quantitative superiority enjoyed by the Warsaw Pact countries in many areas of conventional arms, are likely to reduce the probability of conventional war in Europe in the early 1990s.

Indeed, when writing the first chapter of this book, I found it extremely difficult to imagine a convincing set of political and military circumstances that would trigger a conventional war in Europe today. In spite of the enormous mistrust that still exists between the NATO and the Warsaw Pact countries, both sides are haunted by fears of the catastrophe that a war might bring. It is easy enough, when sitting in the West, to see all those Soviet tanks and artillery pieces, and dream up some nefarious Soviet scheme to conquer Western Europe. But another picture emerges if you try to place yourself in the shoes of Soviet military leaders and confront the same issues from the Soviet perspective. It is my hope that this book has managed to give its readers a somewhat different perspective of the military balance in Europe today.

# GLOSSARY

**ACRV:** Armored command and reconnaissance vehicle, like the Soviet 1V12 armored vehicles.

**AGS-17:** Soviet 30mm automatic grenade launcher. Also called *Plamya* (flame), it is the size of a heavy machine gun, but has a short, stubby barrel. It is comparable to the American Mk.19 40mm grenade launcher.

**AHR:** Attack Helicopter Regiment.

**Akatsiya:** Soviet name for the 2S3 152mm self-propelled howitzer. Means "acacia" in Russian. The Soviets codename their artillery systems with the names of flowers or plants.

**AKS-74:** New standard Soviet assault rifle. The earlier AK-47 and AKM used 7.62mm ammunition; the AK-74 series uses 5.45mm ammunition, which allows the rifleman to carry more rounds.

**AMRAAM:** Advanced medium range air-to-air missile, AIM-120A. A successor to the older American AIM-7 Sparrow.

**Anona:** Soviet name for the 2S9 120mm self-propelled, airmobile mortar/howitzer. Means "anemone" in Russian.

**APFSDS:** Armor-piercing, fin-stabilized, discarding sabot. Acronym for tank ammunition using a kinetic energy penetrator. The round penetrates thick armor by speed and mass (kinetic energy) rather than high-explosive pressure (chemical energy). Also called "hard core" rounds by the Soviets, or "sabot" rounds by American tankers.

**Army:** Soviet term for a military formation consisting of several divisions and their supporting units. Comparable to a NATO corps. A NATO army is comparable to a Soviet front.

**ATGM:** Antitank guided missile. The Russians use their own acronym, PTURS.

**BMD:** Russian acronym for airlanding fighting vehicle, a tracked, armored troop-carrying vehicle used by Soviet paratrooper forces. The BMD-1 is armed with the same turret as the BMP-1, while the BMD-2 is a turretless troop carrier and command vehicle. The BMD-1 resembles a miniature BMP-1 and carries fewer troops.

**BMP:** Russian acronym for infantry fighting vehicle, a tracked armored infantry vehicle with turret-mounted weapon and side firing ports. The BMP-1 is armed with a 73mm low-pressure gun; the BMP-2 is armed with a 30mm automatic cannon.

**Border Guards:** Paramilitary branch of the Soviet KGB security forces used to patrol Soviet frontiers as well as perform basic security and customs duty at airports and harbors.

**BRM:** Russian acronym for armored reconnaissance vehicle. This lightly armored scout vehicle is based on the same chassis as the BMP-1, but has a larger two-man turret, better sighting devices, and carries a smaller crew. The BRM-1 has a "Tall Mike" surveillance radar on a telescoping mount, fitted on the turret rear. BRM-2 uses a revised turret with a 30mm gun, like the BMP-2.

**BTR:** Russian acronym for armored transporter. This wheeled, armored infantry vehicle is a less expensive counterpart to the tracked BMP. Three types of BTR are commonly in service in the Soviet army—the BTR-60, BTR-70, and BTR-80. They are all similar in appearance and armament, and the main change through the series has been evolutionary improvement in the engine and hull design.

**Bundeswehr:** The West German Army.

**Chobham armor:** A type of tank armor developed by a British research establishment in Chobham, hence its name. It consists of spaced layers of steel and non-metallic armors, although the exact composition is still classified. It has been used, in both its original or improved form, on current NATO tanks like the American M1 Abrams, German Leopard II, and British Challenger.

**DOSAAF:** Russian acronym for Volunteer Society for Cooperation with the Army, Air Force, and Fleet. Soviet government organization responsible for pro-military indoctrination and training amongst Soviet youth.

**DPICM:** Dual-purpose improved conventional munitions. A type of American artillery shell containing small submunitions that can be used against armored or unarmored targets, hence dual-purpose. This acronym usually refers to an advanced version of the ICM first introduced in the late 1980s.

**DShB:** Russian acronym for Air Assault Force, a branch of the Soviet Army specializing in airmobile operations.

**Durandal:** Type of runway cratering munition developed by Matra in France, but employed by several NATO air forces including the U.S. Air Force. The Durandal contains a rocket motor which propels it at high speed against concrete runways. The warhead has a time-delay mechanism so that it explodes seconds after impact, making a deep crater which is more difficult to repair.

**ECM:** Electronic countermeasures. Electronic systems designed to defeat enemy electronic sensors like radars and radar-based missile guidance systems.

**ERA:** Explosive reactive armor. A type of added-on armor consisting of small boxes of steel-encased plastic explosive. When hit by a shaped-charge warhead (as on antitank missiles), the explosive detonates, pushing the steel casing into the path of the warhead's explosive jet, thus preventing the warhead from penetrating the main armor of the tank. ERA has been in use on Soviet tanks since the mid-1980s.

**FASCAM:** Family of artillery scatterable mines. This includes the RAAM (remote antiarmor mines), used against tanks, and ADAM (area denial antipersonnel mines), used against troops. Each artillery shell contains several small mines; the projectile opens up in the air, scattering the mines to the ground below.

**FLIR:** Forward looking infrared. Also called thermal imagers, these electro-optical sensors can see in the dark by sensing the temperature (infrared) difference between tanks, soldiers, or military equipment, and the cooler natural background. They are used as surveillance sights on many different NATO weapon systems including tanks, attack helicopters, and antitank missile launchers. They are not commonly used on Soviet systems, except for a more simplified thermal pointer system used on some Soviet fighters like the MiG-29.

**FROG-7:** Free Rocket Over Ground-7. The NATO reporting name for the Soviet ballistic artillery rocket the Russians call Luna-M. It is used by divisional or army artillery units to deliver tactical nuclear or chemical warheads.

**Front:** Soviet military formation consisting of several armies. Comparable to a NATO army. Several fronts make up a theatre of operations.

**Fulcrum:** NATO reporting name for the MiG-29 jet fighter.

**GAU:** Russian acronym for Main Artillery Directorate. The command element of the Soviet artillery force, now called the GRAU (Main Missile and Artillery Directorate).

**GCI:** Ground-controlled intercept; a system of directing fighter airplanes using ground-based radars and command centers.

**Gepard:** A West German armored antiaircraft vehicle consisting of twin, radar-directed 35mm automatic cannon on a Leopard 1 tank chassis.

**GITB:** Guards Independent Tank Battalion.

**Gorbach:** Russian for "hunchback," also nickname for Mi-24 helicopter.

**Grad:** Soviet name for the BM-21 122mm multiple rocket launchers; the Russian word for "hail." The basic BM-21 is a 40-tube rocket launcher on a Ural 375 truck. The BM-21V is an air-portable version on a GAZ-66B truck.

**Great Patriotic War:** Soviet term for the war between the Soviet Union and Germany, 1941–45; used to distinguish the Soviet fighting from the rest of World War II.

**GRU:** Russian acronym for Main Intelligence Command, the Soviet military intelligence service, comparable to the American DIA (Defense Intelligence Agency).

**GSFG:** Group of Soviet Forces, Germany. The Soviet term for their forces in East Germany.

**GSP:** Russian acronym for mechanized tracked ferry. Consists of a pair of tracked, amphibious vehicles with special pontoons, which can be joined together to form a self-propelled ferry to carry tanks or other heavy equipment across rivers.

**GTR:** Guards Tank Regiment.

**Guards:** Russian honorific added to unit designation, such as 11th Guards Tank Division. The Guards title was awarded to units during World War II and the Afghanistan War for exemplary service and has been retained by many units since then.

**Gvozdika:** Soviet codename for the 2S1 122mm self-propelled howitzer; the word means "carnation" in Russian.

**HEAT:** High explosive antitank. Acronym for explosive warheads used to penetrate tank armor. The high explosive is shaped over a metal cone, leading to other names for this type of warhead such as "shaped charge" or "hollow charge."

**Hind:** NATO reporting name for the Soviet Mil Mi-24 attack helicopter.

**Hip:** NATO reporting name for the Soviet Mil Mi-8/Mi-17 transport helicopter.

**Hokum:** NATO reporting name for the Soviet Kamov attack helicopter.

**Hoplite:** NATO reporting name for the Warsaw Pact Mi-2 utility helicopter.

**HOT:** A Franco-German heavy antitank missile similar in performance to the American BGM-71 TOW. The HOT is usually carried by special antitank helicopters or special tank-hunting vehicles. It uses a wire-guidance system.

**Hot Brick:** Nickname for a type of electronic countermeasures system fitted to aircraft or helicopters which is used to prevent infrared guided missiles from homing in on the thermal emissions of the aircraft.

**HUD:** Heads up display. An advanced optical sight system fitted to new fighter aircraft which displays flight and targeting data on a small, transparent optical panel in front of the pilot.

**IAHR:** Independent Attack Helicopter Regiment.

**ICM:** Improved conventional munition. An artillery round containing several dozen small grenades (submunitions) that are scattered over a target rather than the traditional high-explosive filler. This type of round has been in service with the U.S. Army since the early 1970s with projectiles like the 155mm M483.

**IFF:** Identification friend or foe. An electronic interrogation system used to distinguish hostile aircraft from friendly aircraft through use of a coded electronic signal.

**IFV:** Infantry fighting vehicle. An armored vehicle used to transport infantry that also allows the infantry to fight from inside the vehicle, like the U.S. Army M2 Bradley.

**Igla:** Soviet codename for a man-portable antiaircraft missile called SA-16 by NATO. Russian word means "needle."

**INF:** Intermediate nuclear forces; usually referring to nuclear delivery systems covered under the 1987 INF treaty.

**IRM:** Russian acronym for engineer reconnaissance vehicle, an armored vehicle, based on the BMP chassis, that is used by combat engineers to scout for suitable river crossings. It is fully amphibious or can be submerged to drive across river bottoms to test for their suitability for underwater tank crossings.

**Kalashnikov:** Name of the designer of the Soviet AK-47 and AK-74 assault rifles, Mikhail T. Kalashnikov. Sometimes used as a generic name for Soviet assault rifles.

**Katyusha:** Russian nickname for multiple rocket launchers. The name stems from a Russian song about "little Katy" that was popular in 1941 when this type of weapon was introduced.

**KGB:** Russian acronym for Committee for State Security, the Soviet security organization that combines the functions of the American FBI and CIA.

**KHAD:** Afghan acronym for Afghan secret police.

**Khrom Nikel:** Soviet codename for the IFF system called Odd Rods by NATO; in Russian it means "chrome nickel."

**Komsomol:** Russian acronym for a Communist party youth organization for teenagers too young to join the party.

**Konkurs:** Soviet codename for a heavy antitank missile called AT-5 Spandrel by NATO; Russian word for "contest."

**Korshun:** Soviet codename for the BMP-1 infantry fighting vehicle; in Russian it means "kite."

**LuAZ-967:** A small jeep-like amphibious vehicle used by the Soviets mainly as a light ambulance or airmobile transporter.

**LZ:** Landing zone.

**Malyutka:** Soviet codename for 9M113 antitank missile known also by its US/NATO designation, AT-3 Sagger; in Russian it means "little one."

**Marder:** West German infantry fighting vehicle, comparable to U.S. M2 Bradley or Soviet BMP. Armed with a 20mm automatic cannon, and sometimes with a Milan antitank missile.

**Maskirovka:** Russian term meaning deception or concealment.

**Milan:** A NATO medium antitank missile manufactured by France, Germany, and Britain; comparable to the Soviet AT-4 Spigot or American Dragon. The system can be carried by two soldiers and consists of a firing post and missile launch tube.

**MLRS:** Multiple launch rocket system M270. The American equivalent of the Soviet BM-22 Uragan artillery rocket system, also used by other NATO armies.

**MRR:** Motor Rifle Regiment; Soviet term for mechanized infantry regiment.

**MTK:** Soviet acronym for mine clearing system. This consists of a tracked, armored vehicle with a rocket launcher on the top. The rocket pulls an explosive line charge behind it when it is fired over a minefield, breaching the minefield by explosives.

**Mujihadeen:** Afghan insurgents, usually called *dushmani* by the Russians.

**NCO:** Non-commissioned officer; in most armies, a sergeant.

**NKVD:** Russian acronym for Peoples Commissariat of the Interior, forerunner of the KGB.

**Nyemtsi:** Russian word for Germans; also means "dumb" in Russian, as in "unable to speak."

**OGPU:** Russian acronym for Units of the State Political Directorate, forerunner of the NKVD/KGB.

**OMG:** Operational Maneuver Group.

**Panzerfaust:** Generic term for German antitank rockets; literally means "armored fist."

**Panzergrenadier:** German term for mechanized infantry.

**Pechora:** Soviet codename for S-125 air defense missile called SA-3 Goa in NATO; named after river in northern Russia.

**PGM:** Precision-guided munition.

**PKM:** Soviet 7.62mm squad light machine gun; armored vehicle version called PKT.

**PKT:** Soviet 7.62mm armored vehicle light machine gun; infantry version called PKM.

**Plamya:** Soviet codename for AGS-17 30mm grenade launcher; in Russian it means "flame."

**PMP:** Russian acronym for pontoon bridge assembly, a type of portable engineer bridge called a "Ribbon Bridge" in the U.S. Army.

**Praporshchik:** Soviet rank corresponding to warrant officer.

**PRP-3:** Soviet acronym for mobile reconnaissance post, an artillery scout vehicle based on the BMP chassis with a turret-mounted surveillance radar and other sensors. Called Little Fred in NATO.

**PTURS:** Russian acronym for antitank guided missile.

**PVO:** Russian acronym meaning Air Defense Force, a branch of the Soviet armed forces.

**RAAM:** Remotely scattered antiarmor mine, an artillery-delivered mine of the FASCAM series.

**Razvedchiki:** Russian name for scout troops.

**RGN:** Russian acronym for a type of concussion hand grenade.

**RGO:** Russian acronym for a type of fragmentation hand grenade.

**RKhM:** Russian acronym for chemical reconnaissance vehicle, a tracked, armored vehicle based on the same chassis as the 2S1 self-propelled howitzer. Used by Soviet chemical defense troops for scouting chemically contaminated areas.

**RPG:** Russian acronym meaning rocket-propelled antitank grenade. Includes types like the RPG-7, RPG-22.

**RPV:** Remotely piloted vehicle, usually referring to a small unmanned drone aircraft used for reconnaissance purposes.

**RSC:** Reconnaissance strike complex. Soviet term for future integrated artillery systems.

**RWR:** Radar warning receiver. An electronic device fitted to aircraft which warns the pilot when the plane is being tracked by enemy radars.

**SADARM:** Sense and destroy armor munition. A type of American artillery projectile that dispenses autonomously guided antiarmor submunitions.

**SAM:** Surface-to-air missile. An antiaircraft missile.

**Spetsnaz:** Russian abbreviation for "special purpose." Used to refer to Soviet special forces.

**Su-24:** Soviet codename for the Sukhoi strike aircraft known as Fencer in NATO. This is a large, high capability two-man strike aircraft similar in configuration to the U.S. Air Force F-111.

**Su-25K:** Soviet codename for the Sukhoi ground attack aircraft known as Frogfoot in NATO. This is a single-seat, subsonic attack aircraft, roughly comparable to the U.S. Air Force A-10 Warthog.

**SVD:** Russian acronym for a 7.62mm sniper rifle.

**Syrena:** Soviet codename for a RWR (radar warning receiver) mounted on a Soviet combat aircraft; means "siren" in Russian.

**TGW:** Terminally guided weapon. A NATO program to develop an autonomously guided submunition for the MLRS artillery rocket system.

**TOW:** Tube-launched, optically tracked, wire-guided antitank missile. The American BGM-71 heavy antitank missile, comparable to the Franco-German HOT or Soviet Konkurs.

**Tyulpan:** Soviet codename for the 2S4 240mm self-propelled mortar vehicle; in Russian it means "tulip flower."

**UAC:** Unified Army Corps; a new Soviet formation somewhat larger than a division and smaller than an army, used as the OMG or exploitation force of a Soviet front.

**UAZ-469:** A Soviet jeep.

**Uragan:** Soviet codename for the BM-22 multiple launch rocket system; means "hurricane" in Russian.

**VDV:** Russian acronym for Air Assault Force; a semi-independent branch of the Soviet army specializing in paratroop operations.

**Villiys:** Soviet slang for a jeep, stemming from "Willys."

**VTA:** Russian acronym for Military Transport Aviation, a branch of the Soviet Air Force responsible for transport aircraft.

**VV:** Russian acronym for Interior Army, a paramilitary state police force of the Ministry of the Interior.

**VVS:** Russian acronym for the Soviet Air Force.

**Yozh:** Soviet codename for the BMP-2 infantry fighting vehicle; means "hedgehog" in Russian.

**ZiL-130:** Soviet medium truck.

**ZU-23:** Soviet towed, twin-barrelled antiaircraft 23mm automatic cannon.

# BIBLIOGRAPHY

## Chapter 1

Detailed investigations of Soviet operational art and war planning are a fairly recent trend in military studies. As a result, there are few generally available books on the subject. Some of the most interesting and influential articles on Soviet operations and tactics have appeared in the monthly defense magazine *International Defense Review*. The scenarios presented here have been heavily influenced by the work of Col. David Glantz and the studies prepared by the Soviet Army Studies Office of the U.S. Army Combined Arms Center in Fort Leavenworth, Kansas. These studies are not generally available, but fortunately in 1988, a new journal devoted to these subjects, the *Journal of Soviet Military Studies*, began publication. The editors of this magazine are Col. David Glantz and Christopher Donnelly, two of the most influential of the new generation of Soviet military scholars. The following list, while hardly exhaustive, includes some of the books that deal with issues raised in this chapter.

Baxter, William. *Soviet AirLand Battle Tactics*. Novato, CA: Presidio Press, 1986.

Donnelly, Christopher. *Red Banner: The Soviet Military System in Peace and War*. London: Jane's Publishing, 1988.

Erickson, John, et al. *Soviet Ground Forces: An Operational Assessment*. Boulder, CO: Westview Press, 1986.

Isby, David. *Weapons and Tactics of the Soviet Army*. London: Jane's Publishing, 1988.

Johnson, A. Ross, et al. *East European Military Establishments: The Warsaw Pact Northern Tier*. New York: Crane, Russak & Co., 1982.

Monks, Alfred L. *Soviet Military Doctrine: 1960 to the Present*. New York: Irvington Publishers, 1984.

Suvorov, Viktor. *Inside the Soviet Army*. London: Hamish Hamilton, 1982.

U.S. Army. *Soviet Army Operations*. Washington, DC: U.S. Army Intelligence and Security Command, 1978.

U.S. Army. *The Soviet Army*. Field Manual 100-2-1. Washington, DC: HQ, Department of the Army, 1984.

Vigor, P. H. *Soviet Blitzkrieg Theory*. New York: St. Martin's Press, 1983.

## Chapter 2

Alexiev, Alexander. *Inside the Soviet Army in Afghanistan.* Santa Monica, CA: Rand Corporation, 1988.

Alexiev, Alexander, and S. Enders Wimbush. *Ethnic Minorities in the Red Army: Asset or Liability?* Boulder, CO: Westview Press, 1988.

Defense Intelligence Agency. *The Soviet Motorized Rifle Battalion.* Washington, DC: DIA, 1978.

Defense Intelligence Agency. *The Soviet Motorized Rifle Company.* Washington, DC: DIA, 1976.

Jones, Ellen. *Red Army and Society: A Sociology of the Soviet Military.* Boston: Allen & Unwin, 1985.

Suvorov, Victor. *The Liberators.* London: Hamish Hamilton, 1981.

U.S. Army. *BMP AICV Operator's Manual.* Aberdeen Proving Grounds, MD: 519th MI Bn, 1977.

U.S. Army. *The BMP: Capabilities and Limitations.* Fort Monroe, VA: U.S. Army TRADOC, 1977.

Williams, E. S. *The Soviet Military: Political Education, Training & Morale.* New York: St. Martin's Press, 1986.

Zaloga, Steven. *Inside the Soviet Army Today.* London: Osprey Publications, 1987.

Zamascikov, Sergei. *Political Organizations in the Soviet Armed Forces—The Role of the Party and Komsomol.* Falls Church, VA: Delphic Associates, 1982.

## Chapter 3

Much of the material for this chapter was collected by the author during research on the book on Soviet tanks listed below. There is very little English language material on the training and experiences of Soviet tankers except for internal U.S. Army and DIA studies. A valuable source of information is the Soviet émigrés living in the United States, many of whom served in the Soviet Ground Forces.

Baskalov, Yu. D., et al. *Spravochnik serzhanta motostrelkovikh (tankovikh) voisk* (Handbook for Sergeants of the Motor Rifle/Tank Forces). Moscow: Voenizdat, 1987.

Defense Intelligence Agency. *Soviet Tank Regiment Tactics.* Washington, DC: DIA, 1979.

Dragunskiy, D. A., *Motostrelkoviy (tankoviy) batalon v boyu* (The Motor Rifle/Tank Battalion in Combat). Moscow: Voenizdat, 1986.

Evans, T. C. *Current Objectives and Deficiencies in the Training of Soviet Tankers*. Garmisch, FRG: U.S. Army Institute for Advanced Russian Studies, 1975.

Noskov, A. S. (ed.). *Motostrelkovaya (tankovaya) rota v boyu* (The Motor Rifle/Tank Company in Combat). Moscow: Voenizdat, 1988.

Zaloga, S. J., and J. W. Loop. *Soviet Tanks and Combat Vehicles 1946 to the Present*. London: Arms & Armour Press, 1987.

## Chapter 4

Alexiev, Alexander. *Inside the Soviet Army in Afghanistan*. Santa Monica, CA: Rand Corporation, 1988.

Beitler, Stephen. *Spetsnaz: The Soviet Union's Special Operations Forces*. Master's Thesis, Defense Intelligence College, June 1985.

Buffardi, Louis N. *The Soviet Naval Infantry*. Washington, DC: Defense Intelligence Agency, 1979.

Glantz, David M. *The Soviet Airborne Experience*. Fort Leavenworth, KS: U.S. Army Command and General Staff College, 1984.

Hansen, James. "Soviet Vanguard Forces-Spetsnaz." *National Defense*, March 1986.

Isby, David C. *Soviet Special Operations Forces in Afghanistan*. Proceedings of the Light Infantry Conference, Boeing Corporation, 1985.

Isby, David C. "The Spetsnaz in Afghanistan: Soviet special operation forces in action." *Military Technology*, October 1985.

Isby, David C. "The Vertical Threat: Air Assault and Airmobile Brigades of the Soviet Army." *Amphibious Warfare Review*, August 1985.

Knight, Amy W. *The KGB: Police and Politics in the Soviet Union*. Boston: Unwin Hyman, 1988.

Kohler, David R. "Spetsnaz." *U.S. Naval Institute Proceedings*, August 1987.

Kuth, Robert. *Soviet Airborne Anti-Armor Tactics in the Defense*. Garmisch, FRG: U.S. Army Russian Institute, 1981.

Lewis, Edward. *A Comprehensive Examination of the Soviet Naval Infantry*. Garmisch, FRG: U.S. Army Russian Institute, 1977.

Suvorov, Viktor (pseud.). "Spetsnaz: The Soviet Union's special forces." *International Defense Review*, September 1983.

Suvorov, Viktor (pseud.). *Spetsnaz: The Story of the Soviet SAS*. London: Hamish Hamilton, 1987.

Zaloga, Steven, and James Loop. *Soviet Bloc Elite Forces*. London: Osprey Publications, 1985.

## Chapter 5

Chaiko, Lev. *Helicopter Construction in the USSR*. Falls Church, VA: Delphic Associates, 1985.

Cook, Maj. Charles B. *An Assessment of the Soviet Combat Helicopter Threat*. Master's Thesis, U.S. Army Command and General Staff College, 1982.

Stapfer, Hans-Heiri. *The Mi-24 Hind in Action*. Carrollton, TX: Squadron-Signal Publications, 1988.

Stepniewski, W. Z. *A Comparative Study of Soviet vs. Western Helicopters*. Washington, DC: NASA Scientific and Technical Information Branch, 1982.

U.S. Army. *Air-to-Air (Helicopter) Combat. FM 1-107*. Washington, DC: HQ, Department of the Army, 1984.

U.S. Army. *OPFOR Attack Helicopter Field Pocket Reference*. Fort Hood, TX: U.S. Army Forces Command Opposing Forces Training Detachment, 1986.

U.S. Army. *The Soviet Army: Specialized Warfare and Rear Area Support*. Fort Monroe, VA: U.S. Army TRADOC, 1984.

Zaloga, Steven, and George Balin. *Anti-Tank Helicopters*. London: Osprey Publications, 1986.

## Chapter 6

Anashkin, I. N., and M. N. Belokur. *Spravochnik serzhanta artillerii* (Handbook for Artillery Sergeants). Moscow: Voenizdat, 1981.

Bellamy, Chris. *Red God of War: Soviet Artillery and Rocket Forces*. London: Brassey's Defence Publishers, 1986.

Betit, Eugene D. *Soviet and Warsaw Pact River Crossing: Doctrine and Capabilities*. Washington, DC: Defense Intelligence Agency, 1976.

Lebedev, V. Ya. *Spravochnik ofitsera nazemnoi artillerii* (Handbook for Officers of Land Artillery). Moscow: Voenizdat, 1984.

Peredelskiy, G. E. (ed.). *Otechesvennaya artilleriya* (Artillery of the Homeland). Moscow: Voenizdat, 1986.

U.S. Army. *Threat Monograph: A Comparison of Selected NATO and Warsaw Pact Engineer Organizations and Equipment*. Fort Monroe, VA: TRADOC, 1977.

Zaloga, Steven. "Bog voiny: The Russian God of War." *Combat Weapons*, spring 1986.

## Chapter 7

The following bibliography accents recent articles on the MiG-29 Fulcrum. For readers interested in Soviet Air Force developments, one of the more interesting unclassified sources on current trends is the annual Soviet Aerospace Almanac issue of *Air Force Magazine* devoted to Soviet affairs.

General Dynamics. *F-16/MiG-29 Comparative Analysis.* Fort Worth, TX: General Dynamics, 1988.

Mason, R. A., and J. W. R. Taylor. *Aircraft, Strategy and Operations of the Soviet Air Force.* London: Jane's Publishing, 1986.

"Mig Impresses Western Observers." *Flight International,* 17 September 1988.

"MiG-29: Stealing the Show." *Interavia,* October 1988.

"MiG-29 Design Merges Old, New Technologies." *Aviation Week and Space Technology,* 26 September 1988.

Nordeen, Lon. *Air Warfare in the Missile Age.* Washington, DC: Smithsonian Institution Press, 1985.

Pawloski, Dick. *Changes in Soviet Air Combat Doctrine and Force Structure.* Fort Worth, TX: General Dynamics, 1987.

Pennington, Rana. "Closing the Tactics Gap: Initiative and Independence Are the New Buzzwords in Soviet Air Tactics." *Air Force Magazine,* Volume 67, No. 3, March 1984.

Price, Alfred. *Air Battle: Central Europe.* New York: The Free Press, 1986.

"The Show Stopper, MiG-29 at Farnborough." *International Defense Review,* October 1988.

Sweetman, B., and B. Gunston. *Soviet Air Power.* London: Salamander Books, 1978.

## Chapter 8

Defense Intelligence Agency. *The Soviet Chemical Weapons Threat.* Washington, DC: DIA, 1985.

Heller, Maj. Charles. *Chemical Warfare in World War I.* Fort Leavenworth, KS: Combat Studies Office, USAC & GSC, 1984.

Segal, David. "Better Killing through Chemistry." *Combat Weapons,* winter 1986.

U.S. Army. *Identification Guide to Chemical, Biological and Radiological Equipment of the Warsaw Pact Countries.* APO NY: USAEUR, 1973.

U.S. Army. *Soviet-Warsaw Pact Chemical Threat Briefing.* 70th Ordnance Detachment, 1985.

USSR Ministry of Foreign Affairs. *Information on the Presentation at the Shikany*

*Military Facility of Standard Chemical Weapons and of the Technology for the Destruction of Chemical Weapons at a Mobile Unit.* Moscow: Soviet Ministry of Foreign Affairs, 1987.

Zaloga, Steven J. "NBC Defense: Protecting Soviet Armored Vehicles." *NBC Defense & Technology International*, Vol. 1, No. 4, September 1986.